IT Architectures
and Middleware

Second Edition

IT Architectures and Middleware
Second Edition

Strategies for
Building Large,
Integrated Systems

Chris Britton
Peter Bye

♦♦Addison-Wesley

Boston • San Francisco • New York • Toronto • Montreal
London • Munich • Paris • Madrid • Capetown
Sydney • Tokyo • Singapore • Mexico City

The publisher offers discounts on this book when ordered in quantity for bulk purchases and special sales. For more information, please contact:

U.S. Corporate and Government Sales
(800) 382-3419
corpsales@pearsontechgroup.com

For sales outside of the U.S., please contact:

International Sales
(317) 581-3793
international@pearsontechgroup.com

Visit Addison-Wesley on the Web: www.awprofessional.com

Library of Congress Cataloging-in Publication Data

CIP Data on file.

ISBN 0-321-24694-2
Text printed on recycled paper
3 4 5 6 7 8 DOC 09 08 07
3rd printing, July 2007

To my wife, Judy,
and children, Katie and Alice.

—CB

To my wife, Alison.

—PB

Contents

Figures

Boxes

Preface

All large organizations have complex, heterogeneous IT systems. All of them need to integrate their applications to support faster, more accurate business processes and to provide meaningful, consistent management information. All organizations are struggling to achieve this.

One reason for their struggle is that they are caught in the crossfire of an IT vendor war. In one corner is Microsoft Corporation, whose strength is its consistent technical strategy based on the .NET set of software technologies and the Windows operating system. In the other corner, ranged against Microsoft, is a group that includes IBM Corporation, Sun Microsystems, Oracle Corporation, and BEA Systems. This group is focusing its resources on the Java environment. This is a battle about who will rule over middleware technology, a battle about how to implement distributed systems. Given the importance of the subject matter, it is a battle for the hearts and souls of IT for the next decade. Why? Because all large organizations have complex, heterogeneous IT systems that need to be brought together.

Vendor wars are only part of the problem. Scratch the surface of a large IT department and you will see many camps, for example, workstation/departmental server "decentralizers" and mainframe "centralizers." Look from another angle and you will see two kinds of people—"techies" and "modelers." A techy will start a project by deciding what platform and software to use and will eventually get around to the boring bit, which is writing application code. A modeler will design the application with a modeling tool, generate a few programs and a database, and will eventually confront the (to him or her) trivial question of what platform it will run on. Modeling to a techy seems abstract and disconnected from reality. Technical issues to a modeler are tedious, and surely, soon we will be able to generate the application from the model at the press of a button, won't we? One key to developing large distributed systems is to bring these people together.

Computer professionals generally are comfortable with developing applications on a single platform to a well-defined set of requirements. The reason is that the technology is well understood; the modelers know that what they design can be implemented, and the techies know they can make it work. Large distributed systems are not like that. A system designed without consideration for the distributed implementation will not work. Even worse, it will only become apparent that it doesn't work when scaling up to production capacity starts. To add to our woes, we are now considering integrating multiple systems, each of which was a challenge to develop in the first place, and each of which is changing at a different speed, driven ever faster by the business. The notion of a "well-defined set of requirements" is not realistic; requirements will always be changing.

It is our contention that modelers need to know something about technology, techies need to know something about modeling, and while we are about it, vendors, commentators, consultants, academics, and marketers need to know why their "solutions" aren't quite the panaceas they claim.

This book is about IT architecture. IT architecture provides a framework for discussing implementation design, and it is in these discussions where techies and modelers should meet. Anyone whose roles and responsibilities include IT architect should know everything in this book. (Note we said "know," not "agree with.")

Although IT architects are an important audience for this book, we have tried to write a book for IT management. We have assumed that the IT managers in our readership come from an IT background not a business background; this book is not an introduction to IT. So why do IT managers need a book about IT architecture? It is because here so many of their concerns come together—application flexibility, information quality, resiliency, scalability, and so on. One of our aims is to give IT management the knowledge to call the IT architects to account.

This book gives an overview of the whole subject of building and running large distributed systems. It is a deliberate attempt to step above the detail and the in-fighting to examine what is important, what isn't important, and what we need to do differently from the way we did it 10 years ago. Our contention is that the difference between then and now is much more than simply that there are new tools to play with. Building integrated systems is substantially different from building standalone applications, and it affects everything we do in IT.

A major theme of this book is enterprise computing. In the list of terms abused by the industry, "enterprise computing" has to be somewhere near the top. This book takes the view that enterprise computing is about being able to build systems that support the whole enterprise, which in large organizations means many thousands of users. It's obvious that systems that support thousands of users must have resiliency, scalability, security, and manageability as major concerns. The enterprise computing mentality is not prepared to compromise on these objectives. An old mainframe application written in COBOL that gives you resiliency, scalability, security, and manageability is far superior to any implementation that does not.

This is not to say that you cannot build enterprise-capable applications with modern tools, such as Web services. But to succeed you must understand the principles of building large, resilient systems. The principles that served us well for standalone applications do not all apply for distributed systems and vice versa.

Many people in IT find discussions of principles too abstract and dry, so we have tried to enliven the presentation with many examples.

Many organizations today are trying to avoid all these issues by buying third-party application packages. This is partially successful. When you buy a package, you buy an IT architecture, albeit only in the context of the package's functionality. If you buy many packages, it is likely that you must lash them together somehow, and for this you need an IT architect. If the packages are from different vendors, integration is a challenge. In this book, we give you the principles that should help in this task, but we have chosen not to address the challenge directly. Because there are so many packages, to do the subject justice would require another book.

This book is not for everyone. You will find this book short on product detail. It does not tell you anything about installation, there are no proper coding examples, there is no survey of products, and there is little in the way of product comparisons. We make no apologies for any of these omissions. There are many books on coding, and product details change so fast the best place for comparisons is on the Internet. This book does not teach application design. There are many books for this as well. But we hope application designers will read this book because the discussion on the principles for building enterprise systems is vital for them also. Finally, this book is not an academic book. It contains little mathematics except for the back-of-the-envelope calculations to illustrate a few points. We offer a practical, wide-ranging discussion for IT professionals to help them understand what is going on so they can pick out the real issues from the imaginary issues and start building complex distributed systems with confidence.

Changes in the second edition

Changes that led to the second edition fall into three categories: new author, new technology, new approaches to design.

First, authorship has now become a team—Peter Bye has joined Chris. Peter brings a long-standing expertise in integration, networking, systems management, and all matters concerned with designing an IT architecture. Although Peter has concentrated on adding to the technical content in the first part of the book, all parts are mulled over by both of us and authorship is shared. Compare the new text with the old and you will notice small changes scattered everywhere. As befits Peter's additional expertise, where there was one chapter on systems management and security, there are now two.

Second, the book has been updated to take into account new technology, in particular Web services, and consequently new ways of thinking about IT architecture, in particular loosely coupled architectures.

Chris was in the final stages of writing the first edition of the book when Microsoft announced .NET and he had no time to digest the merits of the announcement and incorporate it into the text. When Web services moved toward center stage, it became clear that a fundamental driver was a desire for a more loosely coupled architecture or, more specifically, a loosely coupled integration of tightly coupled archipelagos of system. The integrated applications architecture described in the first edition of this book was a quintessentially tightly coupled approach. When many people said that they could never reach enough agreement across an organization to impose a tightly coupled architecture, we could see some truth to these complaints. But loosely coupled integration is impossible without some common standards, and Web services are now providing them.

However, "loosely coupled" is a fuzzy term, easily bandied about by sales-people and consultants, and you can't just apply Web services pixie dust to create loosely coupled integrated applications. One of our aims with this new edition is to identify when loosely coupled works and when it doesn't, and to lay out the advantages and disadvantages of the different approaches to architecture. In consequence, our approach to IT architecture is very flexible and we present a range of architectural options such as middleware bus architectures, hub and spoke architectures, and Web services architectures. The common theme throughout is the notion of service-oriented architectures.

In concrete terms, describing Web services and other new technology has led to one new chapter and substantial changes to three others.

The third major area of change in this book has to do with design. As in the technology chapters, the changes in the design chapters are partly in response to changes in the industry. In particular, we have felt the need to discuss agile approaches to development and how they can cooperate with an architectural approach. But the wider reason for change is that the authors' understanding has developed in the intervening years. In particular, we have been able to describe a lightweight approach to integration design and to provide a better view on how the IT architecture supports business processes. These changes have led to one new chapter and substantial changes to two others.

We have also tidied up some of the material on changing existing systems and in the process eliminated one chapter. Also, two of the earlier chapters that discuss the history of middleware have been merged since some of the technology has sunk in importance.

Of course, with all these changes to the body of the book, we needed to rewrite the first and last chapters.

In spite of all the changes in the IT industry, it is gratifying to observe how much of the book has remained useful. Although there are substantial changes, we have retained the original structure. The first few chapters are about technology; the middle chapters are about using the technology to meet performance, resilience, security, and system management goals; and the last few chapters are about design.

Organization of this book

You can read this book straight through or use it as a reference. This section explains the structure of the book. If you intend to use it for reference and don't intend to read it through first, we encourage you to read at least Chapters 1, 6, 11, and 16.

In addition to introductory and concluding information, the body of the book falls into four main sections:

- Middleware technology alternatives
- IT architecture guidelines and middleware
- Distributed systems technology principles
- Distributed systems implementation design

The thread that holds these topics together is the focus on IT architecture and implementation design.

Introduction

Chapter 1, The Problem, is an introduction to the rest of the book. Using an example, it points out the main concerns of IT architecture.

Middleware technology alternatives

Chapter 2, The Emergence of Standard Middleware, and the following two chapters are a historical survey of middleware technology. Chapter 2 covers remote procedures calls, remote database access, distributed transaction processing, and message-queuing technologies. It ends with a comparison of message queuing and distributed transaction processing.

Chapter 3, Objects, Components, and the Web, is an overview of the concept of object-oriented interfaces and components. The technologies discussed are DCOM, CORBA, COM+, and Enterprise JavaBeans. The impact of the Web is discussed and the chapter ends with an examination of the concept of sessions.

Chapter 4, Web Services, brings the history of middleware up-to-date with an overview of Web services technology, in the context of service and service-oriented architecture concepts.

IT architecture guidelines and middleware

Chapter 5, A Technical Summary of Middleware, discusses middleware as a whole, beginning with the parts that make up middleware, with an emphasis on

Web services. It also looks at vendor architectures, such as Microsoft .NET and Sun's J2EE, and at the issues surrounding middleware interoperability.

Chapter 6, Using Middleware to Build Distributed Applications, takes an application designer's view of middleware. It examines the major questions, what is middleware for and what is the role of middleware in architectural design? This chapter also proposes some basic architectural patterns—middleware bus, hub, and Web services architectures—and discusses the difference between tight and loose coupling of distributed applications.

Distributed systems technology principles

These four chapters examine architecture design for nonfunctional requirements—performance, resiliency, and so on. We believe that the overall architecture of the system can greatly assist in providing good performance, resiliency, and so on. You cannot just rely on faster, more resilient hardware to get you out of any hole you happen to dig yourself into. These chapters explain why and give some solutions to common problems.

Chapter 7, Resiliency, explains the principles of resiliency in distributed systems. There is discussion on how to use backup systems effectively and on how to write applications so as not to lose vital transactions.

Chapter 8, Performance and Scalability, explains the principles of performance and scalability in distributed systems. It describes the crucial importance of looking at the network traffic and the distribution of the data.

Chapter 9, Systems Management, deals with the principles of systems management in distributed systems. It discusses what centralized system management tools can and cannot do for you.

Chapter 10, Security, addresses the principles of security in so far as they impact on architectural design. The emphasis in on access control and where to implement it in the system. Web services security standards are explained, especially the differences between Web services security and earlier forms of security.

Distributed systems implementation design

Chapter 11, Application Design and IT Architecture, is about where architectural design belongs in the context of application design. It proposes an approach based on the idea of levels of design where each level includes some analysis to identify and correct flaws in the design. The following two chapters discuss the top levels in more detail. (Detailed design is well covered in many other books.)

Chapter 12, Implementing Business Processes, describes business processes and why they are important to IT architecture. Four large-scale designs for implementing business processes are discussed: Single Centralized server, Multiple Centralized servers, Pass Through, and Copy out/Copy in.

Chapter 13, Integration Design, discusses integration design at the task or dialogue level. A technique called task/message diagrams for highlighting integration design issues is presented, as are some integration design analysis techniques. The chapter ends with a further discussion of differences between loosely coupled and tightly coupled applications.

Chapter 14, Information Access and Information Accuracy, addresses two information topics that are particularly important for large-scale architectural design. (This book does not try to describe all aspects of design, and database design is well covered in many other books.) The information accuracy section is largely about whether to share data between applications or whether to implement some form of controlled data duplication. Retrofitting a data strategy on existing applications is also covered.

Chapter 15, Changing and Integrating Existing Applications, covers creating a new presentation layer for existing applications, integrating existing applications in a service-oriented architecture, and reducing reliance on batch processing.

Conclusion

Chapter 16, Building an IT Architecture, summarizes the contents of the book and reviews a few case studies.

Boxes

Throughout the book you will see references like this: (see the box entitled A box). They refer to the text set apart in screened boxes with a boldface heading. These boxes contain more information about the topic under discussion, perhaps a subject that is more technical than the body of the text or that is an esoteric area we couldn't resist writing about.

The Web site

This book draws on many sources. One problem with the subject, as with most of IT, is the rapidly changing nature of the technology and the ideas behind it. We therefore decided that we would not put a list of sources and pointers to further information in the book itself, as there would no doubt be much additional material available within a few weeks of publication. Indeed, there would probably be new material at the time of publication!

We decided that the best way to provide readers with sources of information, and further case studies and examples, would be to use the Internet. Therefore, this book has an associated Web site, where readers can find additional material: http://eCommunity.unisys.com/Books/ITArchitectures.

On your first visit, you will be asked to complete a simple registration. You will then be forwarded to the appropriate Web page.

This Web site will be maintained after publication to keep it up to date.

We would appreciate any comments you may have on the value of this Web site.

Acknowledgments

CHRIS: I must first thank Peter Gordon from Addison-Wesley Professional and Dot Malson, then at Unisys, for persuading me to embark on the second edition. Peter Bye was coopted to help. I have known Peter ever since Burroughs merged with Sperry to form Unisys and have often had long interesting discussions about IT architecture, classical music, and cricket. The book is better for Peter's involvement. His enthusiasm for the project and his attention to detail have been particularly appreciated.

Since the first edition of this book, I left Unisys and most of the more recent influences on my thinking have come from outside Unisys. It's hard to pick out individuals, especially as I have been more influenced by disagreement than by agreement.

As the book was being written we had valuable comments from Bob Vavra, Nick Smilonich, and Lynne Thompson from Unisys and from Kirk St. Amant from James Madison University.

We would also like to thank the Addison-Wesley team, in particular Joan Flaherty, who was the copy editor, and Patrick Cash-Peterson, who guided us through the production process.

Finally, I thank my family—Judy, Katie, and Alice—who have no interest at all in the contents of this book but had to put up with my taking time out to write it. Katie and Alice will still tell anyone who asks that the book is incredibly boring and can't possibly be of interest to anybody.

PETER: First, I would like to thank Chris for inviting me to join him as co-author of the second edition. I had been discussing the ideas with him over a long period and reviewed parts of the first edition, so I am delighted to be contributing to the new edition. I join Chris in thanking Addison-Wesley Professional for their help and support and Joan Flaherty for the additional task of having to convert two, different English English styles into American English!

I would like to thank my management, Colin Hicks and Norman Talbot, for their support.

Chris acknowledges many of the people to whom I also owe a debt of gratitude, either specifically in the context of this book or more generally as sources of ideas and discussion over an extended period. In particular, I would like to thank

Rudi Chati, Bob Gambrel, Ron Q. Smith, Bertie van Hinsbergen, and Bob Vavra, all of Unisys, for many hours of discussion and comment. In particular, Bob Vavra has always been an assiduous commenter and sounding board for ideas. I would also like to thank Mike Lawrence, Steve Schuppenhauer, and Curt Wicklund of Unisys for their specific assistance with the AirCore example in Chapter 16.

Finally, I thank my wife, Alison, for her continued support, which has extended to the practical in reviewing parts of what I have written and providing valuable comments on content and style.

1

The Problem

This book makes the link between business problems and IT solutions. It is about turning functional requirements into an implementation design, deciding how to spread the functionality across programs, and choosing the technology to make it happen. But any set of functional requirements is accompanied by what may be called nonfunctional requirements, which have to do with ensuring that the system not only does what is expected, but does it with the required performance, reliability, scalability, manageability, and security. We therefore address these issues as well.

We believe that a key ingredient for success in all of the above is taking an IT architectural approach. What does this mean? Architecture in IT normally means high-level design. There is application architecture, infrastructure architecture (network, system management, etc.), security architecture, and many other architectures. IT architecture is the overarching high-level design of all of these. Our view is that caring about the high-level design, trying to get it right, and ensuring that all the technical aspects (application, infrastructure, security, etc.) fit together are important and are much neglected in IT design.

As an aside, *architecture* is unfortunately one of those words in the ITer's lexicon that has been severely mangled by overuse. *Architecture* sometimes means a generic design pattern, for example, an "*n*-tier architecture." Sometimes it is vaguer than that, like "RISC architecture" (meaning some generic properties like a small instruction set). Then there are the "markitectures" such as IBM's SAA (Systems Application Architecture, which was much promoted around 1990) and Microsoft's DNA (Distributed interNet applications Architecture). When we talk about architecture, we usually mean high-level design. When we mean something vaguer and more generic, we hope that is obvious from the context.

So why is high-level design so important? In a word—integration. Integration turns many small applications into one large application. Whole sections of the IT industry are built on the premise that small applications can be easily assembled into larger ones; it's just a relatively straightforward technology problem. Well, you can create a large boat by lashing together many small boats, and on a flat calm sea it will work just fine. So how about lashing together IT applications?

To answer this question, we use an example of an imaginary but realistic company to illustrate the things many organizations are trying to do.

1.1 Example: Moving to e-business

Our example concerns a company that markets and sells, but does not manufacture, a range of products. It now wants to sell over the Internet. This represents a significant departure because the only Internet presence up to this time is a Web server with static information pages about the company and its products.

The IT applications of the sample company are illustrated in Figure 1-1.

The original idea is to get an expert in Web development, build an interface to the Order Entry system and then launch it on the world. A moment's thought, however, and it's obvious that more is necessary. To start, we need a number of additional interfaces, which are shown in Figure 1-2.

But building the interfaces is only part of the problem. The Web interface has now exposed to the outside world all the inconsistencies and complexities of

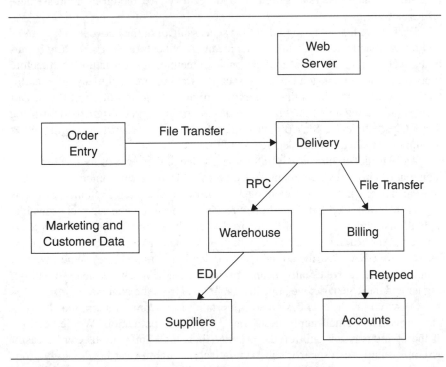

Figure 1-1 IT applications before marketing via the Internet

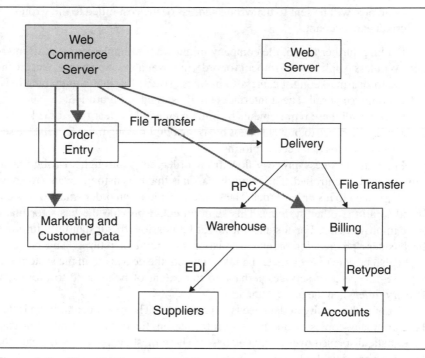

Figure 1-2   IT applications after adding a Web commerce server

the system that until now only the internal users had to contend with. Even if the Web interface is a good one, some fundamental issues go much deeper, for instance:

- When the order information is being sent from the Order Entry to the Delivery system, there comes a time when it has been completed on one system but is still unknown on the other. The order has gone into limbo. The online user is left wondering what happened to it.
- Previously, payment was received after delivery. On the Internet there probably will be a need to take credit card details and process the payment before delivery. This means changes to the Order Entry, Delivery, and Billing applications.
- Product information is dispersed via the Order Entry, Warehouse, Delivery, Billing, Static Web Server, and Marketing applications. There is great potential for inconsistencies of information and therefore a danger that an online customer will order an unavailable product or be unable to order an available product.
- Customer information is dispersed via the Order Entry, Delivery, Billing, and Marketing applications. There is a possibility that the customer's goods

or invoice will be sent to the wrong address or the cost billed to the wrong credit card account.

Looking further ahead, the company might want to implement a WAP interface (Wireless Application Protocol for ordering over a mobile phone), a call center, one-to-one marketing, business to business (B2B) Internet communications, and a commerce portal. These interfaces are illustrated in Figure 1-3.

How can all these requirements be implemented? It's clear that some kind of structure is necessary to prevent chaos breaking out. Looking more closely, we see three generic issues that need exploring.

First, the business process flow from order entry through distribution to billing must be controlled. The primary reason is that the customer wants to know what happened to his or her order. The solution could be an order-tracking system linked to all the other systems. This solution could provide the basis for many other improvements. For instance, it might be possible to substantially improve the business process for order cancellation and product returns. The business might also be able to get a better handle on where the delays are in the system and improve its speed of service, perhaps to the extent of being able to promise a delivery time when the order is made.

Second, the quality of data needs improvement. The fundamental issue is that there are many copies of one piece of information, for instance, product or customer data, dispersed over many databases. There must be a strategy to share the data or control data duplication or both.

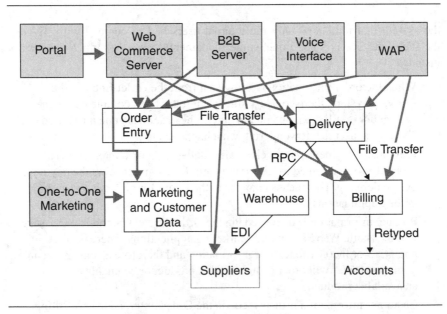

Figure 1-3   IT applications after adding interfaces

Third, an existing application needs to be opened up to additional end-user devices. Figure 1-3 shows the Order Entry application being called from a Web Commerce server, from a WAP server, from the Call Center workstations, and from a B2B server. Not only should the Order Entry application be able to handle all these forms of access, it should also be possible to start entering an order on a Web Commerce server and finish entering the same order over the telephone.

These three challenges—improve cross-functional business process control, provide accurate online information, and support multiple presentation devices—are typical of many IT organizations. IT architecture is a primary tool for solving all these problems.

Of course, these problems are not the only IT management concerns. Three other issues that stand out are:

- Making applications more responsive to change—in other words, building for the future
- Keeping costs down
- Finding skilled staff

IT Architecture has a direct impact on the first of these problems and an indirect but considerable impact on the other two.

So what is IT architecture? Why is it different from what we did before? And how does it help us tackle the issues just outlined?

1.2   What is IT architecture?

IT architecture is a solution to the problem "How do I structure my IT applications to best suit the business?" Technically, an architecture identifies the components of a problem space, shows the relationships among them, and defines the terminology, rules, and constraints on the relationships and components. This notion of architecture has been widely and successfully used, starting in the 1970s with communications architecture, first by vendors such as Burroughs, IBM, and Sperry Univac, and then by various standards bodies.

The main purpose of defining an architecture is to try to impose order on chaos, or potential chaos. Architecture is an essential first step to orderly solutions to problems. It does this by establishing a framework within which to solve both current and anticipated problems. Consider again the sample company. The initial business requirement was to add an Internet sales channel. This could be tackled as a one-off, by installing a Web commerce server of some kind, without too many problems. However, the initial requirement implies a need for a number of other connections, which introduces more complexity. And the requirements are not likely to stop there but will extend to new channels and services. If every requirement is tackled as a one-off, the environment quickly becomes chaotic, as can be

Access Channels

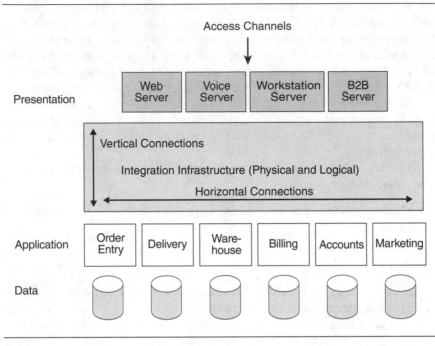

Figure 1-4   Typical IT architecture

seen in Figure 1-3. It shows the connections among the various parts of the system and how functions are implemented—file transfer, Remote Procedure Call (RPC), and electronic data interchange (EDI)—as well as the connections that would be required to introduce various new channels. In many cases, these connections are implemented ad hoc, leading in the extreme (a documented case) to several thousand unique point-to-point connections.

So what does a typical architecture look like? Figure 1-4 shows such an architecture as it might be defined, for example. Although variations are possible, the structure in Figure 1-4 should serve as a useful starting point for discussing the ideas behind architecture.

Figure 1-4 identifies the various components of the architecture. The environment is split into three parts, or tiers: presentation, application, and data. The presentation tier manages the interface with the various connections to the system—the access channels—and is responsible for ensuring that information is delivered in the right way to whatever device is being used. The application tier represents the business logic, operating on the various databases in the data tier.

The key to tying the parts together is in the rectangle in Figure 1-4 labeled Integration Infrastructure. It describes the hardware and software required to make the desired connections—the presentation tier to the applications and the applications to each other. What happens inside the rectangle is crucial. The following paragraphs sketch the main elements, which are discussed in detail throughout the book.

A critical part of the software content is called middleware. The IT industry is a bit of a fashion industry. Some middleware vendors have expunged the word *middleware* from their vocabularies because they think it is associated too closely with now unfashionable approaches. However, we'll carry on using the word because it is helpful.

A simple definition of *middleware* is "software that is necessary in practice to build distributed applications." But why does the application have to be distributed? It does not; the middleware could easily be used to integrate applications in one machine. In fact, it is important that middleware be able to integrate two applications in one machine; first, for testing purposes, and second, because it is sometimes a convenient way to implement an application that might be distributed later. However, we don't want to widen the definition to include every piece of integration software that cannot operate over a network. An important characteristic of middleware software is that it is capable of operating over a network.

Middleware is more complex than most IT people recognize (and certainly a good deal more complex than most middleware vendors would have you believe). For a complete solution, there are at least eight elements to consider, although many of these elements are seen as part of the network infrastructure and not middleware. (It is hard to draw a line between networking software and middleware software, so we will consider it in its totality.) The total picture is illustrated in the Figure 1-5.

In the context of the example, A and B are two elements: either one from the presentation tier and one from the application tier or two applications. For the

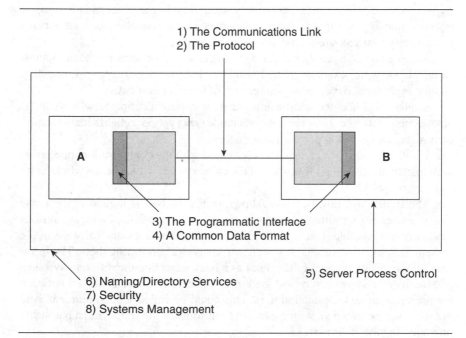

Figure 1-5   Middleware and associated elements

purpose of this discussion, suppose that the two are in different physical systems. The box around both indicates a complete environment. There are eight numbered elements in the diagram, collectively providing the necessary facilities for effective collaboration.

The first two, the *communication link* and the *protocol,* enable A and B to send data to each other through a physical communications link, either local or wide area. There are two sets of protocols: a network protocol to carry data over the link and a middleware protocol to handle the dialog between A and B. The two sets of protocols are complementary and together provide the required degree of reliability, performance, and so on. Different middleware protocols provide a wide variety of connection types, for example, in terms of response time and guarantee of delivery.

The *programmatic interface* and the *common format for data* together define the way that A and B communicate with the middleware. The common format for data describes how the data should be structured so that both A and B understand it, and the programmatic interface specifies the way the data are presented to the middleware.

These four elements together are sufficient to ensure the required communication between A and B. The other four elements are technical and are concerned with ensuring the required degree of performance, reliability, and so on. Insufficient attention to these four items will result in a system that functions but is unsuitable for production.

Server process control concerns the way that the operating system, middleware, and other software manage the scheduling and execution of the applications and is crucial to performance, particularly scalability. For instance, a failure to use resource pooling for threads, database connections, and application components can severely restrict system capacity and performance.

Naming and Directory Services provide the means of locating the communicating elements, for example, for A to find B. These services may be rudimentary or very sophisticated, depending on the size of the environment.

Security is concerned with ensuring that the communication between A and B is safe enough to meet requirements; it includes encryption, reliable identification of systems, and granting permission for access.

Finally, *Systems Management* is concerned with the configuration, operation, fault management, and performance of the environment—it keeps the whole thing working properly.

The Integration Infrastructure (shown in Figure 1-4) is logical in the sense that it makes no specific assumptions about its physical deployment. Various structures are possible. One approach is to deploy the necessary software in the presentation and application tiers, with just a network connecting them. The infrastructure in this case may be thought of as a bus connecting the different systems. Alternatively, a separate physical system or systems could be deployed between the presentation and application tiers. This could be called a hub approach. And the two can be combined, with a hub handling some of the traffic and a bus structure handling the other parts.

A critical point about the architecture discussed here, including its various deployment strategies, is that the access channels are managed in the presentation tier while the business logic resides in the applications. Their role can be viewed as providing *services* to whoever requests them, independently of the characteristics of any ultimate requester. It is up to the presentation tier to manage device dependencies. The Integration Infrastructure ties the presentation and applications together. Applications can also request services of each other, again without regard to characteristics of the requester. An architecture in this form is referred to as a *service-oriented architecture (SOA)*. Web services technology, which is discussed in detail in Chapter 4, is a current approach to standardization of SOA across multiple organizations on the Internet, although it can be used within a single organization as well. We strongly support the concept of service-oriented architecture with or without Web services technology.

The architectural model is a framework for deciding which parts need to communicate with which, how they do it, where any new logic should reside, how existing applications are to be incorporated, how the databases are to be handled, and how to deal with all the various technical issues, such as performance. There are quite a few variations to juggle. It is therefore essential to develop a number of alternatives, based on the patterns just described. Each model has to be matched with the business requirements, used as a framework for analyzing the kind of technology required, and ultimately used to guide the choice of specific technologies and products in those cases where there is a choice.

1.3   Why is this different from what we did before?

If you look at the IT configurations of most organizations today, you will see many standalone applications, each with its own presentation layer, business processing logic, and database. We will call these *silos*. Silo applications are represented in Figure 1-6.

The example company has six silos: Order Entry, Delivery, Warehouse, Billing, Accounts, and Marketing. The problems described in this example are typical: inconsistencies in the data, difficulties in creating a single user view across multiple silos, and the lack of business process integration. Sixty silos, not six, would be more typical of a large commercial organization.

Silo applications were bought or built on behalf of departments in the organization and were tuned to their requirements. Typically, those requirements were to computerize paper-based systems and designed to make that single department's life easier. Now, several reorganizations later, the departmental boundaries are different. What worked then does not work now.

Observe that new tools and clever techniques such as reuse make it easier to develop new silos even faster. In the past we might have developed a few hundred applications using old tools; given the new tools, we could have developed a few

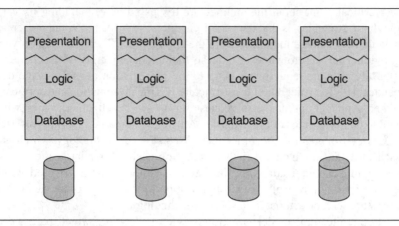

Figure 1-6   Silo applications

thousand more applications. Yes, the business would have more functionality in its IT applications, but the problems of fast response to business change and information accuracy would be just as intractable.

Silo thinking is deeply embedded. Reasons include:

- Departments don't want to lose power.
- Project management wants self-contained projects to control, often for budgetary reasons.
- Development methodologies are silo based.
- There is a fear of large integrated systems.
- There is a fear of changing large existing applications.

Clearly, we think the fears are to some extent unjustified; otherwise, we would not be writing this book. Nonetheless, there is genuine fear and uncertainty.

Organizations are loathe to change their applications and are therefore looking for ways to gain the benefits of integration without the pain of touching the existing code. One alternative we call the "Surround Architecture." It is illustrated in Figure 1-7. The idea is to surround the existing applications with a front end and a back end.

Before going further, let us point out that in some cases this kind of architecture is inevitable. If the application is bought from an external software vendor and can be changed by only the vendor, then this kind of integration may be the only choice. If the application actually resides in a different organization—in other words, the organization is part of an alliance—this kind of architecture may also be inevitable. And silos are a natural consequence of mergers and acquisitions.

But the surround technique should be kept to a minimum. A front-end hub can be easily built to cope with 5 transaction types from one application and 20 from another. But if you try to reshape the interface for 200 transaction types in

one application and 400 in another, the list of rules will balloon to enormous pro-
portions. Furthermore, recovery issues make the front-end hub much, much more
complex. For instance, suppose your new presentation interface takes one input
and processes 10 back-end transactions. What happens if the sixth in the set fails?
You have to programmatically reverse the transactions of the previous five.

Note, it is not that hubs are inherently wrong. The problems arise because the
applications being called by the hubs are not service oriented.

Turning to the back end, we are not against data warehouses, but a data warehouse is much more effective if the data is clean. The notion of taking data from
multiple sources and reconstructing the correct form is unrealistic. How can
you take the name from one database, the address from another, the phone number from a third, and reconstruct a correct record? How do you know John Smith
in one database is J. Smith in another? If there are two phone numbers for a person, which is the correct one? Of course, the last input data is the most likely to
be correct, but how do you know which one is the last by looking at the data?
You can't!

An alternative strategy is to replace silos by packages. Many organizations
have a policy that they will use third-party application packages for IT applications as much as is reasonably possible.

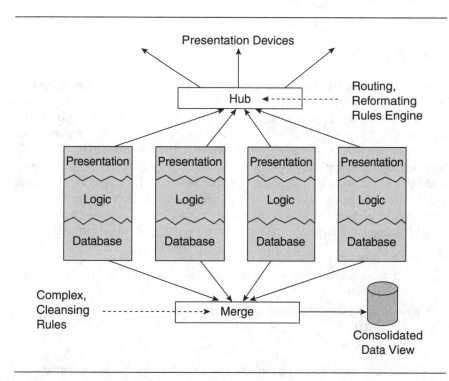

Figure 1-7   Surround architecture

All the problems described with silo applications can exist with applications packages and for exactly the same reason—they are essentially stand-alone silo applications. Fortunately, many more packages these days are taking a service-oriented approach and can be integrated well with the rest of the organization's IT. It is rare that an organization can run using only one package, so some level of integration is likely to be necessary.

Many of the techniques described in this book can be used on packages as well as standalone applications. The big difference is that technology choices are constrained. Since the architecture principles we describe do not rely on a single technology or even a short list of technologies, most of them apply for packages. For instance, in Chapter 14 on information we describe the notion of achieving data accuracy by having a primary database and controlled duplication of the data to one or more secondary databases. This technique can often be implemented with packages. For instance, let us suppose the data in question is the customer information. You might have to write some code to create the flow of messages from the primary database to the package applications, and you might have to write code to process these messages as updates on the package database, but it can be done. It is probably harder to make the package database the primary, but of course, how much harder depends on the package.

1.4   Rewrite or evolve?

Given a decision to take an IT architectural approach, how can it be implemented? There are two options: rewrite or evolve.

It is wise to be cautious about the notion of rewriting simply to keep up with technology. If you had done so in the past, you would have first rewritten the application into DCE, then again into CORBA, and again into J2EE, and would now be looking to implement Web services. One reason that IT architecture got a bad name is because many organizations have had their IT architecture evaluated; the resulting studies are sitting on a shelf gathering dust. A major problem with such exercises has been their recommendation of technology-driven change.

What about occasional rewrites? There are again good reasons to be cautious:

- The existing application works.
- All those concerns about scalability, resiliency, and security may have been solved already.
- Rewriting is expensive and lengthy, during which time the business cannot move forward.
- Rewriting is risky.

In the long term, rewriting can never be a strategy for success; at some stage or other the organization will have to embrace evolutionary change. To understand why, look at the graph in Figure 1-8.

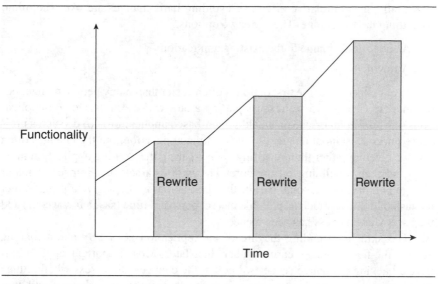

Figure 1-8   The cost of rewriting

Over time, a system's functionality will increase and improve and the rewrite will become larger and longer. The only escape occurs if the rewrite can use new tools that are an order of magnitude better than their predecessors. Suppose ten analysts and programmers have spent 10 years extending an application; they have spent 100 staff years on the application. For the same ten people to rewrite the system in 1 year would require tools that deliver ten times the productivity of their old tools.

So when should you rewrite? First, rewrite when the technology is so old that there are serious issues with support, such as a lack of skills. Second, rewrite when the business functionality has changed so much that it's probably easier to rewrite than to modify.

It seems to be a fact of life that all of an organization's important applications need to change, and often organizations feel held back by their inability to change their key applications fast enough. Changes run along a continuum. At one end of the continuum there are changes with the flow—changes that affect only a small, localized part of the existing application, although they may add a large amount of new code. At the other end of the continuum are changes against the flow—changes that cause widespread alterations to the code. A simple example of changes against the flow is increasing the size of an important field (e.g., product code) where the field length has been hard coded in many places. During the life of an application, changes against the flow are avoided, either by not being done entirely or by developing a new module in the application that overlaps in func-tionality and holds the same data. Sometimes a new silo application is developed.

Eventually, the cumulative effects of avoiding hard changes are overwhelming; something has to be done. There are two options:

1. A substantial change to the existing application

2. A rewrite

In our experience, the first option is often easier than many people realize. For instance, in Chapter 15 we discuss putting a new end-user interface on applications (e.g., a Web interface on an old screen-based application). To do such a project requires substantial changes to the existing application, but the changes often involve deleting rather than rewriting code—paring the existing application to its core and then rebuilding on the core. The way to assess the impact of major change is to try it on a small part of the application. Perhaps give a programmer the task of doing as much as possible in a set period of time (say, a few weeks) and then see what progress has been made.

The skill in extending the life of an application is largely about making against-the-flow changes earlier rather than later. Most important applications have a backlog of change requests. Look at the changes and assess whether they go with the flow or against the flow. Take the against-the-flow changes and consider what needs to be done to the overall architecture of the application to make them possible. Then decide whether you need to rewrite.

If you do need to rewrite and the application is large, the rewrite will have to be done in stages. Often a good preliminary to doing a rewrite is to divide the existing application into chunks that are then replaced one at a time. A huge advantage of such an approach is that if the project is stopped for any reason, you will still have the benefit of a partial rewrite.

What does this have to do with architecture? Against-the-flow changes are often changes to the architectural design. A key characteristic of a good architecture is that it is designed for evolution. Applications today are not islands; they are integrated. Against-the-flow changes can have ramifications across many applications, especially, for instance, changes to the database. We are looking therefore for an overall architecture that is designed for evolution. The architecture itself is not implemented once and then forgotten. It is something that should continually be kept up to date.

From a technical point of view, design for evolution largely means that the parts of the system have clearly defined functionality and work together in the simplest way possible. A good starting point is following the principles of a service-oriented architecture, which is discussed in Chapters 4, 5, and 6. But this is only a start. Often the biggest stumbling block is aligning the services with the business functionality and the business information. We discuss this issue in detail in Chapters 11, 12, and 13.

1.5   Who develops the architecture?

As we work on architectures across the world, we often find that the person nominally in charge of the IT architecture is (a) a technician through and through and (b) somewhat detached from the rest of the organization. Often that person or group is not really concerned with architecture, but rather is the organization's technology leader, the person or group who searches out new stuff and tells the organization what might be interesting. This job is important; it just isn't architecture. Architecture should not be described in a big document that is put on a shelf; It is the high-level design that is developed during a project's inception phase and should be used throughout the project. The architecture is valuable only when real problems are considered.

Trying to implement a design with knowledge only of the technology is fraught with danger. It's a bit like making a decision whether to go to work by train, car, or bicycle without knowing how far you have to travel. If the technologists know little about the application, they will be forced to overengineer, to build a Rolls Royce when a Mini would do.

Trying to design an application without concern about the technology is also dangerous. Suppose you program your application and demonstrate it on a portable PC. It may work wonderfully, but try to scale it to work with 1,000 users and all kinds of problems arise. A specific example may make this clear.

One of us attended a conference on architecture where one of the presentations was a case study of an application to process sales figures from a large number of retail outlets. A core part of the application was a data-collection process, followed by a daily batch run to update the sales database. An architecture was defined and a fashionable run-time environment technology chosen. The development progressed, and a test was set up to run a representative daily run against the database; it took over 24 hours. After a lot of work, the figure was reduced, but it was still not very good. The matter was made worse by the fact that the technology had minimal batch facilities. If sufficient attention had been paid to the technical aspects of the chosen environment at the architectural stage, a lot of the problems could have been avoided.

These points are explored in Chapters 7 through 10 on resiliency, performance, systems management, and security.

So during the inception phase both technologists and application designers are required, as are, for much of the time, representatives of the business. Looking again at the example, notice that a service-oriented architecture solves only one of the problems—the need for channel independence. Another problem was keeping track of a business process, in this case the status of an order. There is no technological solution to this; it is a high-level application design problem. It requires aligning the services with the business processes. Another problem was the quality of the data and the major question of whether we want one or multiple copies of a piece of information. These are application architectural issues and are discussed in detail in Chapter 12 on business processes level design. Essentially the argument is about distributed versus centralized applications and databases. Only by building up a picture of how applications and databases support the business processes can we derive or discern detailed performance and resiliency requirements. This in turn influences technology decisions, which also relate to distribution decisions. For example, a particular configuration may need a high-speed network that is prohibitively expensive. Finding this out early allows the opportunity to choose another architectural design and avoid spending time and money that cannot be recouped.

One of the main aims of this book is to teach the application designers enough about the technology and to teach the technologists enough about application design so that they can all participate in these discussions.

1.6 Summary

In this chapter, we set the scene for the rest of the book by explaining the most important concepts concerning architecture and its implementation.

The key points are:

- When faced with implementing new requirements such as those in the example, avoid one-off solutions. Instead, develop an architecture as a framework for matching requirements against design and discussing technology options. The architecture should address current requirements and anticipate future needs. Expect a number of iterations at this stage before arriving at a workable solution.

- The architecture separates the applications logic from any presentation required by access channels. It is a service-oriented architecture, where the applications deliver services regardless of the requester. This is the goal.

- Follow an evolutionary approach when implementing the architecture, avoiding large-scale rewriting unless there are extremely good reasons (e.g., the business is now run on entirely different lines). Rewriting for the sake of technology alone is a mistake. If a rewrite is absolutely necessary, it is best to do it gradually, introducing new functionality in stages.

- Ensure that the technical issues are addressed up front to avoid developing systems that work functionally but are operationally unusable. Do this by making sure that architects work with people who understand the technology and the applications, and who can refer to and consult those who understand the business.

- Finally, do not finish the architecture and then leave it on a shelf to gather dust. It should be regarded as a living document, updated and revised as necessary so that it continues to be useful.

2

The Emergence of
Standard Middleware

The aim of this chapter and the next two is to give a short introduction to the range of middleware technologies from a historical point of view and afford an insight into some of the factors that have been driving the industry. This background knowledge is vital for any implementation design that uses middleware, which today is practically all of them.

So far as we know, the first use of the word *middleware* was around 1970, but it was an isolated case. In the early days there didn't appear to be a need for middleware. (In the 1970s many organizations didn't see much point in database systems either.) The awareness came gradually, and we will review how this came about. The following sections look at various technologies, all of which are still in use in various production systems around the world.

2.1 Early days

Distributed systems have been with us for a long time. Networking originally meant "dumb" green-screen terminals attached to mainframes; but it wasn't very long before, instead of a terminal at the end of a line, organizations started putting computers there, thus creating a network of computers. Figure 2-1 illustrates the difference between attaching a terminal and talking to a computer.

The first distributed systems were implemented by large organizations and by academia. The U.S. Department of Defense's Advanced Research Projects Agency (DARPA) built a four-node network, called ARPANET, in 1969. By 1972, ARPANET had grown to include approximately 50 computers (mainly universities and research sites).

An early need for a kind of middleware was for communication between companies in the same industry. Two outstanding examples of this are the financial

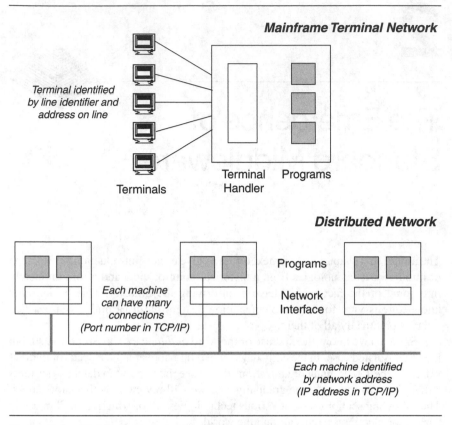

Figure 2-1   Distributed networking. **A.** Terminals linked to a mainframe and **B.** Computer workstations linked to one another.

community for interbank money transfers and the airline industry for handling functions such as reservations and check-in that involve more than one airline (or more precisely, more than one system). The Society for Worldwide Interbank Financial Telecommunication (SWIFT) was established to provide the interbank requirements; it defined the standards and provided a network to perform the transfers. The International Air Transport Association (IATA), an organization representing the airline industry, defined a number of standards. Another airline industry group, the Société Internationale de Télécommunications Aeronautiques (SITA), also defined standards and, in addition, provided a global network for airline use. Airlines in particular were pioneers, largely out of necessity: They needed the capabilities, and as no suitable open standards were available, they defined their own.

During the 1970s most major IT hardware vendors came out with "network architectures" that supported large networks of distributed computers. There was IBM's System Network Architecture (SNA), Sperry's Distributed Communication

Architecture (DCA), Burroughs' Network Architecture (BNA), and DEC's Distributed Network Architecture (DNA). These products provide facilities for programs to send and receive messages, and a number of basic services:

- File transfer
- Remote printing
- Terminal transfer (logging on to any machine in the network)
- Remote file access

The vendors also developed some distributed applications, the most prevalent of which by far was e-mail.

In organizations that bought all their IT from a single vendor, such network architectures worked fine; but for organizations who used or wanted to use multiple IT vendors, life was difficult. Thus the open systems movement arose.

The key idea of the open systems movement, then as now, is that forcing all IT vendors to implement one standard will create competition and drive down prices. At the lower levels of networking, this always worked well, perhaps because the telephone companies were involved and they have a history of developing international standards. (The telephone companies at the time were mostly national monopolies, so standards didn't hold the same threat to them as they did for IT vendors.) For instance, standards were developed for electrical interfaces (e.g., RS232) and for networking protocols (e.g., X.25). The chief hope of the early open systems movement was to replicate this success and widen it to include all distributed computing by using the International Organization for Standardization (ISO) as the standards authority. (We did get that right, by the way. ISO does not stand for International Standards Organization, and it's not IOS.) The fruit of this work was the Open Systems Interconnection (OSI) series of standards. The most influential of these standards was the OSI Basic Reference Model—the famous seven-layered model. The first draft of this standard came out in December 1980, but it was several more years until the standard was formally ratified. Since then, numerous other standards have fleshed out the different parts of the OSI seven-layer model. The seven-layer model itself isn't so much a standard as it is a framework in which standards can be placed. Figure 2-2 shows the model.

It was apparent early on that there were problems with the OSI approach. The most obvious problem at first was simply that the standardization process was too slow. Proprietary products were clearly way ahead of standard products and, the longer the delay, the more code would need to be converted later. The next problem was that the standards were so complex. This is a common failing of standards organizations. Standards committees have a major problem with achieving consensus and a minor problem with the cost of implementation. The simplest way to achieve a consensus is to add every sound idea. The OSI seven-layer model probably exacerbated the situation because each committee had to look at a tiny slice of the whole problem (e.g., one layer) and it was hard for them to make compromises on technology. However, the problem is by no means unique to networking standardization.

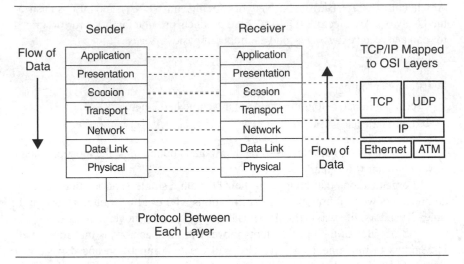

Figure 2-2   The OSI seven-layer model

The ISO's System Query Language (SQL) standardization effort has also suffered from runaway function creep—a function avalanche perhaps! A clear example of an OSI standard that suffered from all the problems of complexity and lateness was the OSI virtual terminal standard, which was tackling one of the simpler and, at the time, one of the most important requirements—connecting a terminal to an application.

So the industry turned away from OSI and started looking for alternatives. Its attention turned to UNIX and suddenly everyone was talking about "open systems," a new marketing buzzword for UNIX-like operating systems. These products were meant to deliver cheap computing that was driven by portable applications and a vigorous software market.

Although UNIX originated in AT&T, it was extensively used and developed in universities. These organizations, when viewed as IT shops, have several interesting characteristics. First, they are very cost conscious—so UNIX was cheap. Second, they have a nearly unlimited supply of clever people. UNIX then required lots of clever people to keep it going, and these clever people were quite prepared to fix the operating system. Consequently, UNIX developed into many versions, one of the most well-known being the Berkeley version. Third, if the system goes down, the only people complaining are students, so UNIX went down, often. Of course, given time, the IT vendors could fix all the negative points but, being IT vendors, they all fixed them in different ways.

But this cloud had a silver lining. Along with UNIX came, not SNA or OSI, but TCP/IP. The Transmission Control Protocol/Internet Protocol (TCP/IP) was developed in the mid-1970s for the U.S. military and was deployed in 1983 in ARPANET. The military influence (and money) was key to TCP/IP's success. It has been said that the resilience and flexibility of TCP/IP arose largely because of a requirement to survive nuclear war! In 1983, APRANET split into military and nonmilitary networks, the nonmilitary network in the first instance being academic and research establishments where UNIX reigned supreme. Over the years ARPANET evolved into the worldwide Internet and the explosion of Internet (largely caused by the Web) has made TCP/IP the dominant networking standard. TCP/IP and the Web are examples of what standardization can do. But it will only do it if the technology works well and is relatively easy to use.

TCP/IP is used as a name for a set of standards, even though IP and TCP are just two of them. Internet Protocol (IP) is the network standard. It ensures that messages can be sent from machine to machine. Transmission Control Protocol (TCP) is a connection-oriented transport standard for program-to-program communication over IP. If you want to write a program to use TCP/IP directly, you use Sockets in UNIX and Winsock on Windows. A host of other standards are normally bracketed with TCP/IP such as Telnet (terminal interface), Simple Mail Transfer Protocol for e-mail (SMTP), File Transfer Protocol (FTP), and numerous lower-level standards for network control. Today, TCP/IP is the accepted network standard protocol set, regardless of the operating system and other technology in use.

So far, we have been largely discussing networking evolution. What about building applications over the network, which is, after all, the concern of middleware? Since every network architecture provides application programming interfaces (APIs) for sending messages over the network and a few basic networking services, is anything more necessary? In the early days, the need was not obvious. But when organizations started building distributed systems, they found that they had to build their own middleware. There were four reasons: performance, control, data integrity, and ease of use. It turned out that "rolling your own" was a huge undertaking; but few of the organizations that did it, regret it. It gave them competitive advantage, allowing them to integrate new applications with the existing code relatively quickly. It gave them the flexibility to change the network technology since the applications could remain unchanged. It took a long time for the middleware supplied by outside vendors to catch up with the power of some of these in-house developments. The number one priority of a large organization betting its business on distributed computing is data integrity, closely followed by performance. Not until the middleware software vendors released products with equal data integrity and performance could migration be contemplated, and this has taken time.

2.2 Preliminaries

It will save time in our discussion of middleware if we describe a few concepts now.
First, middleware should provide the following:

- Ease of use (compared to writing it yourself using a low-level API-like sockets)

- Location transparency—the applications should not have to know the network and application address of their opposite number. It should be possible to move an application to a machine with a different network address without recompilation.
- Message delivery integrity—messages should not be lost or duplicated.
- Message format integrity—messages should not be corrupted.
- Language transparency—a program using the middleware should be able to communicate with another program written in a different language. If one program is rewritten in a different language, all other programs should be unaffected.

Message integrity is usually supplied by the network software, that is, by TCP/IP. All of the middleware we describe has location transparency and all, except some Java technology, has language transparency. Ease of use is usually provided by taking a program-to-program feature used within a machine (such as procedure calls to a library or calls to a database) and providing a similar feature that works over a network.

Most of the middleware technology we will describe is *client/server* middleware. This means that one side (the server) provides a service for the other side (the client). If the client does not call the server, the server does not send unsolicited messages to the client. You can think of the client as the program that gives the orders and the server as the program that obeys them. Do not assume that a client always runs on a workstation. Web servers are often clients to back-end servers. The concept of client/server has proved to be a straightforward and simple idea that is enormously useful.

Since during this book we discuss data integrity, we need to ensure some consistency in the database terms we use. To keep it simple, we stick to the terminology of relational databases. *Relational* databases are made up of *tables,* and tables have *columns* and *rows.* A row has *attributes,* or put another way, an attribute is the intersection of a row and a column. A row must be unique, that is, distinguishable from every other row in the table. One of the attributes that make the row unique is the called the *primary key. SQL* is a relational database language for retrieving and updating the database. The structure of the database (table name and layout) is called the database's *schema.* SQL also has commands to change the database schema.

The final preliminary is threads. When a program is run, the operating system starts a *process.* The process has a memory environment (for mapping virtual memory to physical memory) and one or more threads. A *thread* has what is required for the run-time execution of code; it contains information like the position in the code file of the next executable instruction and the procedure call stack (to return to the right place when the procedure is finished). *Multithreading* is running a process that has more than one thread, which makes it possible for more than one processor to work on a single process. Multithreading is useful even when there is only one physical processor because multithreading allows one thread to keep going when the other thread is blocked. (A *blocked thread* is one waiting for something to happen, such as an input/output (IO) sequence to complete.)

2.3   Remote procedure calls

Procedure calls are a major feature of most programming languages. If you need to access a service (e.g., a database or an operating system function) on a machine, you call a procedure. It seems logical therefore that the way to access a remote service should be through Remote Procedure Calls (RPCs), the idea being that the syntax in the client (the caller) and the server (the called) programs remain the same, just as if they were on the same machine.

The best-known RPC mechanisms are Open Network Computing (ONC) from Sun Microsystems and Distributed Computing Environment (DCE) from the Open Software Foundation (OSF). (OSF is the group formed in the late 1980s by IBM, Hewlett-Packard, and DEC, as it then was. Its rationale was to be an alternative to AT&T, who owned the UNIX brand name and had formed a group—which included Unisys—called UNIX International to rally around its brand. OSF was the first of the great "anti-something" alliances that have been such a dominant feature of middleware history.) The basic idea in both ONC and DCE is the same. Figure 2-3 illustrates the RPC architecture.

If you are writing in C and you want to call a procedure in another module, you "include" a "header file" in your program that contains the module's callable procedure declarations—that is, the procedure names and the parameters but not the logic. For RPCs, instead of writing a header file, you write an Interface Definition Language (IDL) file. Syntactically, an IDL file is very similar to a header file but it does more. The IDL generates client *stubs* and server *skeletons,* which are small chunks of C code that are compiled and linked to the client and server programs. The purpose of the stub is to convert parameters into a string of bits and send the message over the network. The skeleton takes the message, converts it back into parameters, and calls the server. The process of converting parameters to message is called *marshalling* and is illustrated in Figure 2-4.

The advantage of marshalling is that it handles differing data formats. For instance, if the client uses 32-bit big-endian integers and the server uses 64-bit small-endian integers, the marshalling software does the translation. (Big-endian format integers have bits in the reverse order of small-endian format integers.)

As an aside, it looks like the word *marshalling* is going to die and be replaced by the word *serialization.* Serialization has more of a feel of taking an object and converting it into a message for storing on disk or sending over the network, but it is also used in the context of converting parameters to messages.

The problem with RPCs is multithreading. A client program is blocked when it is calling a remote procedure—just as it would be calling a local procedure. If

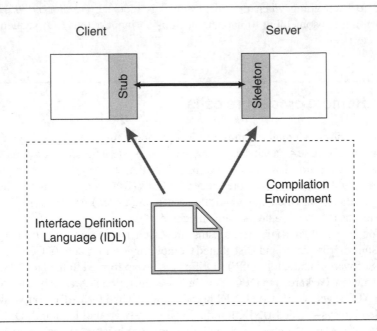

Figure 2-3   Remote procedure call

the message is lost in the network, if the server is slow, or if the server stops while processing the request, the client is left waiting. The socially acceptable approach is to have the client program reading from the keyboard or mouse while asking the server for data, but the only way to write this code is to use two threads—one

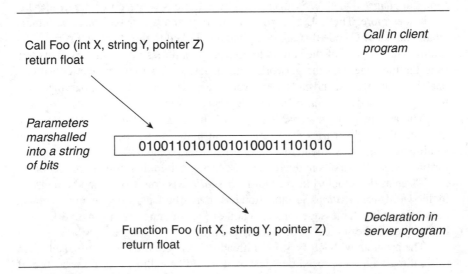

Figure 2-4   Marshalling

thread for processing the remote procedure call and the other thread for processing the user input.

There are similar concerns at the server end. Simple RPC requires a separate server thread for every client connection. (A more sophisticated approach would be to have a pool of server threads and to reuse threads as needed, but this takes us into the realms of transaction monitors, which we discuss later.) Thus, for 1,000 clients, there must be 1,000 threads. If the server threads need to share resources, the programmer must use locks, semaphores, or events to avoid synchronization problems.

Experienced programmers avoid writing multithreading programs. The problems are not in understanding the syntax or the concepts, but in testing and finding the bugs. Every time a multithreading program is run, the timings are a bit different and the actions on the threads are processed in a slightly different order. Bugs that depend on the order of processing are extremely hard to find. It is nearly impossible to design tests that give you the confidence that most such order-dependent bugs will be found.

RPC software dates back to the middle 1980s. RPCs were central to the thinking of the Open Software Foundation. In their DCE architecture they proposed that every other distributed service (e.g., remote file access, e-mail) use RPCs instead of sending messages directly over the network. This notion of using RPCs everywhere is no longer widely held. However, the notions of marshalling and IDL have been brought forward to later technologies.

2.4 Remote database access

Remote database access provides the ability to read or write to a database that is physically on a different machine from the client program. There are two approaches to the programmatic interface. One corresponds to dynamic SQL. SQL text is passed from client to server. The other approach is to disguise the remote database access underneath the normal database interface. The database schema indicates that certain tables reside on a remote machine. The database is used by programs in the normal way, just as if the database tables were local (except for performance and maybe additional possible error messages).

Remote database access imposes a large overhead on the network to do the simplest of commands. (See the box entitled "SQL parsing" at the end of this chapter.) It is not a good solution for transaction processing. In fact, this technology was largely responsible for the bad name of first-generation client/server applications. Most database vendors support a feature called stored procedures. You can use remote database access technology to call stored procedures. This turns remote database access into a form of RPC, but with two notable differences:

- It is a run-time, not a compile-time, interface. There is no IDL or equivalent.
- The procedure itself is typically written in a proprietary language, although many database vendors allow stored procedures to be written in Java.

In spite of using an interpreted language, remote database access calling stored procedures can be many times faster than a similar application that uses remote database access calling other SQL commands.

On the other hand, for ad hoc queries, remote database access technology is ideal. Compare it with trying to do the same job by using RPCs. Sending the SQL command would be easy; it's just text. But writing the code to get data back when it can be any number of rows, any number of fields per row, and any data type for each field would be a complex undertaking.

There are many different technologies for remote database access. Microsoft Corporation has at one time or another sold ODBC (Open Database Connectivity), OLE DB (Object Linking and Embedding DataBase), ADO (Active Data Objects), and most recently ADO.NET. In the Java environment are JDBC (Java Database Connectivity) and JDO (Java Data Objects). Oracle has Oracle Generic Connectivity and Oracle Transparent Gateway. IBM has DRDA (Distributed Relational Database Architecture). There is even an ISO standard for remote database access, although it is not widely implemented. Why so many products? It is partly because every database vendor would much rather you use its product as the integration engine, that is, have you go through its product to get to other vendors' databases. The situation is not as bad as it sounds because almost every database supports ODBC and JDBC.

2.5   Distributed transaction processing

In the olden days, transactions were initiated when someone pressed the transmit key on a green-screen terminal. At the mainframe end, a transaction monitor, such as IBM's CICS or Unisys's TIP and COMS, handled the input. But what do you do if you want to update more than one database in one transaction? What if the databases are on different machines? Distributed transaction processing was developed to solve these problems.

By way of a quick review, a *transaction* is a unit of work that updates a database (and/or maybe other resources). Transactions are either completed (the technical term is *committed*) or are completely undone. For instance, a transaction for taking money out of your account may include writing a record of the debit, updating the account balance, and updating the bank teller record; either all of these updates are done or the transaction in its entirety is cancelled.

Transactions are important because organizational tasks are transactional. If an end user submits an order form, he or she will be distressed if the system actually submits only half the order lines. When customers put money in a bank, the bank must both record the credit and the change account balance, not one without the other. From an IT perspective, the business moves forward in transactional steps. Note that this is the business perspective, not the customer's perspective. For instance, when a customer gives a bank a check to pay a bill, it seems to him to be one atomic action. But for the bank, it is complex business processing to ensure the payment is made, and several of those steps are IT transactions. If the process fails when some of the IT transactions are finished, one or more reversal transactions are processed (which you might see in your next statement). From the IT point of view, the original debit and the reversal are two different atomic transactions, each with a number of database update operations.

Transactions are characterized as conforming to the *ACID* properties:

A is for atomic; the transaction is never half done. If there is any error, it is completely undone.

C is for consistent; the transaction changes the database from one consistent state to another consistent state. Consistency here means that database data integrity constraints hold true. In other words, the database need not be consistent within the transaction, but by the time it is finished it must be. Database integrity includes not only explicit data integrity (e.g., "Product codes must be between 8 and 10 digits long") but also internal integrity constraints (e.g., "All index entries must point at valid records").

I is for isolation; data updates within a transaction are not visible to other transactions until the transaction is completed. An implication of isolation is that the transactions that touch the same data are "serializable." This means that from the end user's perspective, it is as if they are done one at a time in sequence rather than simultaneously in parallel.

D is for durable; when a transaction is done, it really is done and the updates do not at some time in the future, under an unusual set of circumstances, disappear.

Distributed transaction processing is about having more than one database participate in one transaction. It requires a protocol like the *two-phase commit* protocol to ensure the two or more databases cooperate to maintain the ACID properties. (The details of this protocol are described in a box in Chapter 7.)

Interestingly, at the time the protocol was developed (in the early 1980s), people envisaged a fully distributed database that would seem to the programmer to be one database. What killed that idea were the horrendous performance and resiliency implications of extensive distribution (which we describe in Chapters 7 and 8). Distributed database features are implemented in many databases in the sense that you can define an SQL table on one system and have it actually be implemented by remote access to a table on a different database. Products were also developed (like EDA/SQL from Information Builders, Inc.) that specialized in creating a unified database view of many databases from many vendors. In practice this technology is excellent for doing reports and decision-support queries but terrible for building large-scale enterprise transaction processing systems.

Figure 2-5 is a simple example of distributed transaction processing.

The steps of distributed transaction processing are as follows:

1. The client first tells the middleware that a transaction is beginning.

2. The client then calls server A.

3. Server A updates the database.

4. The client calls server B.

5. Server B updates its database.

6. The client tells the middleware that the transaction has now ended.

If the updates to the second database failed (point 5), then the updates to the first (point 3) are rolled back. To maintain the transaction's ACID properties (or more precisely the I—isolation—property), all locks acquired by the database software cannot be released until the end of the transaction (point 6).

There are an infinite number of variations. Instead of updating a database on a remote system, you can update a local database. Any number of databases can be updated. At point (3) or (5) the server update code could act like a client to a further system. Subtransactions could also be processed in parallel instead of in series. But, whatever the variation, at the end there must be a two-phase commit to complete all subtransactions as if they are one transaction.

Looking more closely at the middleware, you will see that there are at least two protocols. One is between the middleware and the database system and the other is from the client to the server.

Distributed transaction processing was standardized by the X/Open consortium, in the form of the X/Open DTP model (X/Open subsequently merged with the Open Software Foundation to form the Open Group, whose Web address is www.opengroup.org. We will therefore refer to the standard throughout this book as Open Group DTP.) Open Group's standard protocol between the middleware and the database is called the XA protocol. (See the box entitled "Open Group DTP" at the end of this chapter.) Thus, if you see that a database is "XA compliant," it means

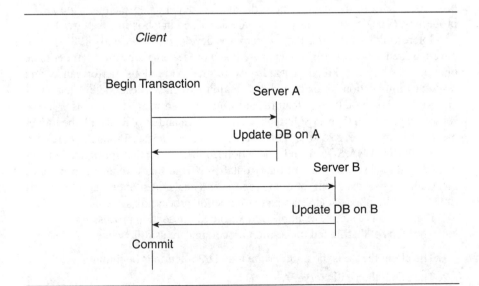

Figure 2-5   Example of distributed transaction processing

that it can cooperate with Open Group DTP middleware in a two-phase commit protocol. All major database products are XA compliant.

Efforts to standardize the client/server protocol were less successful, resulting in three variations. From IBM came a protocol based on SNA LU6.2 (strictly speaking this is a peer-to-peer, not a client/server, protocol). From Encina (which was subsequently taken over by IBM) came a protocol based on DCE's remote procedure calls. From Tuxedo (originally developed by AT&T, the product now belongs to BEA Systems, Inc.) came the XATMI protocol. (The Tuxedo ATMI protocol is slightly different from XATMI; it has some additional features.) In theory, you can mix and match protocols, but most implementations do not allow it. BEA does, however, have an eLink SNA product that makes it possible to call an IBM CICS transaction through LU6.2 as part of a Tuxedo distributed transaction.

These protocols are very different. LU6.2 is a peer-to-peer protocol with no marshalling or equivalent; in other words, the message is just a string of bits. Encina is an RPC, which implies parameter marshalling as previously described and threads are blocked during a call. Tuxedo has its own ways of defining the format of the message, including FML, which defines fields as identifier/value pairs. Tuxedo supports RPC-like calls and unblocked calls (which it calls asynchronous calls) where the client sends a message to the server, goes off and does something else, and then gets back to see if the server has sent a reply.

To confuse matters further, Tuxedo and Encina were developed as transaction monitors as well as transaction managers. A transaction monitor is software for controlling the transaction server. We noted the disadvantages of having one server thread per client in the section on RPCs. A major role of the transaction monitor is to alleviate this problem by having a pool of threads and allocating them as needed to incoming transactions. Sharing resources this way has a startling effect on performance, and many of the transaction benchmarks on UNIX have used Tuxedo for precisely this reason. Transaction monitors have many additional tasks, for instance, in systems management, they may implement transaction security and route by message content. Since transaction monitors are a feature of mainframe systems, mainframe transactions can often be incorporated into a managed distributed transaction without significant change. There may be difficulties such as old screen formatting and menu-handling code, subjects we explore in Chapter 15.

2.6   Message queuing

So far the middleware we have discussed has been about program-to-program communication or program-to-database communication. Message queuing is program-to-message queue.

You can think of a message queue as a very fast mailbox since you can put a message in the box without the recipient's being active. This is in contrast to RPC or distributed transaction processing, which is more like a telephone conversation; if the recipient isn't there, there is no conversation. Figure 2-6 gives you the general idea.

To put a message into the queue, a program does a Put; and to take a message out of the queue, the program does a Get. The middleware does the transfer of messages from queue to queue. It ensures that, whatever happens to the network, the message arrives eventually and, moreover, only one copy of the message is placed in the destination queue. Superficially this looks similar to reading from and writing to a TCP/IP socket, but there are several key differences:

- Queues have names.
- The queues are independent of program; thus, many programs can do Puts and many can do Gets on the same queue. A program can access multiple queues, for instance, doing Puts to one and Gets from another.
- If the network goes down, the messages can wait in the queue until the network comes up again.
- The queues can be put on disk so that if the system goes down, the queue is not lost.
- The queue can be a resource manager and cooperate with a transaction manager. This means that if the message is put in a queue during a transaction and the transaction is later aborted, then not only is the database rolled back, but the message is taken out of the queue and not sent.
- Some message queue systems can cross networks of different types, for instance, to send messages over an SNA leg and then a TCP/IP leg.

It's a powerful and simple idea. It is also efficient and has been used for applications that require sub-second response times. The best-known message queue software is probably MQSeries (now called WebSphere MQ) from IBM. A well-known alternative is MSMQ from Microsoft.

A disadvantage of message queuing is that there is no IDL and no marshalling; the message is a string of bits, and it is up to you to ensure that the sender

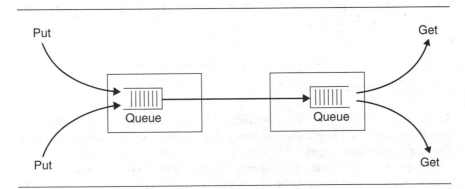

Figure 2-6   Message queuing

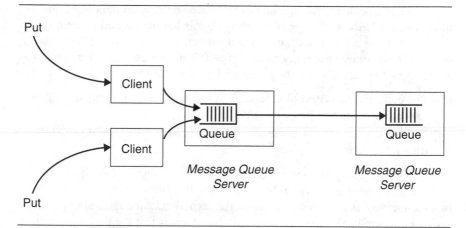

Figure 2-7   Client/server message queuing

and the receiver know the message layout. MQSeries will do character set translation, so if you are sending messages between different platforms, it is simplest to
put everything into characters. This lack of an IDL, however, has created an add-
on market in message reformatting tools.

Message queuing is peer-to-peer middleware rather than client/server middleware because a queue manager can hold many queues, some of which are sending
queues and some of which are receiving queues. However, you will hear people
talk about clients and servers with message queuing. What are they talking about?

Figure 2-7 illustrates message queue clients. A message queue server physically stores the queue. The client does Puts and Gets and an RPC-like protocol to
transfer the messages to the server, which does the real Puts and Gets on the queue.

Of course, some of the advantages of message queuing are lost for the client. If
the network is down between the client and the server, messages cannot be queued.

Message queuing products may also have lightweight versions, targeted at
mobile workers using portable PCs or smaller devices. The idea is that when a
mobile worker has time to sit still, he or she can log into the corporate systems and
the messages in the queues will be exchanged.

2.7   Message queuing versus distributed
transaction processing

Advocates of message queuing, especially of MQSeries, have claimed that a complete distributed transaction processing environment can be built using it. Similarly, supporters of distributed transaction processing technology of one form or
another have made the same claim. Since the technologies are so different, how is
this possible? Let us look at an example.

Suppose a person is moving money from account A to account B. Figure 2-8 illustrates a solution to this problem using distributed transaction processing. In this solution, the debit on account A and the credit on account B are both done in one distributed transaction. Any failure anywhere aborts the whole transaction—as you would expect. The disadvantages of this solution are:

- The performance is degraded because of the overhead of sending additional messages for the two-phase commit.
- If either system is down or the network between the systems is down, the transaction cannot take place.

Message queuing can solve both these problems. Figure 2-9 illustrates the solution using message queuing. Note the dotted line from the disk. This indicates that the message is not allowed to reach the second machine until the first transaction has committed. The reason for this constraint is that the message queuing software does not know the first transaction won't abort until the commit is successful. If there were an abort, the message would not be sent (strictly speaking, this can be controlled by options—not all queues need to be transaction synchronized); therefore, it cannot send the message until it knows there won't be an abort.

But this scheme has a fatal flaw: If the destination transaction fails, money is taken out of one account and disappears. In the jargon of transactions, this schema fails the A in ACID—it is not atomic; part of it can be done.

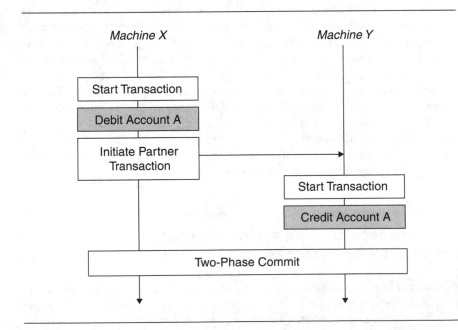

Figure 2-8　Debit/credit transaction using distributed transaction processing

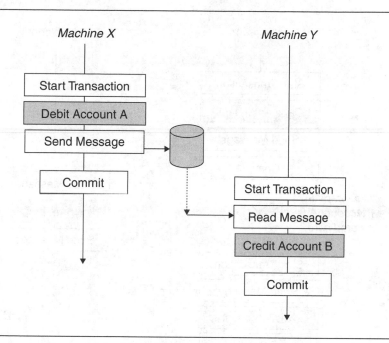

Figure 2-9   Debit/credit transaction using message queuing

The solution is to have a reversal transaction; the bank can reverse the failed debit transaction by having a credit transaction for the same amount. Figure 2-10 illustrates this scenario.

But this fails if account A is deleted before the reversal takes effect. In the jargon of transactions, this scheme fails the I in ACID—it is not isolated; other transactions can get in the way and mess it up. The reason for the debit and the account deletion could be to close account A. In this system, the account number for B could be entered by mistake. It is not going to happen very often, but it could, and must therefore be anticipated.

In a real business situation, many organizations will throw up their hands and say, we will wait for a complaint and do a manual adjustment. Airlines are a case in point. If an airline system loses a reservation, or the information about the reservation has not been transferred to the check-in system for some reason, this will be detected when the passenger attempts to check in. All airlines have procedures to handle this kind of problem since there are various other reasons why a passenger may not be able check in and board. Examples include overbooking and cancelled flights, which are far more likely than the loss of a record somewhere. It is therefore not worthwhile to implement complex software processes to guarantee no loss of records.

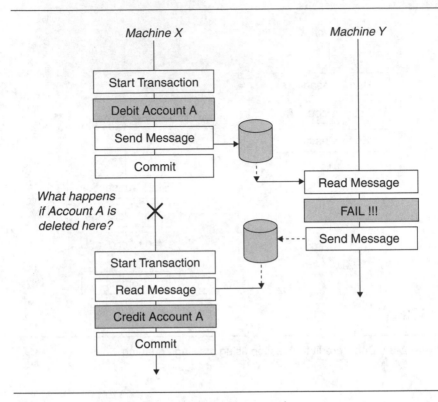

Figure 2-10   Debit/credit transaction with reversal

Often an application programming solution exists at the cost of additional complexity. In our example it is possible to anticipate the problem and ensure that the accounts are not deleted until all monetary flows have been completed. This results in there being an account status "in the process of being deleted," which is neither open nor closed.

Thus the choice between what seems to be esoteric technologies is actually a business issue. In fact, it has to be. Transactions are the steps that business processes take. If someone changes one step into two smaller steps, or adds or removes a step, they change the business process. This is a point we will return to again and again.

2.8   What happened to all this technology?

With remote database access, remote procedure calls, distributed transaction processing, and message queuing you have a flexible set of middleware that can do most of what you need to build a successful distributed application. All of the technologies just described are being widely used and most are being actively developed and promoted by their respective vendors. The market for middleware is still wide open. Many organizations haven't really started on the middleware trail and, as noted in the first section, some large organizations have developed their own middleware. Both organizational situations are candidates for the middleware technologies described in this chapter. In short, none of this technology is going to die and much has great potential to grow.

Yet most pundits would claim that when we build distributed applications in the twenty-first century, we will not be using this technology. Why? The main answer is that new middleware technologies emerge; two examples are component middleware and Web services. It is generally believed that these technologies will replace RPCs and all the flavors of distributed transaction middleware. Component middleware and Web services are discussed in the next two chapters.

Message queuing will continue to be used, as it provides functions essential to satisfy some business requirements, for example, guaranteed delivery and asynchronous communication between systems. Message queuing is fully compatible with both component middleware and Web services, and is included within standards such as J2EE.

It looks like remote database access will always have a niche. In some ways it will be less attractive than it used to be because database replication technology will develop and take away some of the tasks currently undertaken by remote database access. But new standards for remote database access will probably arise and existing ones will be extended.

In summary, although we may not see these specific technologies, for the foreseeable future we will see technologies of these three types—real-time transaction-oriented middleware, message queuing, and remote database access—playing a large part in our middleware discussions.

2.9 Summary

This chapter describes the early days of distributed computing and the technologies RPC, remote database access, distributed transaction processing, and message queuing. It also compares distributed transaction processing and message queuing.

Key points to remember:

- You can build distributed applications without middleware. There is just a lot of work to do.
- There are broad categories of middleware: real-time, message queuing, and remote database access. Each category has a niche where it excels. The real-time category is good for quick request/response interaction with another application. Remote database access can have poor performance for

production transaction processing but is excellent for processing ad hoc queries on remote databases. Message queuing excels at the secure delivery of messages when the sender is not interested in an immediate response.

- The most variation lies in the real-time category where there are RPCs and various forms of distributed transaction processing.
- RPC technology makes a remote procedure syntactically the same for the programmer as a local procedure call. This is an important idea that was used in later technologies. The disadvantage is that the caller is blocked while waiting for the server to respond; this can be alleviated by multithreading. Also, if many clients are attached to one server, there can be large overhead, especially if the server is accessing a database.
- Alternatives to RPC discussed in this chapter are Tuxedo and IBM LU6.2, both of which support distributed transaction processing. Distributed transaction processing middleware can synchronize transactions in multiple databases across the network.
- Reading and writing messages queues can be synchronized with database transactions, making it possible to build systems with good levels of message integrity. Message queuing middleware does not synchronize database transactions, but you can often implement similar levels of consistency using reversal transactions.
- The transactions ACID (atomicity, consistency, isolation, and durability) properties are important for building applications with high integrity.
- The emergence of standards in middleware has been long and faltering. But middleware standards are so important that there are always new attempts.

SQL parsing

To understand the strengths and weaknesses of remote database access technology, let us look into how an SQL statement is processed. There are two steps: parsing and execution, which are illustrated in Figure 2-11.

The parsing step turns the SQL command into a query plan that defines which tables are accessed using which indexes, filtered by which expression, and using which sorts. The SQL text itself also defines the output from the query—number of columns in the table and the type and size of each field. When the query is executed, additional data may be input through parameters; for instance, if the query is an inquiry on a bank account, the account number may be input as a parameter. Again the number and nature of the parameters is defined in the SQL text. Unlike RPCs, where for one input there is one output, the output can be any length; one query can result in a million rows of output.

For a simple database application, remote database access technology incurs an enormous amount of work in comparison with other technologies, especially distributed transaction processing. There are optimizations. Since the host software can remember the query plan, the parse step can be done once and the execution step done many times. If the query is a call to a stored procedure, then remote database access can be very efficient because the complete query plan for the stored procedure already exists.

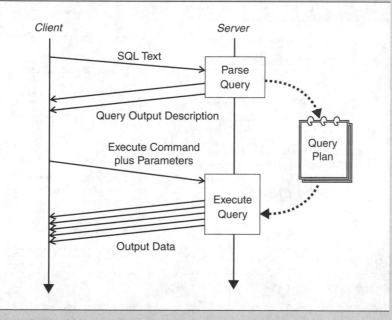

Figure 2-11   Message flow via remote database access

Open Group DTP

The Open Group (formerly X/Open) DTP model consists of four elements, as illustrated in Figure 2-12.

This model can be somewhat confusing. One source of confusion is the terminology. Resource Managers, 999 times out of 1,000, means databases, and most of the rest are message queues. Communications Resource Manager sends messages to remote systems and supports the application's API (for example, XATMI and TxRPC). One reason that CRMs are called Resource Managers is that the protocol from TM to CRM is a variation of the protocol from TM to RM. Another source of confusion is that the TM, whose role is to manage the start and end of the transaction including the two-phase commit, and the CRM are often bundled into one product (a.k.a. the three-box model). The reason for four boxes is that the X/Open standards bodies were thinking of a TM controlling several CRMs, but it rarely happens that way.

Another possible source of confusion is that no distinction is made between client and server programs. An application that is a client may or may not have local resources. An application that is a server in one dialogue may be a client in another. There is no distinction in the model. In fact, the CRM protocol does not have to be client/server at all. Interestingly, this fits quite well with the notions of services and service orientation, which are discussed in Chapter 4. In both Tuxedo and Open Group DTP, the applications are implemented as entities called services.

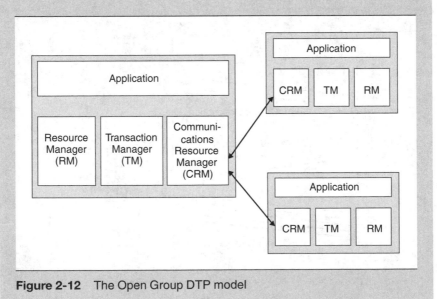

Figure 2-12   The Open Group DTP model

3

Objects, Components, and the Web

This is the second chapter in our historical survey of middleware technology.

All the technologies described in Chapter 2 have their roots in the 1980s. At the end of that decade, however, there was a resurgence of interest in object-oriented concepts, in particular object-oriented (OO) programming languages. This led to the development of a new kind of OO middleware, one in which the requestor calls a remote object. In other words, it does something like an RPC call on an object method and the object may exist in another machine. It should be pointed out at once that of the three kinds of middleware discussed in Chapter 2—RPC/transactional, message queuing, and remote database access—OO middleware is a replacement for only the first of these. (The interest in OO has continued unabated since the first edition of this book, leading to a wide understanding of OO concepts. We therefore do not feel it necessary to describe the basic ideas.)

A notable example of OO middleware is the Common Object Request Broker Architecture (CORBA). CORBA is a standard, not a product, and was developed by the Object Management Group (OMG), which is a consortium of almost all the important software vendors and some large users. In spite of its provenance, it is one of those standards (the ISO seven-layered model is another) that has been influential in the computer industry and in academia, but is seldom seen in implementations. (A possible exception to this is the lower-level network protocol Internet Inter-ORB Protocol (IIOP), which has been used in various embedded network devices.) One reason for the lack of CORBA implementation was its complexity. In addition, interoperability among vendor CORBA implementations and portability of applications from one implementation to another were never very good. But possibly the major reason that CORBA never took off was the rise of component technology.

The key characteristics of a component are:

- It is a code file that can be either executed or interpreted.
- The run-time code has its own private data and provides an interface.
- It can be deployed many times and on many different machines.

In short, a component can be taken from one context and reused in another; one component can be in use in many different places. A component does not have to have an OO interface, but the component technology we describe in this book does. When executed or interpreted, an OO component creates one or more objects and then makes the interface of some or all of these objects available to the world outside the component.

One of the important component technologies of the 1990s was the Component Object Model (COM) from Microsoft. By the end of the 1990s huge amounts of the Microsoft software were implemented as COM components. COM components can be written in many languages (notably C++ and Visual Basic) and are run by the Windows operating system. Programs that wish to call a COM object don't have to know the file name of the relevant code file but can look it up in the operating system's registry. A middleware known as Distributed COM (DCOM) provides a mechanism to call COM objects in another Windows-operated machine across a network.

In the second half of the 1990s, another change was the emergence of Java as an important language. Java also has a component model, and its components are called JavaBeans. Instead of being deployed directly by the operating system, Java beans are deployed in a Java Virtual Machine (JVM), which runs the Java byte code. The JVM provides a complete environment for the application, which has the important benefit that any Java byte code that runs in one JVM will almost certainly run in another JVM. A middleware known as Remote Method Invocation (RMI) provides a mechanism to call Java objects in another JVM across a network.

Thus, the battle lines were drawn between Microsoft and the Java camp, and the battle continues today.

The first section in this chapter discusses the differences between using an object interface and using a procedure interface. Using object interfaces, in any technology, turns out to be surprisingly subtle and difficult. One reaction to the problems was the introduction of *transactional component middleware*. This term, coined in the first edition of this book, describes software that provides a container for components; the container has facilities for managing transactions, pooling resources, and other run-time functions to simplify the implementation of online transaction-processing applications. The first transactional component middleware was Microsoft Transaction Server, which evolved into COM+. The Java camp struck back with Enterprise JavaBeans (EJB). A more detailed discussion of transactional component middleware is in the second section.

One issue with all OO middleware is the management of sessions. Web applications changed the ground rules for sessions, and the final section of this chapter discusses this topic.

3.1   Using object middleware

Object middleware is built on the simple concept of calling an operation in an object that resides in another system. Instead of client and server, there are client and object.

To access an object in another machine, a program must have a reference pointing at the object. Programmers are used to writing code that accesses objects through pointers, where the pointer holds the memory address of the object. A reference is syntactically the same as a pointer; calling a local object through a pointer and calling a remote object through a reference are made to look identical. The complexities of using references instead of pointers and sending messages over the network are hidden from the programmer by the middleware.

Unlike in earlier forms of middleware, calling an operation on a remote object requires two steps: getting a reference to an object and calling an operation on the object. Once you have got a reference you can call the object any number of times.

We will illustrate the difference between simple RPC calls and object-oriented calls with an example. Suppose you wanted to write code to debit an account. Using RPCs, you might write something like this (We've used a pseudo language rather than C++ or Java because we hope it will be clearer.):

```
Call Debit(012345678, 100) ;     // where 012345678 is the account
                                 // number and 100 is the amount
```

In an object-oriented system you might write:

```
Call AccountSet.GetAccount(012345678)    // get a reference to
    return AccountRef;                   // the account object
Call AccountRef.Debit(100);              // call debit
```

Here we are using an AccountSet object to get a reference to a particular account. (AccountSet is an object that represents the collection of all accounts.) We then call the debit operation on that account. On the face of it this looks like more work, but in practice there usually isn't much to it. What the client is more likely to do is:

```
Call AccountSet.GetAccount(X) return AccountRef;
Call AccountRef.GetNameAndBalance(....);
...display information to user
...get action to call - if it's a debit action then
Call AccountRef.Debit(Amt);
```

In other words, you get an object reference and then call many operations on the object before giving up the reference.

What this code segment does not explain is how we get a reference to the AccountSet object in the first place. In DCOM you might do this when you first connect to the component. In CORBA you may use a naming service that will take a name and look up an object reference for you. The subtleties in using objects across a network are discussed in more detail in the box entitled "Patterns for OO middleware."

Patterns for OO middleware

All middleware has an interface, and to use most middleware you must do two things: link to a resource (i.e., a service, a queue, a database), and call it by either passing it messages or call functions. OO middleware has the extra complexity of having to acquire a reference to an object before you can do anything. Three questions come to mind:

1. How do you get an object reference?
2. When are objects created and deleted?
3. Is it a good idea for more than one client to share one object?

In general, there are three ways to get an object reference:

1. A special object reference is returned to the client when it first attaches to the middleware. This technique is used by both COM and CORBA. The CORBA object returned is a system object, which you then interrogate to find additional services, and the COM object is an object provided by the COM application.
2. The client calls a special "naming" service that takes a name provided by the client and looks it up in a directory. The directory returns the location of an object, and the naming service converts this to a reference to that object. CORBA has a naming service (which has its own object interface). COM has facilities for interrogating the register to find the COM component but no standard naming service within the component.
3. An operation on one object returns a reference to another object. This is what the operation `GetAccount` in `AccountSet` did.

Broadly, the first two ways are about getting the first object to start the dialogue and the last mechanism is used within the dialogue.

Most server objects fall into one of the following categories:

- Proxy objects
- Agent objects
- Entrypoint objects
- Call-back objects

As an aside, there is a growing literature on what are called patterns, which seeks to describe common solutions to common problems. In a sense what we are describing here are somewhat like patterns, but our aims are more modest. We are concentrating only on the structural role of distributed objects, not on how several objects can be assembled into a solution.

A proxy object stands in for something else. The AccountRef object is an example since it stands in for the account object in the database and associated account processing. EJB entity beans implement proxy objects. Another example is objects that are there on behalf of a hardware resource such as a printer. Proxy objects are shared by different clients, or at least look as if they are shared to the client.

A proxy object can be a constructed thing, meaning that it is pretending that such and such object exists, but in fact the object is derived from other information. For instance, the account information can be dispersed over several database tables but the proxy object might gather all the information in one place. Another example might be a printer proxy object. The client thinks it's a printer but actually it is just an interface to an e-mail system.

Agent objects are there to make the client's life easier by providing an agent on the server that acts on the client's behalf. Agent objects aren't shared; when the client requests an agent object, the server creates a new object. An important subcategory of agent objects is iterator objects. Iterators are used to navigate around a database. An iterator represents a current position in a table or list, such as the output from a database query, and the iterator supports operations like MoveFirst (move to the first row in the output set) and MoveNext (move to the next output row). Similarly, iterator objects are required for serial files access. In fact, iterators or something similar are required for most large-scale data structures to avoid passing all the data over the network when you need only a small portion of it. Other examples of agent objects are objects that store security information and objects that hold temporary calculated results.

An Entrypoint Object is an object for finding other objects. In the example earlier, the AccountSet object could be an entrypoint object. (As an aside, in pattern terminology an entrypoint object is almost always a creational pattern, although it could be a façade.)

A special case of an entrypoint object is known as a singleton. You use them when you want OO middleware to look like RPC middleware. The server provides one singleton object used by all comers. Singleton objects are used if the object has no data.

Call-back objects implement a reverse interface, an interface from server to client. The purpose is for the server to send the client unsolicited data. Call-back mechanisms are widely used in COM. For instance, GUI Buttons, Lists, and Text input fields are all types of controls in Windows and controls fire events. Events are implemented by COM call-back objects.

Some objects (e.g., entrypoint objects and possibly proxy objects) are never deleted. In the case of proxy objects, if the number of things you want proxies for is very large (such as account records in the earlier example), you may want to create them on demand and delete them when no longer

(continued)

Patterns for OO middleware (*cont.*)

needed. A more sophisticated solution is to pool the unused objects. A problem for any object middleware is how to know when the client does not want to use the object. COM provides a reference counter mechanism so that objects can be automatically deleted when the counter returns to zero. This system generally works well, although it is possible to have circular linkages. Java has its garbage-collection mechanism that searches through the references looking for unreferenced objects. This solves the problem of circular linkage (since the garbage collector deletes groups of objects that reference themselves but no other objects), but at the cost of running the garbage collector. These mechanisms have to be extended to work across the network with the complication that the client can suddenly go offline and the network might be disconnected.

From an interface point of view, object interfaces are similar to RPCs. In CORBA and COM, the operations are declared in an Interface Definition Language (IDL) file, as illustrated in Figure 3-1.

Like RPCs, the IDL generates a stub that converts operation calls into messages (this is marshalling again) and a skeleton that converts messages into operation calls. It's not quite like RPCs since each message must contain an object reference and may return an object reference. There needs to be a way of converting an object reference into a binary string, and this is different with every object middleware.

Unlike existing RPC middleware, the operations may also be called through an interpretive interface such as a macro language. There is no reason that RPCs shouldn't implement this feature; they just haven't. An interpretive interface requires some way of finding out about the operations at runtime and a way of building the parameter list. In CORBA, for instance, the information about an interface is stored in the interface repository (which looks like another object to the client program).

In object middleware, the concept of an interface is more explicit than in object-oriented languages like C++. Interfaces give enormous flexibility and strong encapsulation. With interfaces you really don't know the implementation because an interface is not the same as a class. One interface can be used in many classes. One interface can be implemented by many different programs. One object can support many interfaces.

In Java, the concept of an interface is made more explicit in the language, so it isn't necessary to have a separate IDL file.

So why would you think of using object middleware instead of, say, RPCs? There are two main reasons.

The first is simply that object middleware fits naturally with object-oriented languages. If you are writing a server in C++ or Visual Basic, almost all your data and logic will (or at least should) be in objects. If you are writing your server in

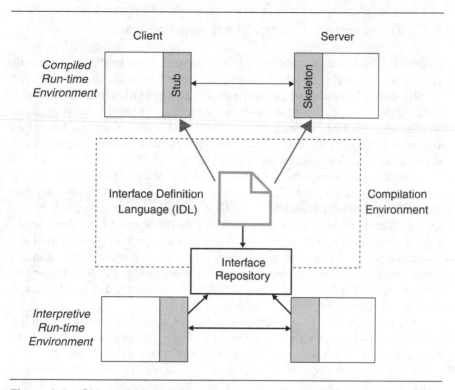

Figure 3-1   Object middleware compilation and interpretation

Java, all your data and code must be in objects. To design good object-oriented programs you start by identifying your objects and then you figure out how they interact. Many good programmers now always think in objects. Exposing an object interface through middleware is more natural and simpler to them than exposing a nonobject interface.

The second reason is that object middleware is more flexible. The fact that the interface is delinked from the server program is a great tool for simplification. For instance, suppose there is a single interface for security checking. Any number of servers can use exactly the same interface even though the underlying implementation is completely different. If there is a change to the interface, this can be handled in an incremental fashion by adding an interface to an object rather than by changing the existing interface. Having both the old and new interfaces concurrently allows the clients to be moved gradually rather than all at once.

3.2   Transactional component middleware

Transactional component middleware (TCM) covers two technologies: Microsoft Transaction Server (MTS), which became part of COM+ and is now incorporated in .NET, from Microsoft; and Enterprise JavaBeans (EJB) from the anti-Microsoft camp. OMG did release a CORBA-based standard for transactional component middleware, which was meant to be compatible with EJB, but extended the ideas into other languages. We will not describe this standard further since it has not attracted any significant market interest.

Transactional component middleware (TCM) is our term. TCM is about taking components and running them in a distributed transaction processing environment. (We discuss distributed transaction processing and transaction monitors in Chapter 2.) Other terms have been used, such as *COMWare* and *Object Transaction Manager (OTM)*. We don't like *COMWare* because components could be used in a nontransactional environment in a manner that is very different from a transactional form of use, so having something about transactions in the title is important. We don't like *OTM* because components are too important and distinctive not to be included in the name; they are not the same as objects.

Transactional Component Middleware fits the same niche in object middleware systems that transaction monitors fit in traditional systems. It is there to make transaction processing systems easier to implement and more scalable.

The magic that does this is known as a container. The container provides many useful features, the most notable of which are transaction support and resource pooling. The general idea is that standard facilities can be implemented by the container rather than by forcing the component implementer to write lots of ugly system calls.

One of the advantages of Transactional Component Middleware is that the components can be deployed with different settings to behave in different ways. Changing the security environment is a case in point, where it is clearly beneficial to be able to change the configuration at deployment time. But there is some information that must be passed from developer to deployer, in particular the transactional requirements. For instance, in COM+ the developer must define that the component supports one of four transactional environments, namely:

1. Requires a transaction: Either the client is in transaction state (i.e., within the scope of a transaction) or COM+ will start a new transaction when the component's object is created.
2. Requires a new transaction: COM+ will always start a new transaction when the component's object is created, even if the caller is in transaction state.
3. Supports transactions: The client may or may not be in transaction state; the component's object does not care.
4. Does not support transactions: The object will not run in transaction state, even if the client is in transaction state.

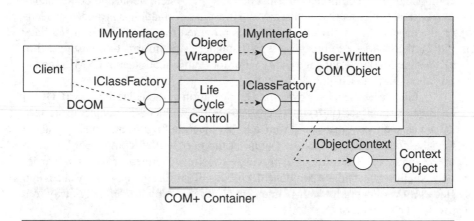

Figure 3-2   Transactional components in Microsoft COM+

In general, the first and third of these are commonly used. Note that the client can be an external program (perhaps on another system) or another component working within COM+. EJB has a similar set of features. Because the container delineates the transaction start and end points, the program code needs to do no more than commit or abort the transaction.

Figure 3-2 illustrates Microsoft COM+ and Figure 3-3 illustrates Enterprise JavaBeans. As you can see, they have a similar structure.

When a component is placed in a container (i.e., moved to a file directory where the container can access it and registered with the container), the administrator provides additional information to tell the container how to run the

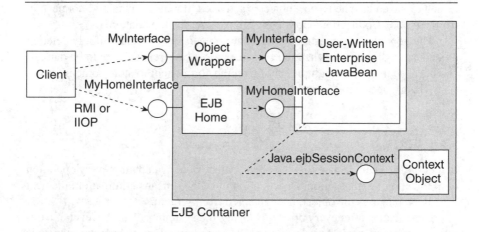

Figure 3-3   Transactional components in Enterprise JavaBeans

component. This additional information tells the system about the component's transactional and security requirements. How the information is provided depends on the product. In Microsoft COM+, it is provided by a graphical user interface (GUI), the COM+ Explorer. In the EJB standard, the information is supplied in eXtensible Markup Language (XML). For more information about XML, see the box about XML in Chapter 4.

A client uses the server by calling an operation in the IClassFactory (COM+) or MyHomeInterface (EJB) interface to create a new object. The object's interface is then used directly, just as if it were a local object. In Figures 3-2 and 3-3 you see that the client reference does not point at the user written component but at an object wrapper. The structure provided by the container provides a barrier between the client and the component. One use of this barrier is security checking. Because every operation call is intercepted, it is possible to define security to a low level of granularity.

The other reason for the object wrapper is performance. The object wrapper makes it possible to deactivate the component objects without the client's knowledge. The next time the client tries to use an object, the wrapper activates the object again, behind the client's back, so to speak. The purpose of this is to save resources. Suppose there are thousands of clients, as you would expect if the application supports thousands of end users. Without the ability to deactivate objects, there would be thousands of objects, probably many thousands of objects because objects invoke other objects. Each object takes memory, so deactivating unused objects makes an enormous difference to memory utilization.

Given that objects come and go with great rapidity, all the savings from the efficient utilization of memory would be lost by creating and breaking database connections, because building and breaking down database connections is a heavy user of system resources. The solution is connection pooling. There is a pool of database connections, and when the object is deactivated the connection is returned to the pool. When a new object is activated, it reuses an inactive connection from the pool. Connection pooling is also managed by the container.

The next obvious question is, when are objects deactivated? Simply deleting objects at any time (i.e., when the resources are a bit stretched) could be dangerous because the client might be relying on the component to store some information. This is where COM+ and EJB differ.

3.2.1   COM+

In COM+, you can declare that the object can be deactivated after every operation or at the end of a transaction. Deactivation in COM+ means elimination; the next time the client uses the object, it is recreated from scratch.

Deactivating after every operation brings the system back to the level of a traditional transaction monitor, because at the beginning of every operation the code will find that all the data attributes in the object are reset to their initial state.

Deactivating at the end of every transaction allows the client to make several calls to the same object, for instance, searching for a record in the database in one call and updating the database in another call. After the transaction has finished, the object is deactivated.

A traditional feature of transaction monitors is the ability to store data on a session basis, and you may have noticed that there is no equivalent feature in COM+. Most transaction monitors have a data area where the transaction code can stash data. The next time the same terminal runs a transaction, the (possibly different) transaction code can read the stash. This feature is typically used for storing temporary data, like remembering the account number this user is working on. Its omission in COM+ has been a cause of much argument in the industry.

3.2.2   EJB

Enterprise JavaBeans is a standard, not a product. There are EJB implementations from BEA, IBM, Oracle, and others. The network connection to EJB is the Java-only Remote Method Invocation (RMI) and the CORBA interface IIOP. IIOP makes it possible to call an EJB server from a CORBA client.

EJB components come in two flavors, session beans and entity beans. Each has two subflavors. Session beans are logically private beans; that is, it is as if they are not shared across clients. (They correspond roughly to what we describe as agent objects in the previous box entitled "Patterns for OO middleware.") The two subflavors are:

- Stateless session beans: All object state is eliminated after every operation invocation.
- Stateful session beans: These hold state for their entire life.

Exactly when a stateful session bean is "passivated" (the EJB term for deactivated) is entirely up to the container. The container reads the object attributes and writes them to disk so that the object can be reconstituted fully when it is activated. The stateful bean implementer can add code, which is called by the passivate and activate operations. This might be needed to attach or release some external resource.

The EJB container must be cautious about when it passivates a bean because if a transaction aborts, the client will want the state to be like it was before the transaction started rather than what it came to look like in the middle of the aborted transaction. That in turn means that the object state must be saved during the transaction commit. In fact, to be really safe, the EJB container has to do a two-phase commit to synchronize the EJB commit with the database commit. (In theory it would be possible to implement the EJB container as part of the database software and manage the EJB save as part of the database commit.)

Entity beans were designed to be beans that represent rows in a database.

Normally the client does not explicitly create an entity bean but finds it by using a primary key data value. Entity beans can be shared.

The EJB specification allows implementers to cache the database data values in the entity bean to improve performance. If this is done, and it is done in many major implementations, it is possible for another application to update the database directly, behind the entity bean's back so to speak, leaving the entity bean cache holding out-of-date information. This would destroy transaction integrity. One answer is to allow updates only through the EJBs, but this is unlikely to be acceptable in any large-scale enterprise application. A better solution is for the entity bean not to do caching, but you must ensure that your EJB vendor supports this solution.

The two subflavors of entity beans are:

- Bean-managed persistence: The user writes the bean code.
- Container-managed persistence: The EJB automatically maps the database row to the entity bean.

Container-managed persistence can be viewed as a kind of 4GL since it saves a great deal of coding.

3.2.3   Final comments on TCM

When EJBs and COM+ first appeared, there was a massive amount of debate about which was the better solution. The controversy rumbles on. An example is the famous Pet Store benchmark, the results of which were published in 2002. The benchmark compared functionally identical applications implemented in J2EE (two different application servers) and .NET. The results suggested that .NET performed better and required fewer resources to develop the application. This unleashed a storm of discussion and cries of "foul!" from the J2EE supporters.

In our opinion, the controversy is a waste of time, for a number of reasons. A lot of it arose for nontechnical reasons. The advocates—*disciples* might be a better word—of each technology would not hear of anything good about the other or bad about their own. The debate took on the flavor of a theological discussion, with the protagonists showing all the fervor and certainty of Savonarola or Calvin. This is ultimately destructive, wasting everyone's time and not promoting rational discussion. Today there are two standards, so we have to live with them. Neither is likely to go away for lack of interest, although the next great idea could replace both of them. And is it bad to have alternatives? Many factors contribute to a choice of technology for developing applications (e.g., functional requirements, performance, etc.). The two technologies we have been discussing are roughly equivalent, so either could be the right choice for an enterprise. The final decision then comes down to other factors, one of which is the skill level in the organization concerned. If you have a lot of Java expertise, EJB is the better choice. Similarly, if you have a lot of Microsoft expertise, choose COM+.

There are, of course, legitimate technical issues to consider. For example, if you really do want operating system independence, then EJB is the correct choice; the Microsoft technology works only with Windows. If you want language independence, you cannot choose EJBs because it supports Java only. There may also be technical issues about interworking with existing applications, for which a gateway of some form is required. It could be that one technology rather than the other has a better set of choices, although there are now many options for both.

Both technologies have, of course, matured since their introduction, removing some reasonable criticisms; the holes have been plugged, in other words. And a final point we would like to make is that it is possible to produce a good application, or a very bad one, in either of these technologies—or any other, for that matter. Producing an application with poor performance is not necessarily a result of a wrong choice of technology. In our opinion, bad design and implementation are likely to be much greater problems, reflecting a general lack of understanding both of the platform technologies concerned and the key requirements of large-scale systems. Addressing these issues is at the heart of this book.

Transaction component middleware is likely to remain a key technology for some time. COM+ has disappeared as a marketing name but the technology largely remains. It is now called Enterprise Services and is part of Microsoft .NET. More recent developments, which have come very much to the fore, are service orientation and service-oriented architectures in general, and Web services in particular, which we discuss in the next chapter.

3.3 Internet Applications

In the latter part of the 1990s, if the press wasn't talking about the Microsoft/Java wars, it was talking about the Internet. The Internet was a people's revolution and no vendor has been able to dominate the technology. Within IT, the Internet has changed many things, for instance:

- It hastened (or perhaps caused) the dominance of TCP/IP as a universal network standard.
- It led to the development of a large amount of free Internet software at the workstation.
- It inspired the concept of thin clients, where most of the application is centralized. Indeed, the Internet has led to a return to centralized computer applications.
- It led to a new fashion for data to be formatted as text (e.g., HTML and XML). The good thing about text is that it can be read easily and edited by a simple editor (such as Notepad). The bad thing is that it is wasteful of space and requires parsing by the recipient.

- It changed the way we think about security (discussed in Chapter 10).
- It liberated us from the notion that specific terminals are of a specific size.
- It led to a better realization of the power of directories, in particular Domain Name Servers (DNS) for translating Web names (i.e., URLs) into network (i.e., IP) addresses.
- It led to the rise of intranets—Internet technology used in-house—and extranets—private networks between organizations using Internet technology.
- It has to some extent made people realize that an effective solution to a problem does not have to be complicated.

Internet applications differ from traditional applications in at least five significant ways.

First, the user is in command. In the early days, computer input was by command strings and the user was in command. The user typed and the computer answered. Then organizations implemented menus and forms interfaces, where the computer application was in command. The menus guide the user by giving them restricted options. Menus and forms together ensure work is done only in one prescribed order. With the Internet, the user is back in command in the sense that he or she can use links, Back commands, Favorites, and explicit URL addresses to skip around from screen to screen and application to application. This makes a big difference in the way applications are structured and is largely the reason why putting a Web interface on an existing menu and forms application may not work well in practice.

Second, when writing a Web application you should be sensitive to the fact that not all users are equal. They don't all have high-resolution, 17-inch monitors attached to 100Mbit or faster Ethernet LANs. Screens are improving in quality but new portable devices will be smaller again. And in spite of the spread of broadband access to the Internet, there are, and will continue to be, slow telephone-quality lines still in use.

Third, you cannot rely on the network address to identify the user, except over a short period of time. On the Internet, the IP address is assigned by the Internet provider when someone logs on. Even on in-house LANs, many organizations use dynamic address allocation (the DHCP protocol), and every time a person connects to the network he or she is liable to get a different IP address.

Fourth, the Internet is a public medium and security is a major concern. Many organizations have built a security policy on the basis that (a) every user can be allocated a user code and password centrally (typically the user is given the opportunity to change the password) and (b) every network address is in a known location. Someone logging on with a particular user code at a particular location is given a set of access rights. The same user at a different location may not have the same access rights. We have already noted that point (b) does not hold on the Internet, at least not to the same precision. Point (a) is also suspect; it is much more likely that user code security will come under sustained attack. (We discuss these points when we discuss security in Chapter 10.)

Fifth and finally, it makes much more sense on the Internet to load a chunk of data, do some local processing on it, and send the results back. This would be ideal for filling in big forms (e.g., a tax form). At the moment these kinds of applications are handled by many short interactions with the server, often with frustratingly slow responses. We discuss this more in Chapters 6 and 13.

Most nontrivial Web applications are implemented in a hardware configuration that looks something like Figure 3-4.

You can, of course, amalgamate the transaction and database server with the Web servers and cut out the network between them. However, most organizations don't do this, partly because of organizational issues (e.g., the Web server belongs to a different department). But there are good technical reasons for making the split, for instance:

- You can put a firewall between the Web server and the transaction and database server, thus giving an added level of protection to your enterprise data.
- It gives you more flexibility to choose different platforms and technology from the back-end servers.
- A Web server often needs to access many back-end servers, so there is no obvious combination of servers to bring together.

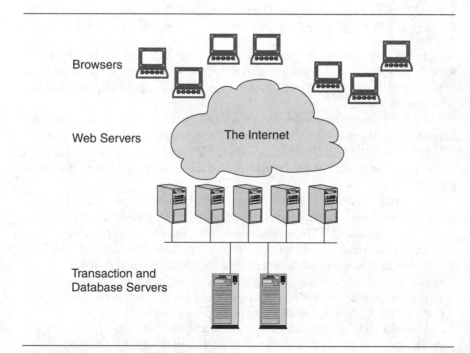

Figure 3-4   Web hardware configuration

Web servers are easily scalable by load balancing across multiple servers (as long as they don't hold session data). Others, for example, database servers, may be harder to load balance. By splitting them, we have the opportunity to use load balancing for one and not the other. (We discuss load balancing in Chapter 8.)

The Transactional Component Middleware was designed to be the middleware between front- and back-end servers.

Many applications require some kind of session concept to be workable. A session makes the user's life easier by

- Providing a logon at the start, so authentication need be done only once.
- Providing for traversal from screen to screen.
- Making it possible for the server to collect data over several screens before processing.
- Making it easier for the server to tailor the interface for a given user, that is, giving different users different functionality.

In old-style applications these were implemented by menu and forms code back in the server. Workstation GUI applications are also typically session-based; the session starts when the program starts and stops when it stops. But the Web is stateless, by which we mean that it has no built-in session concept. It does not remember any state (i.e., data) from one request to another. (Technically, each Web page is retrieved by a separate TCP/IP connection.) Sessions are so useful that there needs to be a way to simulate them. One way is to use applets. This essentially uses the Web as a way of downloading a GUI application. But there are problems.

If the client code is complex, the applet is large and it is time consuming to load it over a slow line. The applet opens a separate session over the network back to the server. If the application is at all complex, it will need additional middleware over this link.

A simple sockets connection has the specific problem that it can run foul of a firewall since firewalls may restrict traffic to specific TCP port numbers (such as for HTTP, SMTP, and FTP communication). The applet also has very restricted functionality on the browser (to prevent malicious applets mucking up the workstation).

Java applets have been successful in terminal emulation and other relatively straightforward work, but in general this approach is not greatly favored. It's easier to stick to standard HTML or dynamic HTML features where possible.

An alternative strategy is for the server to remember the client's IP address. This limits the session to the length of time that the browser is connected to the network since on any reconnect it might be assigned a different IP address. There is also a danger that a user could disconnect and another user could be assigned the first user's IP address, and therefore pick up their session!

A third strategy is for the server to hide a session identifier on the HTML page in such a way that it is returned when the user asks for the next screen (e.g., put the session identifier as part of the text that is returned when the user hits a link). This works well, except that if the user terminates the browser for any reason, the session is broken.

Finally, session management can be done with cookies. Cookies are small amounts of data the server can send to the browser and request that it be loaded on the browser's disk. (You can look at any text in the cookies with a simple text editor such as Notepad.) When the browser sends a message to the same server, the cookie goes with it. The server can store enough information to resume the session (usually just a simple session number). The cookie may also contain a security token and a timeout date. Cookies are probably the most common mechanism for implementing Web sessions. Cookies can hang around for a long time; therefore, it is possible for the Web application to notice a single user returning again and again to the site. (If the Web page says "Welcome back <your name>", it's done with cookies.) Implemented badly, cookies can be a security risk, for instance, by holding important information in clear text, so some people disable them from the browser.

All implementations of Web sessions differ from traditional sessions in one crucial way. The Web application server cannot detect that the browser has stopped running on the user's workstation.

How session state is handled becomes an important issue. Let us take a specific example—Web shopping cart applications. The user browses around an online catalogue and selects items he wishes to purchase by pressing an icon in the shape of a shopping cart. The basic configuration is illustrated in Figure 3-4. We have:

- A browser on a Web site
- A Web server, possibly a Web server farm implemented using Microsoft ASP (Active Server Pages), Java JSP (JavaServer Pages), or other Web server products
- A back-end transaction server using .NET or EJB

Let us assume the session is implemented by using cookies. That means that when the shopping cart icon is pressed, the server reads the cookie to identify the user and displays the contents of the shopping cart. When an item is added to the shopping cart, the cookie is read again to identify the user so that the item is added to the right shopping cart. The basic problem becomes converting cookie data to the primary key of the user's shopping cart record in the database. Where do you do this? There are several options of which the most common are:

- Do it in the Web server.
- Hold the shopping cart information in a session bean.
- Put the user's primary key data in the cookie and pass it to the transaction server.

The Web server solution requires holding a lookup table in the Web server to convert cookie data value to a shopping cart primary key. The main problem is that if you want to use a Web server farm for scalability or resiliency, the lookup table must be shared across all the Web servers. This is possible, but it is not simple. (The details are discussed Chapter 7.)

Holding the shopping cart information in a session bean also runs into difficulties when there is a Web server farm, but in this case the session bean cannot be shared. This is not an insurmountable problem because in EJB you can read a *handle* from the object and store it on disk, and then the other server can read the handle and get access to the object. But you would have to ensure the two Web servers don't access the same object at the same time. Probably the simplest way to do this is to convert the handle into an object reference every time the shopping cart icon is pressed. Note that a consequence of this approach is that with 1,000 concurrent users you would need 1,000 concurrent session beans. A problem with the Web is that you don't know when the real end user has gone away, so deleting a session requires detecting a period of time with no activity. A further problem is that if the server goes down, the session bean is lost.

The simplest solution is to store the shopping cart information in the database and put the primary key of the user's shopping cart directly in the cookie. The cookie data is then passed through to the transaction server. This way, both the Web server and the transaction server are stateless, all these complex recovery problems disappear, and the application is more scalable and efficient.

In our view, stateful session beans are most useful in a nontransactional application, such as querying a database. We can also envisage situations where it would be useful to keep state that had nothing to do with transaction recovery, for instance, for performance monitoring. But as a general principle, if you want to keep transactional state, put it in the database.

On the other hand, keeping state during a transaction is no problem as long as it is reinitialized if the transaction aborts, so the COM model is a good one. To do the same in EJB requires using a stateful session bean but explicitly reinitializing the bean at the start of every transaction.

But you needed session state for mainframe transaction monitors, why not now? Transaction monitors needed state because they were dealing with dumb terminals, which didn't have cookies—state was related to the terminal identity. Also, the applications were typically much more ruthless about removing session state if there was a recovery and forcing users to log on again. For instance, if the network died, the mainframe applications would be able to log off all the terminals and remove session state. This simplified recovery. In contrast, if the network dies somewhere between the Web server and the browser, there is a good chance the Web server won't even notice. Even if it does, the Web server can't remove the cookie. In the olden days, the session was between workstation and application; now it is between cookie and transaction server. Stateful session beans support a session between the Web server and the transaction server, which is only part of the path between cookie and transaction server. In this case, having part of an implementation just gets in the way.

Entity beans, on the other hand, have no such problems. They have been criticized for forcing the programmer to do too many primary key lookup operations on the database, but we doubt whether this performance hit is significant.

3.4   Summary

Key points to remember:

- Transaction Component Middleware (TCM) is the dominant technology today for transaction processing applications. The two leading TCMs are Enterprise JavaBeans (EJB) and .NET Enterprise Services (formerly COM+).

- These two dominant TCM technologies both use OO interfaces. OO interfaces have greater flexibility than older interface styles like RPC and fit well with OO programming languages. But there is a cost in greater complexity because there are objects to be referenced and managed.

- TCMs are preferable to older OO middleware styles like DCOM and CORBA because developing transactional applications is easier (there is much less to do) and the software provides object and database connection pooling, which improves performance.

- Web browsers are significantly different from older GUI applications or green-screen terminals. The browser user has more control over navigation, the server can make far fewer assumptions on the nature of the device, and session handling is different. In particular, the Web application server has no idea when the browser user has finished using the application.

- While there are many fancy features for session handling in EJBs, a simple approach using stateless sessions is usually best. The old adage, KISS— Keep it Simple, Stupid—applies.

- In large organizations, the chances are you will have to work with both .NET and Java for the foreseeable future.

4

Web Services

This chapter completes our brief history of middleware technology by discussing Web services. Although the notion of service orientation has been around for a long time (e.g., the Open Group DTP model and Tuxedo construct applications from what are called services), the ideas have come into prominence again because of the great interest in Web services.

The notion of a service is attractive because it is familiar and easy to understand; it does not, at least on the surface, require an understanding of arcane concepts and terminology. A service requires a requester, who wants the service, and a provider, who satisfies the request. Seeking advice from a financial expert and consulting a doctor are services. Buying something requires a service from the vendor. This notion extends easily to IT: Parts or all of a service can be automated using IT systems. The requester may use a human intermediary, for example, a travel agent to book a flight; the agent handles the IT on behalf of the customer. Another example of an intermediary is a financial advisor, who uses an IT system to analyze financial trends and prices. An alternative is self-service, where the requester does the IT, for example, using an Internet-based reservation system or an investment analysis application.

This chapter discusses the technology and application of Web services. Because Web services technology builds on earlier ideas, and the notion of service orientation is not confined to Web services technology, an understanding of service concepts is necessary before moving to the particular case of Web services.

4.1 Service concepts

The concern in this chapter is where services are provided by software. And although the requester of a service may ultimately be a person (e.g., travel agent, financial advisor, or customer), it is, of course, software (e.g., a Web browser and other software in a PC) that acts as a proxy on his or her behalf. The software providing services may also be thought of as a proxy for humans, although the connection is less direct than a person using a program in a PC. The organization providing the service has chosen to deliver it using software, which acts as the provider's proxy. In the rest of this chapter, when we use the words *requester* and *provider,* we mean a program—a software system or chunk of code, not people or organizations—that requests or provides a service. If we want to refer to an organization or person using or providing the software, we will make it clear, for example, by talking about the provider's organization.

So in the IT context, programs can be providers of services to other programs. Taking it further, a service may be broken down into one or more parts. For example, the service invoked by the requester could itself require another service from somewhere else. In the airline reservation example, the customer may be asked to provide a frequent flyer number at the time of booking. The reservation application could then send it to a frequent flyer application, which is therefore seen by the reservation application as providing a service. There are thus three roles for programs: requesters of services, providers of services, or both.

The example of the airline reservation system as the provider of a reservation service to a customer, and in turn acting as the requester of services from a frequent flyer application, can be thought of as service cascade. In theory this cascading could continue to any depth, where one provider calls another, which calls another, and so on. Alternatively, a requester could request the services of a number of providers in parallel, which can be called parallel cascading. And the requesters and providers need not be confined to a single organization: Organizations interact and have been doing so in various ways for many years.

Consider, for example, a retail bank, which offers a service to its customers to obtain the status (e.g., balance, recent transactions, etc.) of all the products they hold, without having to request each one individually. The service is provided via the Internet using a browser. A customer information system is the provider of this service; it would contain a record of the customer and all the products held and is invoked by customers through PCs. However, the details of each product (e.g., checking accounts, savings accounts, mortgages, etc.) are likely to be in specific product systems, probably (but not necessarily) in other servers. These product systems would be invoked as providers by the customer information system (requester). It is also possible that the bank offers products that are provided by other companies, for example, insurance products. An external service request would therefore be needed to get the status.

This service model, illustrated by the bank example, is shown schematically in Figure 4-1. The requester is the software used by the customer (browser and so on), Organization Y is the bank, and Organization X the insurance company. The provider of Service 1 is the customer information system; Services 2, 3, and 4 are provided by the product management systems, either internal or external to the bank. The provider of Service 1 is also the requester of Services 2, 3, and 4. This is an example of parallel cascading—the requester calls 1, then 1 calls 2, 3, and 4, which is much more efficient that the requester's having to call Service 1, then Service 2, then Service 3, then Service 4.

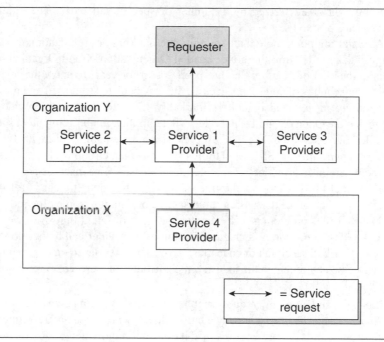

Figure 4-1   Service, requester, and provider relationships

The airline and the bank examples also illustrate two broad types of service invocation: those where an immediate response is required—call it real time; and those where an immediate response is not necessary—call it deferrable. The airline reservation and the banking product status service require an immediate response because someone is waiting for the answer. The frequent flyer number does not have to reach the frequent flyer system immediately, however, as long it gets there before the next statement.

So a provider is a chunk of code providing a service, for example, the banking product information or flight reservation. This raises a number of questions. When should a chunk of code be thought of as a provider of a service? What characteristics must it have? How big or small should it be? Answers to these questions lead to a definition, or at least a better understanding, of *service provider.*

In some ways, it does not matter that there is no general definition, with one big caveat: Great care must be taken to state what is meant when it is used in any particular context. It is dangerous to use terms such as *service, service orientation,* and *service-oriented architecture* with an assumption that everyone knows what you mean. Unless the terms are well defined, different people will interpret them in different ways, leading to confusion. Such confusion will certainly arise in the context of *services* because there are different and conflicting definitions. Some try to tie it to specific technologies or run-time environments, for example, the Internet; others have tried to establish a definition independent of any particular technology but characterized by a number of specific attributes. The latter approach seems best to us.

As a starting point, note that removing the banking or organizational context of Figure 4-1 by deleting the boxes labeled Organization X and Organization Y results in the kind of diagram that has been drawn for years to show the relationships among chunks of code. This goes all the way back to structured and modular programming ideas. It also looks remarkably like the structures provided by Tuxedo and the Open Group DTP model, where application building blocks are in fact called Services. It could equally represent what we could build with J2EE or Microsoft environments. So should things such as Open Group DTP Services and EJBs be regarded as providers of services in the sense we've discussed?

They could be, as long as the rule of making the context clear is followed. However, in much of the discussion about service orientation, something more specific is meant. The problem is, different people mean different things. However, at least a working definition or a characterization of a provider can be developed by stating the attributes a chunk of code must have to be one. Based on our views, and those expressed by others in the industry, the attributes of a provider are:

- It is independent of any requester; it has an existence of its own as a "black box." This means it can be built using any language and run-time environment its creator chooses, and it does not require generation procedures involving other users of the service or service providers it uses. If it did, it would be impossible for independent organizations to cooperate.
- It has a verifiable identity (name) and a precisely defined set of services and ways to invoke them, together with responses—in other words, interfaces.
- It is possible to replace an existing implementation with a new version and maintain backwards compatibility, without affecting existing users. New versions may appear for purely technical reasons, such as fixing problems and enhancing performance, or to add capabilities. The implication is that existing interfaces must be maintained.
- It can be located through some kind of directory structure if necessary.
- It can be invoked by requesters of its services, and it can invoke other services and not be aware of any presentation on a particular device. Communication between requesters and providers should be by exchanging messages, using accepted standard definitions and protocols.
- It contains mechanisms for recovering from errors in the event of a failure somewhere in the environment in which it is invoked. This is not a problem for services where there are no database changes, but it is complicated if there are. To be more specific, if the service requires a database update, it should be treated as a transaction, exhibiting the ACID properties discussed in Chapter 2. If the service provider is part of a wider distributed transaction involving other providers, the ACID properties should be preserved by using two-phase commit or an alternative strategy for maintaining database integrity.

Figure 4-2 represents the kind of architecture that could be created using a services approach. The figure shows Organization Y offering a variety of services through a number of providers. Each provider offers one or more services and is implemented by a number of software components in whatever language and environment the implementer has chosen; they are hidden within the provider—the black box idea, in other words. Defined external interfaces provide the means of accessing the services. As you can see, there are several such providers, deployed across a number of servers. There are also services offered by an external organization (Organization X). Requesters of the various services may use a variety of access channels that require some form of management to get them into the environment. The service definition shown in the figure provides the means of linking the requested services to the provider. The providers can also invoke the services of each other. An interconnecting infrastructure of middleware and networks links the lot together. Putting this into the context of the bank example discussed earlier,

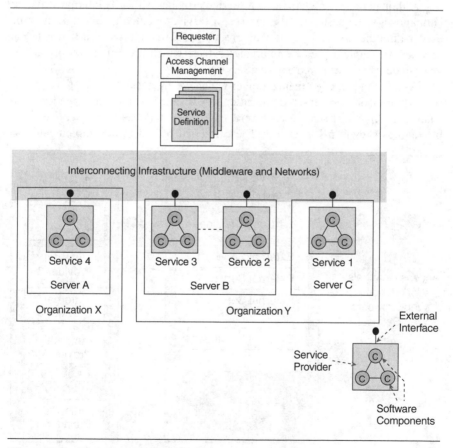

Figure 4-2 Typical service architecture

Server C might contain the customer information application and Server B the product management applications operated by the bank, and the external organization would be the insurance company providing the insurance products—Service 4 in Server A.

In the case of the bank example, the providers—customer information and product systems—are independent, large-scale applications, probably written over an extended period using different technologies. A variety of user channels would access them (e.g., tellers in bank branches) and would request services using branch workstations; software in the workstation is the requester. They also function as providers of services to each other. The insurance company application is also independent and is likely to be a provider of services to a number of organizations. Since the applications are independent, as long as external interfaces do not assume device characteristics, they fit quite well with the characteristics of a service provider listed earlier. Banks have in fact been quite good at producing service-oriented applications, separating the application functions from the access channels.

Although one characteristic of a service provider is that its internal structure is unknown to requesters of its services, a service-oriented architecture may be used within the provider itself. This gives a *two-level* approach in that external services are implemented by internal services, which are combined in various ways to deliver the required external service.

As an example, one organization of which we are aware has adapted a green-screen transaction processing application into a set of callable, independent, and channel-independent service providers, exposing interfaces to the services they provide, as shown in Figure 4-3. These internal providers are implemented as

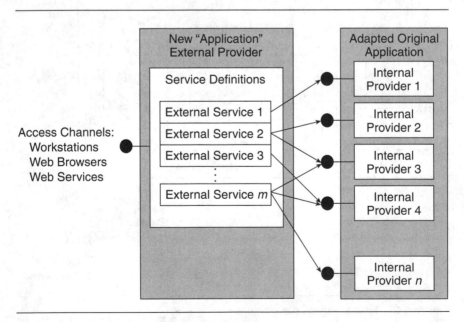

Figure 4-3   Applications and services

Open Group DTP services. A layer between the internal providers in the adapted original application and the external access channels defines which internal service providers are required to implement each external service. The organization concerned now regards this mapping of external service to internal service providers as an application. A high degree of reusability has been achieved, with new applications being a combination of existing and possibly some new internal services. The independence of the internal services means that they can be relocated if required.

4.2   Web services

The previous section assumes no particular technology or standard, just a set of principles. Obviously, to put a service-oriented architecture into practice requires technologies to be defined and implemented. Over the years, a number of organizations have adopted architectures similar to those we have discussed. In some cases, the service orientation has been confined to external connections to other organizations. The standards used for organization-to-organization interaction have included various forms of EDI as well as other bilateral or multilateral definitions, for example, by industry groups such as IATA.

Web services are a specific instance of a service-oriented architecture, of the kind discussed in the previous section. In many senses, the Web is built entirely around the idea of services. A browser or other device is used to find and access information and to execute transactions of some kind. All of the Web sites visited perform services for the requesters. And in many cases they cascade off to other sites or to systems within a specific site. Web services, in the context discussed here, depend on specific concepts, technologies, and standards.

The World Wide Web Consortium (W3C) plays the major role in developing the architecture and standards; its technical committees draw on expertise from all the leading organizations in IT and the academic world. If you are interested in the technical details, you can find all the latest documentation, including published working drafts, on the W3C Web site (www.w3c.org). Of particular value are the Web Services Architecture and Web Services Glossary documents because they explain the principles, the concepts, and the terminology used. The Web Services Architecture Usage Scenarios document is valuable because it explains how the technology can be applied.

The W3C defines a *Web service* (in the Web Services Architecture document, Working Draft 8, which is the current version at the time of writing) as

> a software system designed to support interoperable machine-to-machine interaction over a network. It has an interface described in a machine-processable format (specifically WSDL—Web Services Definition Language). Other systems interact with the Web service in a manner prescribed by its description using SOAP messages, typically conveyed using HTTP with an XML serialization in conjunction with other Web-related standards.

The basic model is much the same as that described in the previous section, with requesters and providers. In the terminology of the Web Services Architecture document, the person or organization offering the service is the *provider entity,* which uses a software system, the *agent,* to deliver it. The *requester entity* is the person or organization requesting the service, which again provides an agent that exchanges messages with the provider's agent. Standards define the various technologies required to support the interactions of requester and provider agents. To provide this interaction with sufficient flexibility, reliability, and so on requires a number of interrelated technologies. Figure 4-4 is a view of the technologies involved, as shown in W3C's current Web Services Architecture document.

As you can see, there are many elements in the complete picture. XML is a fundamental technology—a base technology in the figure—that underpins Web services, for a variety of reasons. It provides the necessary vendor, platform, language, and implementation independence required in the heterogeneous environments envisaged. It is also inherently extensible and widely implemented. XML is not used just for the content of messages—the payload; it is also used for protocol data and as the foundation of the descriptive languages such as WSDL. Using XML for protocol data simplifies mapping onto a variety of communications protocols. (See the box entitled "XML.")

Services are invoked and provide responses via messages, which have to be carried over a communications channel of some sort. Web services architecture

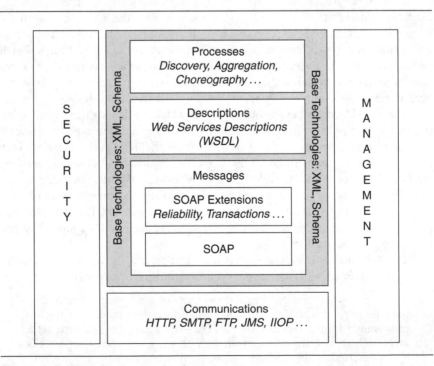

Figure 4-4   Web services technology

makes no assumption about what this channel is, as long as it is capable of carrying the messages. A very wide variety of technologies can be used: HTTP and other Internet protocols, such as SMTP and FTP, as well as others, both old and new. The only assumption is that the layer exists and is capable of carrying the messages.

The key messaging technology is SOAP. (SOAP was originally an acronym for Simple Object Access Protocol, but the acronym expansion is no longer used; it's just called SOAP.) It is relatively simple and can be used over many communications protocols, as discussed in the previous paragraph. Although HTTP is commonly used to carry SOAP messages, it is not required by the protocol. SOAP can be used for simple, one-way transmissions as well as for more complex interactions, ranging from request/response to complex conversations involving multiple request/responses, and multihop, where the message traverses several nodes and each node acts on the message. SOAP has the advantage of widespread support as a standard and is consequently widely implemented. (See the box entitled "XML" for a simple example of SOAP.)

XML

The eXtensible Markup Language (XML) is one of a series of markup languages that includes Standard Generalized Markup Language (SGML) and HyperText Markup Language (HTML). The original problem that needed to be solved was finding a way to share data among different text editors and typesetting programs, and thus SGML was born. Later the concept of SGML was adapted when the first Web browsers were written, resulting in HTML. In both SGML and HTML, documents use only the standard text character sets; tags denote special formatting instructions . For instance, in HTML, to tell the Web browser that some text should be put in italics you write the text like this: "not italics <i>italic text</i> no longer italics". The <i> is a tag and the </i> indicates the end of the tagged element. The universality of HTML, the ease by which the tagged text could be formatted, and the flexibility that allowed the text to be displayed on many different devices are major factors in the popularity of the Web.

XML came about because some Internet applications needed to describe data rather than visual presentation. XML is a formal standard from the World Wide Web Consortium (W3C), the body that controls HTML standards. Rather than start from scratch to define a new way of formatting data, the XML designers adapted the notion of tagged text. HTML had proved the flexibility of tagged text and, furthermore, the designers of XML were interested in embedding XML data in an HTML page (in effect, extending the capabilities of HTML), so it seemed only natural to use a similar format.

To see how it works, consider the following (simplified) example of what a flight itinerary for Mr. Joe Bloggs, going from London to New York, could look like in XML. The content of the message, the payload, has been wrapped in a SOAP envelope. This is the simplest case, where the message is just sent from one system to another, with no complications and no reply

(continued)

XML (*cont.*)

expected—in other words, a "fire and forget." On top of this, there would be the protocol for the transport (e.g., HTTP), the TCP/IP, and the link protocol. It illustrates the amount of data transferred to carry a relatively small payload.

```
A     <?xml version= "1.0"?>
B     <env:Envelope xmlns:env= "http://www.w3.org/2001/09/
        soap-envelope">
C        <env:body>
D           <m:itinerary xmlns:m= "http://airlines.example.
              org/reservations">
                <m:passenger>
                    <m:familyname>Bloggs</m:familyname>
                    <m:firstname>Joe</m:firstname>
                    <m:title>Mr.</m:title>
                </m:passenger>
                <m:flight>
                    <m:flightnumber>AB1234</m:flightnumber>
                    <m:date>29FEB2004</m:date>
                    <m:origin>LHR</m:origin>
                    <m:destination>JFK</m:destination>
                    <m:class>J</m:class>
                    <m:fare>2472</m:fare>
                </m:flight>
E           </m:itinerary>
F        </env:body>
G     </env:Envelope>
```

Line A in the example specifies the version of XML used by the sender. A receiving parser would need to have a compatible version in order to parse the message. If, for example, the receiver had an earlier version than the sender, it might not be able to parse the message. Line B starts the SOAP envelope, which is ended by line G, so the rest of the message is wrapped in the envelope between lines A and G. Line C starts the body of the message, which is ended by line F. Line D identifies the start of the itinerary, which is ended by E. The itinerary contains two elements: passenger information about Mr. Bloggs and flight information.

Unlike HTML, the XML tags specify the name of the data element and have no formatting significance. For different data payloads, different tags must be specified. In lines B and D there are namespace declarations. Taking line D as an example, the text xmlns:m "http://airlines. example.org/reservations" means that m is the namespace prefix defined by the URI http://airlines.example.org/reservations. Namespaces define a collection of names, in the case of this URI (Uniform Resource Identifier). A URI identifies a physical or abstract resource. It can be classified as a locator, a name, or both. The Uniform Resource Locator (URL) is a familiar example. The names are itinerary, passenger, `flight`, and so on. Using `m` as a prefix ensures that the names are unique. Note that the receiver does not have to go over the Web to access the namespace URI; in fact, the URI need not be a valid Web address. All the receiver needs to do is know the names associated with the URI. Line B refers to the namespace used for the SOAP envelope.

To understand an XML document properly, you must understand what the tags mean. In the example, there is a field called `fare`, which is part of a `flight` data element, which in turn is part of an `itinerary` element. The fare is numeric. For a program to do interesting things with an XML document, it must know this information. In other words, it must know the name of the data elements, the structure of the data elements (what fields they may contain), and the type of data in the fields. XML has two mechanisms for describing the structure of an XML document, the *Document Type Definition (DTD)* and the *XML-Data Schema.* (The URI referring to the namespace often points to an XML schema, but it doesn't have to.) DTD is the original mechanism (it was inherited from the earlier SGML standard) and XML data schema was invented later because DTD does not provide all the necessary functionality. You can (but don't have to) include DTD or XML schema in your XML document, or you can point to an external schema somewhere on the Internet. An XML document is considered *well-formed* if it obeys all the rules in the standard. It is considered *valid* if it follows all the additional rules laid down in a DTD or an XML schema.

Note that an XML schema does not provide all the information about the document. In the example, the schema may say the fare is numeric but it does not say that it is a currency field or unit of currency. (Normal airline convention would be to use what are called Fare Currency Units, which are converted to real currencies at the appropriate exchange rate.)

XML is inherently flexible. Because everything is expressed in readable characters, there are no issues about the layout of integer or floating-point numbers, and an XML document can easily be viewed or edited using a simple text editor, such as NotePad. Because data elements have a name, they can be optional (if the schema allows it) or can appear in any order. Data elements can be nested to any level and can be recursive. If there is a list, there is no limit on its length, although the XML schema can specify a limit. It is even possible to have pointers from one field in an XML document to another field in the document.

The disadvantages are equally obvious. Compare formatting information in XML with formatting in a traditional record, and the XML version is almost inevitably many times larger—look at the payload (the data content) in the itinerary, for example. XML does, however, respond well to compaction. The processing overhead in creating and deciphering XML data is also large compared to fix formatted records.

XML is being used increasingly where files or messages hold data. It is being used as a canonical form for output data, which is later formatted for one or several different types of display (or listening) devices. It is used for holding the output of database queries. And it is used for intersystem communication, which is the role of SOAP.

Because SOAP is XML-based, it is flexible and extensible, allowing new features to be added incrementally, as required. A SOAP message comprises an envelope and a mandatory element, the body, which contains the application payload that is to be processed by the destination service provider. The body may be divided into multiple subelements that describe different logical parts of the message payload. The body may be all that is required in many interactions between systems.

An additional, optional element can be included in the envelope: a header. The header is an extension mechanism, providing additional information that is not part of the application payload but context and other information related to the processing of the message (e.g., supporting conversations, authentication, encryption, transactions, etc.). Headers may be divided into blocks containing logical groupings of data. Headers may be processed by intermediaries (e.g., encryption devices) along the path of the message. In short, the header is the means by which complex sequences of interactions can be built.

In order to enable communication across heterogeneous systems, a mechanism to provide a description of the services is required. This mechanism defines the precise structure and data types of the messages, so it must be understood by both producers and consumers of Web services. WSDL provides such a mechanism, where the services are defined in XML documents. It is likely that more sophisticated description languages will be developed; they are discussed in a little more detail later in this chapter.

WSDL, and possible future languages, provide the means of describing specific services. Beyond that, the architecture envisages a variety of process descriptions. They include the means of discovering service descriptions that meet specified criteria, aggregation of processes into higher-level processes, and so on. Some of these functions are much the same in principle as the process orchestration provided by a number of Enterprise Application Integration (EAI) products. This area is much less clearly defined than the others, but a lot of work is going on. One currently defined protocol for advertising and finding services is Universal Discovery, Description and Integration (UDDI).

In spite of all the developments of recent years, the potential of the WWW is only realized in small part. A great deal of work is needed to fulfill expectations. The Web services arena will, of course, continue to be the subject of enormous activity. Many parts of Figure 4-4 clearly need to be fleshed out. These include not only important areas such as security and support of distributed transactions, but also the whole area of service description and process discovery. The ultimate goal is to make the Web look like a single, gigantic data and application environment. Clearly, tiny islands of such a vision could be established within a single organization.

There are significant technical problems. Consider one particular example: semantics. It is not sufficient to be able to encode different types of a thing in XML; for example, order status could be encoded `<orderstatus>confirmed </orderstatus>`. There has to be a consistent interpretation of the data item "confirmed" between the requesting and providing organizations and hence their software implementations. For example, the requester may understand that "confirmed" means that the order has been processed and the thing ordered is on its way, while the provider may think that "confirmed" means that the order has been successfully received and is in the backlog waiting to be processed. This could clearly raise a lot of difficulties in the relationship of the two organizations. There are innumerable other examples where it is essential that all concerned have a precise understanding of exactly what is meant. This is hard enough even within one organization, never mind when two or more organizations are involved.

Establishing such precise meaning is the subject of *ontology,* a term borrowed from philosophy. An ontology, in the sense used here, is a complete and consistent set of terms that define a problem domain. To use Web services to the greatest extent, and bearing in mind that the descriptions of services WSDL provides need to be machine-processed, we need to be able to describe precise meanings as well as the way they are conveyed. The W3C is working on defining a language for this: the Web Ontology Language (for some reason, OWL is the acronym, not WOL).

Finally, the architecture provides for security and management. These are complex areas and are covered in later chapters.

4.3   Using Web services: A pragmatic approach

A long-term vision of Web services is that entrepreneurial application service providers (ASPs) would implement a wide variety of applications, or operate applications provided by others, exposing them as Web services on the Internet. Would-be consumers would then be able to discover the interesting services and use them. The services offered could be implemented in part by invoking other services. For example, a person using a PC with a Web browser as a requester could invoke an application resident in a system somewhere on the Internet as a provider. That system could then use Web services technology to invoke the services of various providers on the Internet, which in turn could do the same thing. The resulting collaboration delivers the required functions to the original requester. Standards such as WSDL provide the required definitions to enable the services to be used, with SOAP as protocol for their invocation, perhaps combined into the kind of complex interactions we discussed in the previous section.

One obvious requirement for this grand vision is a directory structure. UDDI provides the means to publish details of the service and how to access it with a registrar of services, and for the potential requester to find them. The provider describes the service in a WSDL document, which the requester then uses to construct the appropriate messages to be sent, and understand the responses— everything needed to interoperate with the provider of the service. (See the box entitled "Discovery and registries.")

As a number of people have pointed out, great care has to be taken if the results are not to be disappointing. Setting up such a structure on a worldwide basis is a massive undertaking. While certainly possible—some pretty complex

Discovery and registries

A requester and a provider can interact only if the rules for the interaction are unambiguous. The definition includes two parts. The first is a description of the service (the Web Services Description, or WSD), which defines the mechanics of the interaction in terms of data types, message formats, transport protocols, and so on. The second is the semantics governing the interaction, which represent its meaning and purpose and constitutes a contract for the interaction. Ultimately, this definition has to be agreed to by the entities that own them, that is, individuals or the people representing an organization.

The relationship between requester and provider can be established in various ways. At the simplest level, the agreement may be reached between people who represent the requester and the provider, assuming they already know each other. This is common within an organization and also quite likely in the case of bilateral or multilateral groupings, where two or more organizations form a closed group. These groups, such as airlines represented by IATA, hold regular technical meetings where the rules for interaction among the members are discussed and agreed. The resulting agreements are then implemented in the requester and provider software implementations. There is therefore no need for a discovery process. A variation on this is that the semantics are agreed to by people, but the description is provided by the provider and retrieved by the requester. This allows the requester to use the latest version that the provider supports.

If the requester entity does not know what provider it wants, however, there has to be some process of finding, or discovering, an appropriate provider. Discovery is defined (by W3C) as "the act of locating a machine-processable description of a Web service that may have been previously unknown and that meets certain functional criteria." This can be done in various ways, but, ultimately, the requester and provider entities must agree on the semantics of the interaction, either by negotiation or by accepting the conditions imposed by the provider entity.

A person representing the requester, using a discovery tool such as a search engine, for example, could do the discovery. Alternatively, a selection tool of some kind can be used to find a suitable service, without human intervention. In both cases, the provider has to supply the WSD, the semantics, and any additional information needed to allow the desired semantics to be found. The selection could be from an established list of potential services, which are therefore trusted, or a previously unknown service. The latter case may carry significant security risks, so a human intervention may be required.

We have used the terms *discovery tool* and *selection tool* in our discussion. It is the purpose of UDDI and registries to provide a standardized directory mechanism to allow those offering services to publish a description of them and for would-be users to obtain the necessary information about services to be able to find what is required and then establish the interaction. UDDI.org is the organization that has led the development of the UDDI standard. It is backed by a large number of software vendors and other interested parties acting as a consortium.

The idea is that a registry of businesses or other organizations that offer services is established. This is analogous to telephone directories that contain the categories of White Pages, Yellow Pages, and Green Pages, where White Pages provide contact information, Yellow Pages a description of the business according to standard taxonomies, and Green Pages technical information about the services. A long-term vision is a Universal Business Registry of all participating businesses. To set this up on a global basis would be an ambitious undertaking, although some companies have set up such public registries for a limited number of businesses. This can be very useful; it is not necessary to have a directory covering the universe to be valuable. Directories can be set up on a regional or an industry basis, for example. Figure 4-5 shows the relationships of requester, provider, and registry.

However, as was noted in this chapter, the scope can be more restricted but still provide valuable services. Indeed, many of today's Web services applications are not for public use. The services could be for purely internal use, on an intranet, or for external use within a trusted, closed group of users, on an extranet. Registries can be set up in both these cases where the requirements are sufficiently complex and variable that they cannot be managed by simple human agreement, so some discovery is required.

The UDDI standard allows for interaction among registries, using publish-and-subscribe mechanisms. Private registries may publish some information in the public domain. Affiliated organizations (e.g., partners in an alliance, such as one of the airline alliances) can choose to subscribe to each other's registries. And directories may be replicated for performance and resilience reasons.

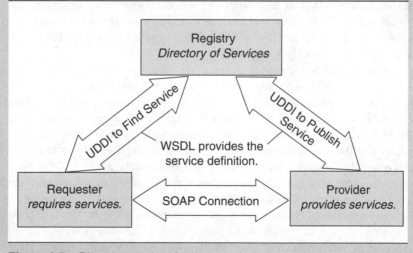

Figure 4-5   Discovery and registries

environments for other things are already in place—doing this with Web services technology poses a significant challenge. The discovery process and the interpretation of the service definition are intended to be performed by software, so the technologies used have to be sufficiently robust and complete to make this possible. There are significant other challenges to overcome, particularly in performance and security, which are discussed later in Chapters 8 and 10, respectively.

As with many other complex technologies, however, there is no need to start with the grand vision. Difficulties might be avoided if implementations are more specific and restricted, certainly initially as experience is gained. One approach would be to use Web services technology inside an organization for collaboration among systems owned by the organization. Depending on the scale of the requirement, it may be possible to use only SOAP and agreed-upon messages for exchange of information, thereby avoiding the need for directory structures and description languages. In effect, the description and locations of the services are worked out by discussions among the people involved, and the software is configured with sufficient information for requesters to find and invoke the service providers. This is still a services-oriented architecture but without the complication of much of the technology, such as directories. It does require that each of the systems involved be able to use SOAP and other related technologies, which may require some modification. An alternative is to group the systems into self-contained, autonomous groups, where each group works internally as it wishes but communicates with the others using Web services technology through a gateway of some kind.

Many analysts view the intra-organization approach as a good way to gain familiarity with the technology. One attraction is that the required standards, specifically SOAP, are widely available on many platforms, or at least committed by their suppliers, thus providing a standard means of communication within heterogeneous environments, which are common in larger organizations. An additional attraction is that, at least within a data center or campus environment, the network bandwidth is likely to be enough to support the somewhat verbose structures of XML with a decent performance. Many organizations are either following this approach or seriously considering it.

Another restricted approach is to use Web services for external connections for e-business (B2B), replacing EDI or other agreed-upon implementations with what is seen as more standard technology. The collaboration could be confined to the members as a closed group, extended to an extranet, or even to two organizations by bilateral agreement. These restrictions remove some of the problems of scale in that the directories are smaller because the number of providers of services is smaller. In some cases, directory structures can be avoided altogether.

As a simple example, consider an organization selling things on the Internet. A customer would be offered a selection of goods, would make a choice, and then be asked for payment, typically by supplying credit card details. The card needs to be verified by a suitable verification agency, which would offer a service to supply the necessary verification and authorization. Web services technology is ideal for this interaction. The credit card verification application therefore functions as the provider of the service, no doubt serving a large number of organizations selling a host of products on the Internet. There would also be a very limited number of such systems, probably just one per country for each credit card type (Visa, MasterCard, etc.), so there is no need for discovery.

The credit card verification application would also serve a very large number of retail outlets using point-of-sale devices through which a card is swiped. Although these could in principle use Web services technology, it is likely that it would take a long time to put in place. The reason is that the retail outlets would have to be supplied with suitable equipment or the software upgraded in existing point-of-sale devices. This is difficult to impose and takes a long time to put in practice. Indeed, the last resting places of many older technologies are in such environments, where the provider of a service cannot easily impose new standards on the users.

The credit card verification service is well defined and is the kind of function the requester would not expect to provide internally. In fact, the requester may already be using the credit card verification agency via a different technology. In other words, it's a well-understood B2B interaction for which Web services technology is ideal. The same is true for the banking example in the connection with the insurance organization. Other examples, among many, include sending purchase orders, invoices, and payments, and requesting and booking transport for delivery of products. Web services are being used in this way and we would expect continuing rapid growth, with increasing levels of sophistication as experience is gained. This could be extended to outsourcing services that are currently performed internally, for example, moving transport logistics to a specialist company.

Taken to an extreme, an organization could outsource all its various IT functions. This is quite common and does not depend on Web services, but typically a single organization provides the outsourcing service. Spreading bits of it around to a variety of organizations, which then collaborate using Web services, is much more complicated. If there are too many small providers requiring a large number of interactions, the problems are severe, not the least of which are in performance and security.

This throws more light on the nature of a service and its suitability as a Web service offered by an ASP on the Internet. It really concerns what the service does, not how much software is required to do it. To be successful, there must be demand, leading to a market for such services, an expectation that did not materialize in the case of objects and components. The credit card application discussed in the example performs a valuable business service that is likely to have many requesters and is easy to incorporate into a complete business process—the process of selling products, in this case. It is also easy to see how it could be advertised and priced. If the services and the associated software providers—the chunks of code—become too much like software components, they are unlikely to become services provided by an ASP. It is just possible, though, that developments in descriptive languages and directory structures could make it easier to find components, which could then be purchased and used internally rather than invoked remotely as Web services.

4.4 Summary

In spite of the current levels of hype about Web services, and the consequent risk of disappointment, the technology will be increasingly important and widely used. The interest in Web services has also highlighted, or revived, the valuable notion of service orientation in general, of which Web services technology is a specific implementation.

Key points to remember:

- The notion of a service has the attraction of being straightforward in principle; it does not require an understanding of obscure terminology. The view that a service is self-contained and provides specific functions to its users through well-defined interfaces, and without revealing details of its internal structure, is good practice. In fact, it is an example of encapsulation.

- Service orientation and service-oriented architectural concepts can be applied at different levels. An application offering external services to others, exposed as Web services, can itself be internally constructed using a service-oriented architectural approach. Web services technology may or may not be used within the application; it depends on what the implementers find convenient.

- Web service technology is in many ways still in its infancy, in spite of all the work that has been done. The full vision will take a long time to mature, but that by no means removes the value of using some of the technology now.

- To avoid disappointment, it is very desirable to approach implementations pragmatically (e.g., use the technology in controlled environments to gain experience). The technology can be used within a single organization, and in B2B environments, either bilaterally or with a group of partners. This approach avoids the complications of extensive discovery of services. It is quite realistic to use only SOAP and messages agreed upon by people in the participating groups. This is already becoming common.

5

A Technical Summary
of Middleware

Chapters 2, 3, and 4 describe in outline form a vast array of technologies. This chapter and the next are about the question, what middleware do we need? This is a key question for implementation design and IT architecture. This chapter approaches the question from a technical angle. First, we discuss the different constituent parts of middleware technology. Second, we examine vendor architectures, such as Microsoft's .NET and Sun's J2EE (Java 2 Enterprise Edition). Finally, we look at middleware interoperability. In the next chapter, we look at middleware from the application developer's point of view.

5.1   Middleware elements

In Chapter 1 we point out that middleware consists of at least eight elements. They are illustrated in Figure 1-5, but for convenience this diagram is repeated in Figure 5-1. In this section we address the elements in more detail with an emphasis on Web services technology.

A and B are different machines. The box around both is meant to indicate the complete systems environment.

5.1.1   The communications link

The first two elements—the communications link and the middleware protocol—enable A and B to send data to each other.

Most middleware is restricted to using one or a few networking standards, the dominant standard at the moment being TCP/IP. The standards offer a set of value added features, which may or may not be useful. For instance, TCP/IP offers

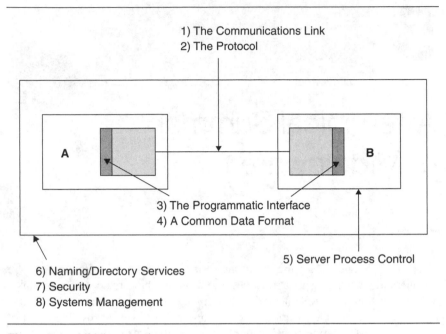

Figure 5-1 Middleware elements

reliable delivery of messages and Domain Name Service (DNS) for converting names into IP addresses.

Networks are implemented in layers (see the next box entitled "Layering") and most layers, including middleware layers, implement a protocol. Protocols are defined by:

- The format of the messages as they travel over the communications link and
- The state transition diagrams of the entities at each end.

Informally, the protocol defines who starts the conversation, how to stop both ends from speaking at once, how to ensure both sides are talking about the same subject, and how to get out of trouble.

Protocols fall into two major categories: protocols with connections and protocols without them. Connection-less protocols are like sending a letter. You chuck the message into the ether with the address on it and hope it reaches its destination. IP (the networking part of TCP/IP) is connection-less, and so are most LAN protocols. As an aside, sessions and connections are very similar concepts; application designers tend to talk about sessions while network specialists tend to talk about connections.

TCP, on the other hand, is a connection protocol. It would be possible to use User Datagram Protocol (UDP), which is basically a (connection-less) raw interface to IP, but TCP is the software of choice for most middleware. The reason is that TCP has some very useful features. In particular it provides:

- No message loss (unless there is an actual break in the link or in a node)
- No messages received in the wrong order
- No message corruption and
- No message duplication

If you don't have these kinds of features implemented by the networking software, then the middleware must fill the gap and provide it.

Note that you can't actually detect message loss or duplication without some kind of connection concept. This has implications for middleware. At some level, there is almost certainly a connection in the middleware implementation. Even in message queuing, which to the programmer looks connection-less, there are underlying connections between the nodes.

The Web services standards do not specify a communications link standard. But there must be a reliable delivery of messages, and in practice most Web services implementations run over HTTP, which in turn uses TCP/IP. However, there is nothing in the standard that prevents Web services from running over another networking protocol or, for that matter, another middleware, such as message queuing.

5.1.2   The middleware protocol

By far the greater number of middleware protocols are connection protocols; they are dialogues rather than signals. Connection protocols can be classified by who starts the dialogue. There are three scenarios: many to one, one to one, or one to many. They are illustrated in Figure 5-2.

The first situation is client/server. Each client initiates the dialogue, and there can be many clients to one server. Normally, the client continues in control of the dialogue. The client will send a message and get back one or more replies. The server does nothing (in the context of the client/server dialogue) until the next client message arrives. The client asks the questions and the server gives the answers.

In peer-to-peer protocols, both sides are equal, and either one initiates a dialogue. TCP is a peer-to-peer protocol. E-mail and directory servers also use peer-to-peer to communicate with each other.

Push protocols are a bit like client/server except that the server initiates the messages. This can be contrasted with client/server, which is sometimes called pull technology. A well-known use of push protocols is within publish and subscribe tools. The subscribe process is standard client/server; a client indicates to the server that it wants to subscribe to a certain information delivery, for instance, to track stock movements. The publish process is a push mechanism, which means that the message is sent to the client without prompting. Push is ideal for broadcasting changes of state. For instance, in a bank, push might be used to publish

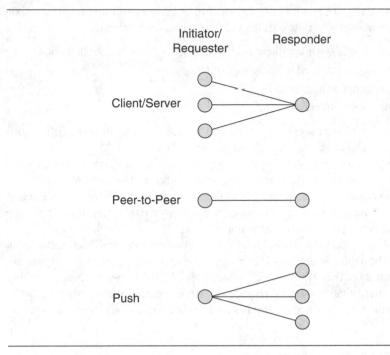

Figure 5-2   Protocol categories

interest rate changes to all interested parties. At the moment. there is no accepted standard for push.

The SOAP protocol for Web services does not define any of these protocols; in fact it is, from the application perspective, connection-less. Any client (including any service) can send a message to any server at any time. To help you build request-response applications with the Connection-less messages, SOAP provides for additional information in the messages headers. For instance, you can link a request with a response by including the requester's message identity in the response. (For more information, see http://www.w3.org/TR/xmlp-scenarios which provides examples of request-response, asynchronous messages, push protocols, and others all implemented in SOAP.)

Another important aspect of protocols is the integrity features they support. As noted earlier, all middleware should provide reliable message delivery, but some middleware has additional integrity features to address the wider issues of application-to-application integrity. For instance, message queuing may store messages on disk and allow the application to read them much later, and transactional middleware may implement the two-phase commit protocol.

The Web services approach to integrity is to make it flexible. You can define integrity features in the message header; for instance, you can ask for delivery confirmation. There is nothing in the standard (at least the SOAP 1.2 version) about storing messages on disk for later retrieval à la message queuing, but nothing preventing it either.

Two-phase commit between requester and provider, however, cannot be implemented only through message header information; it requires additional messages to flow between the parties. There are a number of proposed standards to fill this gap: BTP from OASIS (another independent standards-making body); WS-Coordination and WS-Transaction from BEA, IBM, and Microsoft; and WS-CAF (consisting of WS-Context for the overall description, WS-CF for the coordination framework, and WS-TXM for transaction management) from OASIS again, and supported by Sun, Oracle, Hewlett-Packard, and many other vendors. Obviously, there are overlapping and competing standards, and going into this area in detail is beyond the scope of this book.

5.1.3   The programmatic interface

The programmatic interface is a set of procedure calls used by a program to drive the middleware. Huge variation is possible; the variation lies along three dimensions.

The first dimension is a classification according to what entities are communicating. There is a historical trend here. In the early days, terminals communicated with mainframes—the entities were hardware boxes. Later, process communicated with process (e.g., RPC). Later still, client programs and objects communicate with objects or message queues communicate with message queues.

Observe that this is layering. Objects reside (at runtime at least) in processes. Processes reside in hardware boxes. Underpinning the whole edifice is hardware-to-hardware communication. This is reflected in the network protocols: IP is for hardware-to-hardware communication, TCP is for process-to-process communication, and IIOP is for object-to-object communication (see the box entitled "Layering").

Over much of the history of middleware, the communicating entities (i.e., hardware, then processes, then objects) have become smaller and smaller, more and more abstract, and more and more numerous. To some extent, Web services can be seen as a reversal of this trend because the size and nature of the communicating entities is not defined. Client programs are communicating with services. Services can be of any size. So long as they are reachable, how the service is implemented in terms of objects, processes, or components is not defined by the standard.

The second dimension is the nature of the interface and in this dimension there are two basic categories; we will call them APIs and GPIs. An API (Application Programming Interface) is a fixed set of procedure calls for using the middleware. GPIs (our term, Generated Programming Interfaces) either generate the interface from the component source or from a separated file written in an IDL. (IDLs are discussed in Chapter 2 in the section on RPCs). GPI middleware has compile-time flexibility; API middleware has run-time flexibility.

Layering

Layering is a fundamental concept for building distributed systems. The notion of layering is old and dates back at least to the 1960s. For instance, it features in Dijkstra's 1968 Comm. ACM paper "The Structure of the "THE"-Multiprogramming System," referred to as levels of abstraction. Layering became prominent when the original ISO seven-layer model was published. The seven-layer model itself and the role of ISO in pushing through international standards has diminished, but the concept of layering is as powerful and as obvious as ever. We will illustrate it using TCP/IP but using some ISO terminology. There are basically four layers:

- Physical layer—the wire, radio waves, and pieces of wet string that join two hardware boxes in a network.
- Data link layer—the protocol between neighboring boxes in the network (e.g., Ethernet and Frame relay).
- Network layer—the protocol that allows messages to be sent through multiple hardware boxes to reach any machine in the network. In TCP/IP this is IP, the Internet Protocol.
- Transport layer—the protocol that allows a process in one hardware box to create and use a network session with a process in other hardware box. In TCP/IP this is TCP, the Transmission Control Protocol.

The fundamental notion of layering is that each layer uses the layer below it to send and receive messages. Thus TCP uses IP to send the messages, and IP uses Ethernet, Frame relay, or whatever to send messages. Each layer has a protocol. The system works because each layer has a very well-defined behavior. For instance, when TCP gives IP a message, it expects that the receiving TCP node will be given the message with exactly the same size and content. This might sound trivial, but it isn't when the lower-level protocols might have length restrictions that cause the message to be segmented. When a user program uses TCP, it expects that the receiver will receive the messages in the same order the sender sent them. This also sounds trivial until you realize that IP obeys no such restriction. IP might send two messages in a sequence by an entirely different route; getting them out of order is quite possible.

Middleware software typically starts above the TCP layer and takes all these issues of message segmentation and ordering for granted. Referring to the OSI model, middleware standards live roughly in layers 5, 6, and parts of 7.

Layering is not confined to the network layer. First, it is important as a thinking tool; it is a wonderful technique for structuring complex problems so we can solve them. Second, people are forever layering one technology on another to get around some specific problem. The networking specialists have a special term for this—*tunneling*. For instance, SNA can be used as a data link layer in a TCP/IP network and (not at the same time, we hope)

IP can be used as a data link layer in an SNA network. It is not an ideal solution, but sometimes it is useful tactically. In the middleware context, people rarely talk about tunneling, but the idea comes up often enough, for instance, layering a real time client/server application over a message-queuing infrastructure.

In this book we use terms such as *presentation layer* and *transaction server layer*. We use them in a system context, not a network context, and they have no relationship to the seven-layer model. Since it is not about communication from one network node to another network node, there is no implication that for a presentation entity to talk to a presentation entity, it must send messages down to the database layer and back up the other side. But the implication that the presentation layer cannot jump around the transaction server (or whatever the box in the middle is called) is correct. Basically, the message and the flow of control can move around the layers like a King in chess—one box at a time—and not like a Knight. If we do want to allow layers to be missed out, we will either draw nonrectangular shapes to create touching sides, or we will draw a line to indicate the flows. Strictly speaking, when this is done, it stops being a layered architecture.

Within API middleware there are many styles of interface. A possible classification is:

- *Message-based:* The API sends and receives messages, with associated message types. The server looks at the message type to decide where to route the message. An example is MQSeries where the message type is the queue name.
- *Command-language-based:* The command is encoded into a language. The classic example is remote database access for which the command language is SQL.
- *Operation-call-based—the operation call:* The name of the server operation and its parameters are built up by a series of middleware procedure calls. This is what happens in the interpretative interface for COM+, for instance.

Many middleware systems have both API and GPI interfaces. The API interface is for interpreters and the GPI interface is for component builders.

The third dimension is a classification according to the impact on process thread control. The classification is:

- *Blocked (also known as synchronous):* The thread stops until the reply arrives.
- *Unblocked (also known as asynchronous):* The client every now and then looks to see whether the reply has arrived.
- *Event-based:* When the reply comes, an event is caused, waking up the client.

The Web services standards do not define a programmatic interface. You can if you wish have the program read or write the XML data directly, perhaps using vendor-provided XML facilities to create the actual XML text. This is a form of API. At the other extreme (a GPI approach) are facilities for generating a Web service interface from a set of function and parameter definitions. Take ASP.NET as an example. You can create a Web services project in Microsoft Visual Studio which will generate all the files needed by ASP.NET to run the service and a skeletal source file. Let us suppose you are writing the service in C#. You can then denote that a class provides a Web service, and within the class, designate some public methods to be part of the external interface by prefixing them with the text "[WebMethod]". Visual Studio will generate the relevant code to:

- Convert XML messages into calls on the method with parameter values set from the XML input data.
- Convert the method result to XML output data.
- Build a WSDL service description of the interface.

This kind of approach is clearly easier for the programmer, but is valid only for request-response interactions which, as we have outlined, is far from all Web services can do.

5.1.4   Data presentation

A message has some structure, and the receiver of the message will split the message into separate fields. Both sender and receiver must therefore know the structure of the message. The sender and receiver may also represent data values differently. One might use ASCII, the other Extended Binary Coded Decimal Interchange Code (EBCDIC) or UNICODE. One might have 16-bit, little-endian integers, the other might use 32-bit, big-endian integers. Sender or receiver, or both, may need to convert the data values. Many, but not all, middleware products assemble and disassemble messages and convert data formats for you. Where there is an IDL, this used to be called marshalling, but today is more commonly called serialization. But reformatting does not necessarily need an IDL. Remote database access also reformats data values.

Today XML is more and more a universal data presentation standard, and this is, of course, the approach of Web services.

5.1.5   Server control

Server control breaks down into three main tasks:

1. *Process and thread control.* When the first client program sends its first message, something must run the server process. When the load is heavy, additional processes or threads may be started. Something must route the server

request to (a) a process that is capable of processing it and (b) an available thread. When the load lightens, it may be desirable to lessen the number of processes and threads. Finally, when processes or threads are inactive, they need to be terminated.

2. *Resource management.* For instance, database connection pooling.

3. *Object management.* Objects may be activated or deactivated. Clearly this only applies to object-oriented systems.

Web services standards has nothing to say on server control.

5.1.6   Naming and directory services

The network access point to a middleware server is typically a 32-bit number that defines the network address (IP address) and a port number that allows the operating system to route the message to the right program. Naming services map these numbers to names people can all understand. The best-known naming service, Domain Name Service (DNS), is used by the Internet. Directory services go one step further and provide a general facility for looking things up—a middleware equivalent to the telephone directory. Directory services tend to be separate products, which the middleware hooks into. An example is the Microsoft Active Directory.

If Web services really take off in the way the inventors imagine, UDDI directories will become a major part of many environments, including the Internet. UDDI directories, of course, tell you much more about a service than just its IP address, in particular the details of the interface.

5.1.7   Security

Only valid users must be allowed to use the server resources, and when they are connected, they may be given access to only a limited selection of the possible services. Security permeates all parts of the system. Encryption needs support at the protocol level. Access control needs support from the server control functions, and authentication may need support from a dedicated security manager system.

Web services have a number of security extensions. They are discussed in Chapter 10.

5.1.8   System management

Finally, there needs to be a human interface to all this software for operational control, debugging, monitoring, and configuration control.

Standards and products cover only a few of these issues. In all cases, the solution requires a number of products working together. This broadly is the purpose of standard and vendor architectures—to position the standards and products to show how they can be assembled to create a solution.

Web services standards have nothing to say about system management, but the issue of services management either over the Internet or over an intranet is actively being pursued by many vendors.

5.1.9   Comments on Web services

Middleware is enormously varied mainly because the technologies have been trying to answer two complex questions: What protocol/integrity facilities should it offer, and what should be the programmatic interface? Even in the context of this variability, Web services seems to us to be a break with the past. It has made a separation between the protocol concerns and the programming concerns and has addressed only the former. The latter, the programming concern, has in practice been left to the vendor architectures described in the next section. In the past, the programming concerns largely drove the protocol concerns. There used to be vision that programming in a distributed environment would sometime in the future be as simple as programming for a single machine (and thus there is remote-this and remote-that technology). This vision is gone, largely we believe because there is a new awareness that interoperating across a network with an application you don't control is very different from interoperating in a single machine with an application you do control. For instance, instead of having a reference to an object in another machine and sending read requests and updates to that object, it is often better for the service to send a larger chunk of data in one shot so that the client application can recreate the object locally. This makes it easier to change the applications at either end without breaking the link between them; put another way, it makes them more loosely coupled. As we discuss in the following chapters, we believe that moving to a more loosely coupled approach to distributed systems is to be welcomed.

5.2   Vendor architectures

The discussion in the previous section raises two interesting questions. First, clearly middleware by itself is not enough to create a complete working system, so what other elements are needed? Second, do organizations need just one middleware technology or many, and, if many, how many?

Vendor architectures are about answering these questions for the particular set of products the vendor wishes to sell.

Vendor architectures have been around for many years. The early architectures were restricted to the network, such as SNA from IBM. Later they became more inclusive, such as System Application Architecture (SAA) from IBM. Others have come and gone. The two vendor architectures that are grabbing the attention now are .NET and Java 2 Enterprise Edition (J2EE), from Microsoft and Sun, respectively.

Vendor architectures serve various functions, many of them to do with marketing and image building. We restrict our discussion to platform architectures and distributed architectures.

5.2.1   Vendor platform architectures

If you have a program or a component, then a question you may want answered is, what machines can run this program? The answer depends on the answers to three further questions:

1. What machines can execute the program code? Execute, here, means either run in native mode or interpret.
2. What machines support the system interfaces the program relies on?
3. What machines can run any additional programs or components this program depends on?

The platform architecture addresses the second point and defines the standard interfaces such as access to operating system resources, object and memory management, component management, user interface facilities, transactional facilities, and security facilities.

Both .NET and J2EE include a platform architecture. The .NET platform is illustrated in Figure 5-3.

Going up from the bottom, above the operating system is the Common Language Runtime. The Common Language Runtime defines how different components can be assembled at runtime and talk to each other. The J2EE platform architecture has something very similar—the Java Virtual Machine (JVM).

As an aside, it used to be that Microsoft programs were in machine code and Java components were interpreted. But many JVMs implement a just-in-time (JIT) compilation that turns the Java byte code into machine code. In .NET, compilers create intermediate language, IL, and the .NET framework converts the IL into machine code at runtime. So today, both platform architectures are very close.

Above the Common Language Runtime in Figure 5-3 are three layers of boxes that provide class libraries—in other words, facilities that are invoked by the program as if they were objects provided by just another component. The code behind the class library façade will typically call some Microsoft-provided application. Base class libraries are about accessing operating system facilities (e.g., file IO, time, and date) and other basic facilities (e.g., mathematical functions). ADO.NET is about database access. The XML class library provides routines for creating and reading XML messages and files. A feature of ADO.NET is that it uses XML extensively, which is why the two have been positioned in the same box. ASP.NET is about Web access, and Windows Forms is about using workstation windows. J2EE has a similar set of class libraries.

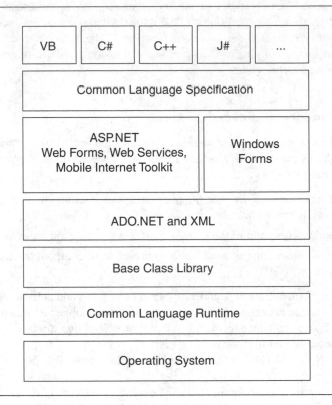

Figure 5-3 .NET framework

At the top are the compilers. Here lies the most striking difference between .NET and Java. .NET supports many languages, J2EE supports only Java—a big advantage for .NET. But J2EE runs on many more platforms than .NET, which is a big advantage for J2EE.

5.2.2 Vendor-distributed architectures

We illustrate a distributed architecture using J2EE in Figure 5-4.
J2EE consists of several tiers:

- The client tier—either browser, possibly with Java Applets, or a stand-alone Java program.
- The Web tier—a Web server running Java Server Pages (JSP) and Java Servlets.
- The Enterprise JavaBeans tier—an EJB container.
- The Enterprise Information Systems tier—a database or a connector to an older application, for instance, on a mainframe.

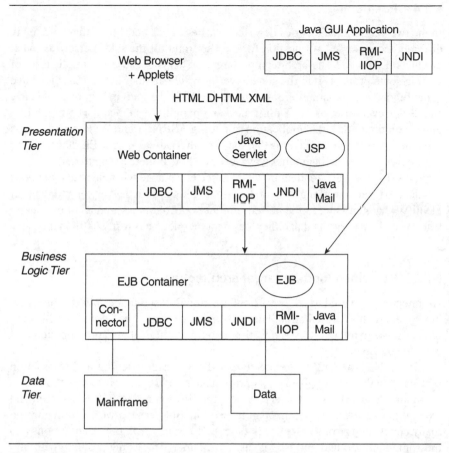

Figure 5-4   A distributed architecture using J2EE

Each tier supports a set of platform APIs. For instance, Java Message Service (JMS), which supports message queuing, and Java DataBase Connectivity (JDBC), which supports remote database access, are supported everywhere except in Java Applets.

The common building blocks everywhere are Java components.

The .NET distributed architecture is very similar except that .NET components, not Java components, are everywhere. Instead of JSP, there is ASP. Instead of EJB, .NET components can have COM+-like features by using .NET Enterprise Services.

5.2.3   Using vendor architectures

Vendor architectures serve a number of functions and we will explore three: positioning, strawman for user architectures, and marketing.

5.2.4   Positioning

In the two vendor architectures described earlier (.NET and J2EE) there are many different technologies. A question for the user (and for the sales person) is, what products do I need? The architecture diagrams helps because the implication of putting some products into the same layer or inside another box is that they have some functions in common. For instance, the .NET diagram in Figure 5-3 clearly shows that every user of .NET must have an operating system and a common languages runtime. Also, the implication of putting ASP.NET and Windows Forms as separate boxes but in one layer is that they are alternatives. The J2EE diagram (see Figure 5-4) is specific in another way; it shows how products map to tiers.

A well-presented architecture lets you see at a glance what elements you need to select to make a working system. Positioning helps both the vendor and the user identify what's missing in the current product portfolio, and architectures usually lead to vendors' ensuring that either they or someone else is ready to fill in the gaps.

5.2.5   Strawman for user target architecture

Architectures are used to tell users how functionality should be split, for instance, into layers such as presentation, business logic, and data. The purpose of this kind of layering is to tell developers how they should partition application functionality between the layers.

Both .NET and J2EE architectures offer message queuing and transaction services, but they aren't given equal prominence. In J2EE, for instance, the EJB is a container and JMS is just a service. The implication is that EJB is essential and JMS might be useful if you happen to need it. But perhaps we are drawing too many conclusions from a picture! In other pictures of J2EE, both transactions and messaging are services and EJB is just a container. That is the problem with pictures; they can hint at things without saying them outright, rather like a politician giving a non-attributable quote.

More pertinent, the implication of architectures is that the set of tools from the .NET bag will work together and the set of tools from the J2EE bag will work together, but if you mix and match from both bags, you are on your own.

There are notable omissions; for instance, J2EE is silent on the subject of batch processing. You should not expect architectures to be comprehensive—none has been yet.

5.2.6   Marketing

An architecture can provide a vision of the future. The architecture is saying: This is how we (the vendor) believe applications should be built and our tools are the best for the job. Using an architecture, the vendor can show that it (possibly with partners) has a rich set of tools, it has thought through the development issues, it has a strategy it is working toward and, above all, it is forward looking.

But there are dangers for a vendor in marketing architectures. The biggest problem is bafflement; by its very nature, when explaining an architecture, you have to explain a range of very complex software. If the architecture is too complex, it's hard to explain. If it's too simple, the vision can seem to have no substance. Unfortunately, the people to whom marketing directs the strategic message are probably senior executives who haven't had the pleasure or pain of reading a book like this to explain what it is all about. Bafflement is only one problem. There are also some fine lines to be drawn between an architecture that is too futuristic and too far ahead of the implementation and one that is so cautious that it's boring. Then there are the dangers of change. You can guarantee that if the architecture changes, most people will have the wrong version.

We often think that the most important audience for the architecture are the vendor's own software developers. It helps them understand where they stand in the wider scheme of things.

5.2.7   Implicit architectures

Arguably every software vendor has an architecture; it is just that many of them don't give it a name. We have described the dangers of too aggressive an approach to marketing architectures, and many vendors choose instead to talk about software strategies and roadmaps. What all vendors need is the positioning, the view on application development, and the visioning.

In practical terms, this means that if your organization buys an application product like SAP or Oracle, then like it or not, your organization has bought into the SAP or Oracle architecture, at least in part. Many of these packages are themselves built around a middleware standard, and all offer a variety of ways to work with other systems using standard middleware technology.

Another example is Enterprise Application Integration (EAI) products. These products provide an approach to application integration. If you go with these products, it pushes you along a certain direction that affects how you develop applications in the future—a vendor architecture in all but name.

A way of accessing the architectural implication of products is to ask yourself three questions:

1. What impact does this product have on the positioning of existing applications? For instance, the product might communicate with your back-end mainframe application by pretending to be a 3270 terminal. This is positioning the back end as a transaction server but one with a load of superfluous formatting code.

2. What impact does this product have on future development? What tools do I use and where? How do I partition the functionality between the tiers?

3. What is the vendor's vision for the future?

A further consequence of this discussion is that large organizations are likely to implement many vendor architectures, which brings us to the next topic.

5.3 Middleware interoperability

It is possible to build a software product to link different middleware technologies. This setup is illustrated in Figure 5-5. We have called this a hub in Figure 5-5, but *gateway* is another common term (albeit in the context of one middleware in, one out). Also, the hub, or gateway, need not be in a separate box but might be packaged with one or more of the applications.

That hubs are practical technology is easily illustrated by the fact that there are widespread implementations. Middleware interoperability is one of the main functions of EAI products (see the box entitled "Enterprise application integration products"). We have decided that this book isn't the place to discuss the differences among EAI products. There are many good EAI products and, unusually for the software business, the market is not dominated by one or two vendors.

When implementing a hub, there are two questions that we believe are of particular interest to IT architects. One question arises because there is an opportunity with hub software to provide all kinds of additional functions such as routing, reformatting, additional security checks, and monitoring. The question is, when should I use an EAI product and what should be implemented in the product rather than in application code? This question is answered in Chapter 6. The second question asks, is middleware interoperability safe? This is the issue we want to address here.

Let us start with a simple scenario. Application A wishes to send a message to application B but it's not bothered about a response. To make it more concrete, let

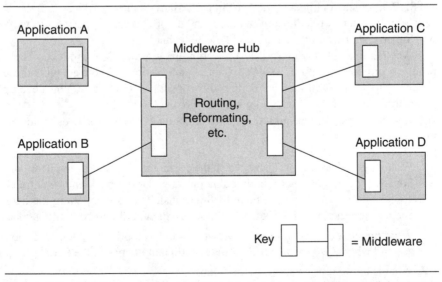

Figure 5-5 Middleware interoperability showing one hub acting as a link to many applications

Enterprise application integration products

The requirement to integrate applications and databases of different types into business processes has led to the development of a wide variety of EAI products from a number of suppliers, many of which are specialists in the field. The products are typically marketed as a core set of functionality with separately priced add-on features, which may be purchased as requirements dictate. They can be used to integrate applications internally in an organization and externally with other organizations—B2B, in other words.

Architecturally, EAI products are hubs, which are connected through local and wide area networks to the various systems involved. Although there are obvious differences in functionality and price among the products, all of them contain a number of common elements.

Starting with their external interfaces, the products have to be able to connect to a wide variety of systems and databases, which may be of various ages and use many technologies. They do this by supplying a selection of gateways or adapters to the most commonly required types, for example:

- Various flavors of Electronic Data Interchange (EDI), such as EDIFACT and X12, which have long formed the basis of B2B communication. These could be transported through basic technologies such as file transfer—FTP is very common.
- Messaging interfaces, for example, using e-mail.
- Middleware-based connections, using MQSeries or other middleware.
- Direct RDBMS connections, for example, to common databases, and general database access technologies such as ODBC and JDBC.
- Increasingly, Web-based technologies, including HTTP and XML, and especially Web services. In the longer term, as the use of Web services technology spreads, it should become the dominant mechanism.
- Interfaces to widely used application suites, such as SAP, Siebel, and Peoplesoft. These may, of course, be based on using middleware.
- Proprietary interfaces. It is likely that some applications will offer only proprietary means of connection. To accommodate these requirements, the products usually offer a development kit to allow users to build their own interfaces, such as screen-scraping, where the application is accessed as though it were talking to terminals.

The products provide the means to connect to the systems or databases involved. Since the different systems will work with different syntax and semantics for the data transferred, the products include a variety of transformation tools to convert from one form to another, as required.

But the real power provided by EAI products lies in the tools to define business processes and orchestrate, or choreograph, the process flow through the whole environment. These tools provide the means to define how traffic is to be routed around the various applications and what to do

(continued)

Enterprise application integration products (*cont.*)

when each step is completed. Some steps may be performed in parallel, such as requesting information from different sources, and others have to be executed in series, in the case where one step depends on the completion of the previous one. The products normally offer sophisticated graphical tools to allow users to define the process and the steps required and to manage the flow. In addition, they may offer services such as transaction management, if the processes require database synchronization, logging, and so on. These facilities make EAI products valuable. If the requirement is simple, with a limited number of connections and transformations, they may be overkill.

Finally, the products have management and monitoring tools, and they contain facilities for reporting and handling exceptions and errors encountered during operation.

The net effect is that the tools allow the user to generate applications built from the various connected systems. Some vendors provide also vertical industry solutions, for example, in healthcare or retailing, using standards defined within that business sector.

A simple example may give a flavor of what can be done. The example, based on a real case, is of a bank that offers mortgages to home buyers. The bank has a mortgage application, as well as other investment and checking account applications. The particular EAI implementation concerned offering mortgages in conjunction with a real estate agent, which also acts as an agent for selling the bank's mortgage products. The following paragraphs describe the process flow before and after the introduction of an EAI product.

The customer would agree on the purchase of a property with the real estate agent. Following this, the agent would offer the customer the prospect of a mortgage product from the bank. If the customer agreed, the agent and customer would together complete a mortgage application form on paper. This was then faxed to the bank, where it would be entered into the bank's system. Following that, the application would be processed by a mortgage verification application, including an external credit check and, subject to approval, an offer in principle (that is, subject to final checks, such as with the customer's employer to confirm salary details) would be sent back to the customer. This took a day or two to complete.

An EAI system was then introduced to automate the whole process. Instead of preparing a paper application form, it is completed on a PC and sent, in XML format, across the Internet to the EAI hub. This invokes the mortgage verification application, including the external credit check; makes an additional check to see if there are any extra conditions applying to the real estate agent; updates the mortgage application database; and sends a letter containing an offer in principle back to the real estate agent, who gives it to the customer. This is completed in a minute or two, so the customer has an answer immediately. Any exceptions or errors are reported to the bank's systems management staff.

It is, of course, theoretically possible that other checks could be made (for example, with the customer's employer to confirm salary details) so the offer sent back would be final rather than in principle. There are technical issues (for example, the employer would need to have its salary system online), but they are not insurmountable from a purely technical point of view; the major difficulties would concern privacy and security.

The functions performed by the EAI product in this and many other cases are, of course, the same as the intentions of Web services. You may recall the Web services technology architecture discussed in Chapter 4, which contains choreography. The potential is to provide the required capabilities using widely accepted open standards rather than a proliferation of different standards and even ad hoc mechanisms.

us assume application A uses message queuing, and the hub receives the message and calls application B using Java Remote Method Invocation (RMI).

Normally, when application A sends a message using message queuing, the message is (a) guaranteed to arrive at its destination and (b) not sent twice. Can a hub provide these guarantees? It is possible for the hub to provide message queuing integrity but not without some work from the hub programmer. One way is for the hub to have a two-phase commit transaction that spans receiving the message from A and calling application B. Alternatively, if the transaction had a special unique identifier (as monetary transactions usually do), you can have the hub call application B again if it lost or never received the reply from the original submission. If the original submission was processed, the resubmission will be rejected. You can think of this as a kind of home-grown message integrity.

Now let's make our example a bit more complex. Suppose application A wants to see the reply from application B and expects to see the reply in a message queue, a different message queue from the sending message queue. If application A is sending many messages simultaneously, it will have to be able to tie the reply to the original sender, which may require the hub to put additional data in the reply message.

There is the possibility that application B processes the transaction but the hub or the link fails before sending the reply message on to A. How can the hub guarantee that if application B sent a reply, one and only one response message gets to application A? Again a simple solution is to put all the hub work—reading in the input from A, calling B, and sending the output to A—in a single transaction, which means using two-phase commit to synchronize the queues and the transaction. The alternative is again to handle it at the application level. A good solution is for application A to send a "is the transaction done?" message if it does not receive a reply within a certain time period. This is discussed more in Chapter 7 on resiliency because it is a common problem with many middleware configurations.

Let us make our scenario more complex. Suppose there is a full-blooded stateful session between application A and application B. Since message queuing has no concept of a session, there must be something in the message that indicates to the applications that this is part of a session. A simple protocol is for application A to ask application B for a session ID and for the session ID to be passed with all subsequent messages. If the hub, not application B, is actually processing the messages, then it is up to the hub to understand the session ID convention and process it appropriately.

Finally, suppose the hub, instead of just calling application B, calls applications B, C, and D, all for one input message. How is integrity maintained? A simple solution is two-phase commit; if any fail, they are all undone. Sometimes though the desired action is not to undo everything but, for instance, to report to application A that B and C were completed but D failed. The problem now arises that if the hub goes down in the middle of all this processing, it must reconstruct how to reassemble the output for A. One ingenious solution is for the hub to send message-queued messages to itself after processing B and C, and let message queue recovery handle all the synchronization issues.

To summarize:

- The integrity issues need to be thought through case by case.
- It can be done.
- If you want the hub to handle everything, you probably have to use techniques like two-phase commit and sending message-queued messages within the hub.
- An alternative is to handle recovery issues at the application level, typically by having the requester repeat requests if it hasn't received a response and having the provider detect and eliminate requests it has already processed.

Whether it is better to implement integrity at the application level depends largely on whether there is existing code for finding out what happened to the last update action. Often in integrity-sensitive applications, the code does already exist or can easily be adapted. If so, then using application integrity checks has the benefit of continuing to work regardless of the complexity of the path through various middleware technologies. Chapter 13 describes a technique called task/message diagrams for, among other things, analyzing protocol integrity issues such as we have discussed.

Finally, why do any of this? Can't Web services handle it all? Is it possible to build a hub that maintains integrity while using Web services as one or all of its middleware connectors? In theory it is possible, but not with any arbitrary implementation of Web services. Most practical implementations of Web services use HTTP as the underlying protocol. This means that the hub could read an HTTP message but fail before doing anything with it, thereby losing the message. What is required is software that can synchronize reading the message within a transaction boundary, as message-queuing technology can. Web service implemented over message queuing, which is allowed in the standard, would be as capable as any other message-queuing implementation.

But perhaps this is less of a problem than it looks on the face of it. The optional information in the SOAP headers, like delivery confirmation and response message identifiers, are designed to make application-to-application integrity easier to implement. As discussed in Chapter 6, for loosely coupled interoperability, implementing integrity at the application level is probably the best way to go.

Looking into the future, we speculate that we will see loosely coupled "choreography" to some extent being used instead of tightly coupled two-phase commits. (*Choreography* is the word used in the Web services architecture document and essentially means assistance in building application-to-application dialogues.)

5.4 Summary

In this chapter, instead of describing middleware technology by technology, we look at the elements that make up a middleware product and describe each of these across the spectrum of middleware technologies. This leads to discussions about vendor architectures and middleware interoperability.

Key points to remember:

- Middleware protocols can be classified into client/server, peer-to-peer, and push protocols. Just as important as these characterizations are the kinds of integrity they support. The integrity can be either message integrity, such as delivery guarantees, or transaction integrity.
- The underlying cause of many of the differences among various middleware technology comes about because of the huge variety of programmatic interfaces.
- The Web services SOAP standard dictates a basic message transfer facility but allows you to enhance it by either specifying message headers or using a protocol layered on top of SOAP (e.g., transaction management or security.) The standard does not specify the programmatic interface, and some existing programmatic interfaces for SOAP restrict the Web services functionality (which is fine if all you need is restricted Web services functionality).
- Whereas in the past there was a desire to make using distributed systems like nondistributed systems (as illustrated by the number of technologies that have "Remote" in their title), Web services goes against this trend. This is a symptom of moving from tightly coupled middleware to loosely coupled middleware (discussed more in Chapter 6).
- Vendor architectures are useful for positioning vendor products. The two most important vendor architectures today (.NET and J2EE) are remarkably similar. One supports more programming languages and the other supports more platforms, but they have the same basic notions of tiering and just-in-time compilation.

- Middleware interoperability is possible and often important. There is a wide range of EAI products to help. An important technical issue is integrity; it is essential to deal with the danger of losing integrity features the application is relying on while converting from one middleware technology to another. Both message and transaction integrity can be implemented by the judicious use of two-phase commit transactions in the middleware hub. In many cases, however, it is also not difficult to manage the integrity at the application level. The building blocks are inquiries to check whether the last transaction was done and reversal transactions to undo some previously processed work. (Chapter 13 discusses a technique called task/message diagrams that helps to analyze distributed application integrity.)

The next chapter looks at interoperability from the application developer's point of view.

6

Using Middleware to Build Distributed Applications

The point of middleware is to make life easier for the distributed systems implementer, but how? In this chapter we try to answer this question. The chapter has three parts. In the first, we look at distributed processing from the point of view of the business. This part is trying to answer the question, what is middleware for? The second part discusses tiers. The path from end user to database typically involves several, distinct logical layers, each with a different function. These are tiers. Note that they are *logical* tiers, which may be implemented in varying numbers of physical systems; one tier does not necessarily mean one physical system. The question is, what tiers should there be? The final part is about distributed architecture. This part is trying to answer the question, how do we assemble the tiered components into a large-scale structure?

6.1   What is middleware for?

From a user's perspective, there are four large groups of distributed processing technology:

1. Transaction technology, or more generally, technology that is part of the implementation of business processes and business services

2. Information retrieval technology, or more generally, technology for supporting management oversight and analysis of business performance

3. Collaborative technology, like e-mail, for helping people work together

4. Internal IT distributed services such as software distribution or remote systems operations

We do not discuss the internal IT needs in this chapter. It is covered to some degree in Chapter 9 on system management.

6.1.1   Support for business processes

Imagine yourself sitting behind a counter and someone comes up and asks you to do something. For example, imagine you are a check-in agent at an airport. The passenger may be thought of as the requester. You, the agent, are equipped with a suitable workstation to interact with the IT systems and act as the provider of the check-in function. (The pattern is similar for self-service check-in, except that the passengers execute the IT operations themselves, using suitable self-service kiosks.)

There are three kinds of action you may be asked to perform:

1. Inquiries.
2. Actions by you, now; you are responsible for seeing them through now.
3. Actions by others (or by you later); you are not responsible for seeing them through now.

Inquiries are straightforward; you can get the information or you can't. For example, a passenger may ask you about obtaining an upgrade using accumulated miles in a frequent flyer program. To answer the question, you would need to make an inquiry into a frequent flyer system to check on the rules for making upgrades and the passenger's available miles.

Actions by you now are required when the person on the other side of the counter is waiting for the action to be done. The desire from both sides of the counter is that the action will be done to completion. Failing that, it is much simpler if it is not done at all; the person in front of the counter goes away unsatisfied but clear about what has happened or not happened. Life gets really complicated if the action is partially done. For instance, in the airport check-in example, you, the agent, cannot take baggage but fail to give a boarding pass. You would perform the interactions necessary to register the passenger on the flight, and print the boarding pass and any baggage tags required.

Actions by others are actions that you would initiate but that would be ultimately processed later. Recording frequent flyer miles is a typical example in the context of a check-in. The frequent flyer number and the appropriate miles for the flight need to be entered, but they do not need to be processed immediately in the frequent flyer system. However, they do need to be reliably processed at some time.

From a purely IT perspective, the concern is with computers of some kind communicating with each other, not people. In the check-in example, the check-in agent's workstation (or the kiosk, for self-service check-in) is the requester, while the check-in system is the provider. Actions that must be performed now are transactions. From the requester's perspective, the transaction must be atomic: If there is failure, nothing is updated on the database and no external device does anything (e.g., no boarding pass or baggage tags are printed).

The messages in the case of inquiries or action now requests are *real-time messages*. The processing of these messages constitutes *real-time transactions*. Thus, the check-in is a real-time transaction in the context of this example.

In the case of action by others, these kinds of messages are *deferrable messages,* and the "actions by another" transactions are *deferrable transactions.* In this example, processing the frequent flyer information is a deferrable transaction. The requester sending the deferrable message could be the check-in application or even a program in the check-in agent's workstation.

Observe that the term is *deferrable,* not *deferred.* The key difference between real-time and deferrable is what happens if the message cannot be sent now, not how long it takes. If a real-time message cannot be sent immediately, the requester must be told; it is an error condition. On the other hand, if a deferrable message cannot be sent immediately, it hangs about in a queue until it can be sent. The distinctions between real-time and deferrable are business process distinctions, not technology distinctions. Some people might refer to real-time messages as synchronous messages, and deferrable messages as asynchronous messages. But these terms, *asynchronous* and *synchronous,* are viewing this issue from the programmer's perspective. With synchronous messages, the requesting program waits for the reply. With asynchronous messages, the program goes off and does something else. But you can build real-time transaction calls with asynchronous calls. The requesting program goes off and does something else, but then checks for the reply (typically in another queue). If the reply does not come, the requester reports the problem. To repeat, the important characteristic of deferrable messages is that they can be deferred. If they cannot be deferred, then the messages are real-time.

There are situations where you want to say, if the action can be done now, I want it done now, but if it cannot, do it later. From a computer perspective, it is best not to think of this as a strange hybrid somewhere between real-time and deferrable messages. It is simpler to think of it as a two-step action by the requester: The requester requests a real-time transaction and, if that fails, it requests a deferrable transaction. With any transaction, someone (or something) must be told whether the transaction failed. With a real-time transaction, that someone is always the requester; with a deferrable transaction, life is not so simple. It may be impossible for the requester to handle the errors because it might not be active. You cannot just turn a real-time transaction into a deferrable transaction without a lot of thought.

What about transactions calling transactions? The distinctions among inquiry, real-time, and deferrable transactions apply here also. Inquires are very common; for instance, reading a common customer or product database. Real-time transaction-to-transaction calls are less common; actually, they are quite rare. An example might be a delivery system asking a warehouse system to reserve some parts for a particular delivery. If the warehouse system cannot reserve the parts, the delivery must be rescheduled. Calling a real-time transaction from within a transaction means using distributed transaction processing technology (in other words, usually using two-phase commits). Many organizations go to great lengths to avoid distributed transaction processing, and you can often do so. For instance, the delivery system might do an inquiry on the warehouse system but only send the actual "reserve" update as a deferrable message. The consequence might be that there is a run on certain parts, and when the "reserve" update message is processed, the part is no longer there. You can handle these errors by building additional business processes, and actually, in this case, the business processes probably already exist; the warehouse computer system is not 100% accurate in any case.

So what middleware best fits these categories?

Middleware choices for real time include RPC, CORBA, EJB, COM+, Tuxedo, and SOAP. In some cases the application must support distributed transaction processing but, in general, as we discuss in later chapters, we avoid two-phase commits unless the advantages are clear-cut.

Many organizations are planning to use message queuing for real-time processing. You can do this by having one queue for input messages and another queue for output messages. We don't recommend this approach for the following reasons:

- If two transaction servers communicate by message queuing, they can't support distributed transaction processing across them (see Figures 2-9 and 2-10).
- Real-time calls have an end user waiting for the reply; if there is no reply, the user eventually gives up and goes away. Put another way, real-time calls always have a timeout. With message queuing, if the end user goes away, a reply message may still be put into the output queue. This message ends up as a "dead message," and the message-queuing software will typically put messages that haven't been read for a long time into a "dead letter box." The administrator now has to look at the message and figure out what to do with it.
- There could be an enormous number of queues. If there are one thousand users, logically you need one thousand output queues. You probably don't want that, and therefore you end up writing some code to share queues.
- Queues have no IDL and no control of the message format.
- For high performance, you will need to write your own scheduler. Imagine again the one thousand users hammering the same transactions. You need multiple programs to empty the input queue and therefore something to initiate the programs and stop them when they are no longer needed. (On some systems you can use the transaction monitor as the scheduler.)

In short, there is a great deal of work to making this approach viable.

But message queuing is the ideal technology for deferrable messages. You can use simple file transfer, but then you have to build the controls to ensure data is sent once and once only, and not sent if the transaction is aborted.

Alternatively, you can take the view that instead of deferring the transaction, why not process it immediately, that is, use real-time transactional software for deferrable transactions? There are several reasons why not to do this:

- It's slower; messages cannot be buffered.
- If the destination server is down, then the calling server cannot operate. Having the flexibility to bring a transaction server offline without bringing down all other applications is a great bonus.
- Message-queuing software has various hooks that can be used to automate operational tasks, for example, by initiating programs to read the messages.

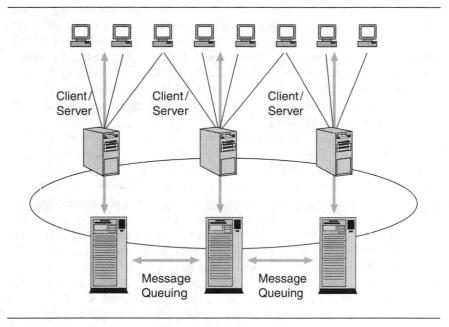

Figure 6-1   Typical use of transactional middleware

In most cases, real-time transactions are used in the path between end user and database; deferrable transactions are used when sending messages between applications. This is illustrated in Figure 6-1.

As always, there are exceptions. We described one earlier; a bank accepting an interbank financial transaction from the SWIFT network. This does not have to be processed in real time, but it must capture the transaction on a secure medium. This is a classic deferrable transaction, but this time from the outside world. Another example mentioned earlier is that if the presentation device is a portable PC, queues are useful for storing data for later processing.

6.1.2   Information retrieval

While transactions are about business operations, information retrieval is about management and customer information.

Information-retrieval requirements are positioned along four dimensions. One dimension is timeliness, the extent to which the users require the data to be current. Some users, such as a production manager trying to find out what has happened to a particular order, need to view data that is 100% up-to-date. Other users, such as a strategic analyst looking at historic trends, will work happily with data that is days, weeks, even months behind.

The second dimension is usability. Raw data tends to be cryptic. Information is held as numeric codes instead of easily understood text. Data about one object is fragmented among many tables or even many databases. Minor inconsistencies, such as the spelling of a company's name, abound. Indexing is geared to the requirements of the production system, not for searching. You can think of this dimension as going from data to information. It is easy to assume that the further you go along the information dimension the better, but people close to the business process and, of course, IT programmers, need access to the raw data.

Putting these two dimensions together and positioning users on the chart gives us something like Figure 6-2.

Clearly timeliness is a matter of toleration rather than an actual requirement. The people to the right of this diagram would probably prefer timely information but are willing to sacrifice some delay for the benefit of more understandable information. We are noticing more and more intolerance to delay and it's probably only a matter of time before any delay is perceived as not dynamic and unacceptable.

The third dimension is the degree of flexibility to the query. Some users want canned queries, for example, I'll give you an order number and you show me what the order looks like. Some users want complete flexibility, the privilege to write arbitrarily complex SQL statements to extract data from the database. There are gradations in between, such as the user who wants to see orders but wants to use a simple search criterion to select the orders he or she is interested in.

The final dimension has (luckily) only three values: time-based push, event-based push, or pull. It is the dimension of whether the user wants to get the data or wants to be informed when something changes. The old-fashioned batch report is a classic example of time-based push technology. Put the report in a spreadsheet and use e-mail for distribution, and suddenly the old system looks altogether more

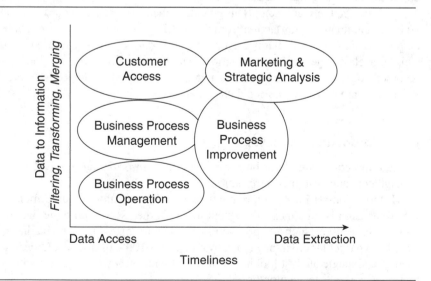

Figure 6-2 Information versus timeliness

impressive. A more sophisticated style of push technology is event-based rather than time-based. An example is sending an e-mail to the CEO automatically when a large order comes in.

With four dimensions, there is clearly the potential for defining a vast range of possible technologies and there certainly is a vast range of technology, although not all of the combinations make much sense; untimely raw data is not of much interest to anybody.

There is a good deal of technology that creates canned inquires and reports and a good deal for ad hoc queries. Ad hoc queries can be implemented with remote database access middleware.

Products available for data replication tend to be database vendor specific. However, storage vendors such as EMC^2 provide products for replication of data at the storage subsystem level. There are many data warehouse and data mart tools for creating a data warehouse and analyzing the data.

6.1.3   Collaboration

A great deal of distributed system software is about helping workers communicate with each other. This includes office software such as e-mail, newsgroups, scheduling systems, and direct communications technology such as online meetings, webcasts, online training, and video conferencing. Whether this fits into the category of middleware is a moot point, but we are slowly seeing convergence, first at the technical level and second at the user interface.

Technical convergence includes shared networks, shared directory services, and common security systems. The driving force is a desire to use the Internet infrastructure.

User interface convergence includes using e-mail as a report distribution mechanism, including multimedia data in databases and using your TV set top box to pay your bills.

It is hard to see where this will end and what the long-term impact will be. At the moment these developments are not important to most IT business applications, but that may not hold true in the future. Meetings are a common part of business processes, and one can envisage an IT system scheduling a meeting and providing an electronic form to be filled in by the participants that will be immediately processed by the next stage in the process. For example, suppose an order cannot be fulfilled because a part is in short supply. The system could schedule a meeting between manufacturing representatives and sales and immediately act on the decisions made. (This book concentrates on transactional and information retrieval systems, so we do not explore this area further.)

6.2   Tiers

When people first started writing online programs, they quickly recognized that such programs had three tiers: a presentation tier to do with formatting and controlling the user interface, a logic tier that decides what to do with the input data, and a database tier that controls access to the data. In a distributed architecture, it is common for these tiers to be run on different physical machines. Furthermore, it was recognized that if the local branch office had a server, which talked to a departmental server, which talked to an enterprise wide server, additional tiers would be defined. So was born the notion of n-tier architectures. In this section we discuss the degree to which these tiers really should be split and why.

6.2.1   The presentation tier

Originally online access was through terminals. Later there were workstations. As a variant on the theme, there were branch office networks with small LANs in each branch and a WAN connection to the central system. Processing in the branch was split between the branch server and the branch workstations. Now of course there is the Internet.

This is only part of the picture. There is telephone access and call centers. There are self-service terminals (such as bank automatic teller machines and airline check-in kiosks). There are EDI or XML transfers for interbusiness communication. There are specialized networks such as the bank SWIFT network and the inter-airline networks.

The banking industry is probably farthest along the path to what is called multichannel access. You can now do a banking transaction by using a check, by using a credit card, by direct interbank transfer, through an ATM, over the Web, on a specialized banking PC product, by using a bank clerk, or over a telephone. We've probably missed a few. It's only a question of time before other industries follow. The Internet is itself is a multichannel interface as it is unlikely that one Web application will be appropriate for all forms of Internet device, for instance, PCs, intelligent mobile phones, and televisions.

This has profound implications on how applications should be built.

Traditional terminals were 20 lines of 80 characters each or similar. Web pages can be much bigger than traditional terminal screens. Telephone communication messages are much smaller. In many existing applications the number and size of the transaction messages are designed to satisfy the original channel. To support a new channel, either a new interface must be built or some intermediary software must map the new messages into the old messages.

We have finally reached our first architectural stake in the ground. We want an architecture to support multiple channels. This defines what is in the presentation layer, namely:

- All end-user formatting (or building voice messages)
- All navigation on the system (e.g., menus and Web links)
- Security authentication (prove the users are who they say they are)
- Build and transmit the messages to the processing tier.

The security is there because authentication depends on the channel. User codes and passwords might be fine internally, something more secure might be appropriate for the Internet and, over the telephone, identification might be completely different.

The presentation layer may be nothing more than a GUI application in a workstation. It may be a Web server and Web browsers. It may be a voice server. It may be a SWIFT network connection box. It may be some old mainframe code handling dumb terminals. It is a logical layer, not a physical thing. It is illustrated in Figure 6-3.

However, whatever the channel, for business processing and business intelligence, there are only a few types of message for the back-end server, namely:

- Real-time
- Deferrable
- Ad hoc queries

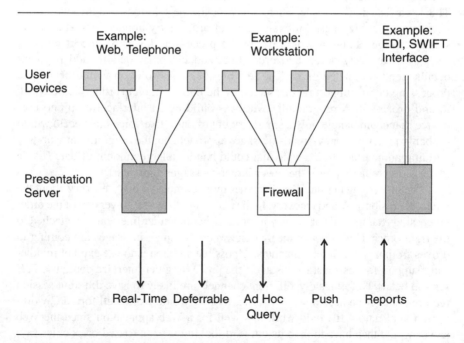

Figure 6-3 The presentation tier

And the backend has two types of unsolicited message for the presentation layer:

- Simple push messages
- Reports

The simple push message normally acts as a wake-up call because the backend system cannot guarantee the user is connected.

6.2.2   The processing tier

The processing tier provides the programming glue between interface and database. It provides the decision logic that takes the input request and decides to do something with it. The processing tier has a major role in ensuring business rules are followed.

The processing tier should have an interface that readily supports a multichannel presentation layer. We have already established that different channels send input and output messages of different sizes and have different dialogues with the eventual end user. Clearly it is undesirable to give to the presentation layer the problems of dealing with the original screen formats, menus, and such. We want a processing tier interface that supports all channels equally well and can be flexibly extended to support any new channels that might come up in the future. This is easier said than done. There are two extreme solutions—many small messages or a few big ones. An example is an order entry application. The many-small-messages solution would be for the processing layer to support requests such as create new order, add order line, add customer details, add payment details, send completed order. The few-big-messages solution would be for the processing tier to support requests such as: here is a complete order, please check it, and process it. A programmer who was building an interface to an end-user device that could handle only a small amount of data (like voice interfaces) would probably prefer the many-small-messages approach, but the programmer who was building an interface to a device that could handle a large amount of data (like a PC) would probably prefer the fewer-larger-messages approach.

The processing tier interface becomes more complex when we worry about the issues of session state and recovery. In the many-small-messages version of the order processing example, it's obviously important that the order lines end up attached to the right order. This is not so easily done when the small messages are coming in droves from many different channels. A possible solution is to use explicit middleware support for sessions; for instance, the processing tier interface could use EJB session beans. Unfortunately, different channels are likely to have different session requirements. A dedicated session for each order would work well for a PC workstation application. It would work less well for a Web application since the Web server would then have to map its outward-looking session (based on cookies say) with its inward-looking sessions to the presentation tier. An end user with a mobile device interface may have an unreliable connection with its presentation-tier server, so outward sessions may come and go. A direct mapping of the outward session to the inward session would mean having some logic in the Web server keeping track of the state of the inward session even if the outward session was temporarily broken. In our experience, it is usually easier to make the inward session—the processing tier interface—session-less. In our example, a simple and flexible solution would be to attach an order number to every processing tier message.

A new concept of user–application interaction is developing. In the past, a user did one task, in one place, at one time. For instance, to submit an order the old way meant typing details to fill in a series of screen forms all in one go. Now envisage the same work being split among different presentation devices. There can be delays. For instance, the order form could be started on the Internet and competed by a voice interface a few days later. Input could be made while the user is on the move. Shortcuts could be taken because information is read from smart cards or picked up from loyalty card systems. This is revolutionary change, and in later chapters we look more into what this means for the application.

6.2.3   The data tier

The data tier is essentially the database. Some vendor architectures have interfaces to old systems as part of the data tier. To our mind, an interface to an old system is just an *n*-tier architecture: one processing tier is communicating with another processing tier.

There are many questions here, most of them capable of stirring up dispute, contention, and trouble. People can get surprisingly emotional about this subject. We will pick on the two key questions.

Question 1 is whether the database should be accessed over a network or whether the database should always reside on the machine that is running the processing tier. The advantage of having the database accessed across the network is that one database can be used by many different applications spread across many locations. Thus, you can have one copy of the product information and one copy of the customer information. This is good, or is it? One disadvantage is that sending database commands over a network has a huge overhead. A second disadvantage is that the database is more exposed to direct access by a malicious user; security is much easier if the user is forced to go through an application to get to the data. A third disadvantage is that if the database schema changes, it may be hard to identify all application programs using the database.

Question 2 is whether the database should be put behind a set of database-handler routines. Variations on this theme come under numerous names: database encapsulation layer, data access objects, persistence layer, persistence framework, and so on. The notion of database-handler routines is practically as old as databases themselves. The original justification was to eliminate the need for programmers to learn how to code the database interface. Today access to the database has largely standardized on SQL, so this reason is barely credible. Instead, database-handlers are justified on programming productivity grounds, the main issue being turning a row in an SQL table into a Java, C#, or C++ object. The opponents of database handlers point out that using SQL is much more productive. Imagine a program that uses a simple SQL statement with a join and perhaps an "order by" clause. The equivalent program that uses a database handler won't be able to use the power of the SQL; instead, it will have to traverse the objects laboriously by following pointers and sort the data itself. (It is not widely known that you can have your cake and eat it too, so to speak, by using an OO database, which not only presents the objects as Java, or C++, or other language objects but also allows SQL-like queries on those objects; but OO databases are probably even more controversial than the two questions outlined here.) A plus point for database handlers is that it allows the database design to change while maintaining the original interface, thus ensuring that the programs can stay the same.

In this book we are mainly interested in transactional services—services that process transactions. A transactional service may process both real-time and deferrable messages. These are not the only important services. A business intelligence service is a service used for retrieval and searching, such as a data warehouse, data mart, decision support system, or management information system. A generic business intelligence server is illustrated in Figure 6-4. The figure illustrates that in addition to transactional real-time and transactional deferrable messages, there are other kinds of interaction between services, such as data extract and push messages.

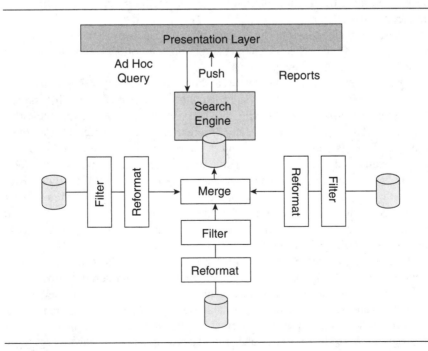

Figure 6-4   Business intelligence servers

The issues of data management and architecture are discussed in more detail in Chapter 14.

6.2.4   Services versus tiers

In the ruthless world of software marketing, tiers are yesterday's concepts. Today, we have services.

Any of the interfaces to a tier could be made into a service. The question is, do they make good services? Two tests for a judging a good service interface are:

1. Is the interface loosely coupled? This is discussed in a later section.

2. Is the interface used by many requesters?

If the processing tier is truly presentation-channel independent, It is likely to make a good service interface since the fact that it supports multiple channels implies that it satisfies at least the second of these tests.

It is not impossible to have a good service interface to the data layer. Sending SQL commands to a database service does not make a service interface since the dependencies between service and requester are tightly coupled. You want an interface that is relatively stable and does not change whenever the database schema changes. It should be like a database view rather than access to database tables, and it should provide the minimum of data. An interface for simple inquiries and common searches may well be useful. An interface for updates is less useful since the update logic is likely to be unique to a particular transaction. The complete transaction logic usually makes a better interface.

6.3   Architectural choices

Categories such as transactional, information retrieval, and so forth don't lead us to different distributed architectures. Rather, the architecture must be capable of working with all of them.

There are three common distributed architecture patterns in use:

1. Middleware bus (or ring) architectures

2. Hub-and-spoke architectures

3. Loosely coupled architectures

They are not mutually exclusive; many organizations have all three. Shades of grey between these categories are also possible.

Perhaps we should a fourth category—ad hoc, or point-to-point architecture. This is what many organizations actually do. They have no plan and solve every problem as it arises, eventually achieving a mish-mash of applications and technologies that not even they understand.

6.3.1   Middleware bus architectures

Many of the organizations that pioneered distributed architectures implemented a form of this architecture, often with middleware software that they wrote themselves. In most cases, the primary aim was to separate the presentation channels from the business services. The architecture achieved this by providing middleware software for accessing the core services. Any new application that needed access to the core systems would then call the middleware software on its local machine, and the middleware software would do the rest. In some organizations, the common middleware implemented real-time messages and in others it implemented deferrable messages. The solution was variously called middleware bus, ring, backplane, or some mysterious organization-specific acronym.

The middleware bus architecture is shown diagrammatically in Figure 6-5.

In implementation terms, it is usual to have something a bit more sophisticated, which is illustrated in Figure 6-6.

The middleware runs in the inner network. The access point can be very lightweight, little more than a router, and indeed the middleware may extend beyond the inner network. Other access points provide gateway functionality to link to other distributed software technologies. Access points are also convenient places to put some security checking functionality, allowing the inner network to be devoted to core production systems. For instance, e-mail traffic can be kept out of the inner network.

There are some almost overwhelming advantages to the middleware bus solution. It is

- Fast. The network hardware and software are tailored for the production workload.
- Secure. There are many barriers to breaking into the core enterprise servers.
- Flexible. New channels can be added easily.

It can also support some unique requirements. For instance, the access point systems may implement failover by routing the traffic to the backup systems in the

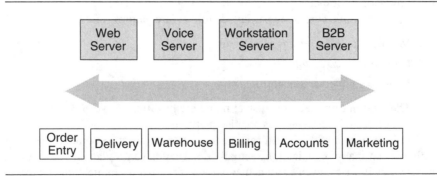

Figure 6-5   Middleware bus architecture

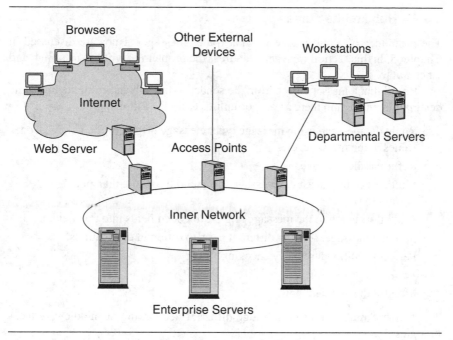

Browsers

Other External
Devices

Workstations

Internet

Departmental Servers

Web Server

Access Points

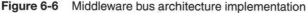

Inner Network

Enterprise Servers

Figure 6-6 Middleware bus architecture implementation

event of a crash on the primary. Enhancing the basic functionality of the middleware bus infrastructure has been a mixed blessing. Functionally it has been superb, allowing the organizations to have facilities that others can only envy. The downside is that it makes it more difficult to migrate to off-the-shelf standard middleware.

If today you asked organizations that have this architecture what they think about it, we think most would say that their major worry is the maintenance of the middleware code. As noted, often they had written the code themselves many years ago. If you were setting out to implement the same architecture today, using off-the-shelf software would be a better idea, if only because of the availability of application development tools that support the best of today's middleware. It must be said, however, that if you had developed a middleware bus, say, 5 years ago, it would already be looking out-of-date simply because the fashions have been changing too fast. Furthermore, the state of the art of middleware is such that for a demanding environment you would still have had to supplement the out-of-box middleware functionality with your own development. (The next few chapters explain why.)

The middleware bus architecture is a high-discipline architecture. Core applications in the enterprise servers must adhere to strict standards that cover not only the interface to the outside world but also how to manage security, system management, and failover. Applications outside the core can access core resources only one way.

6.3.2   Hub architectures

The basic idea of a hub is a server that routes messages. Hubs are discussed in Chapter 5. In this section we want to address the problem of when to use a hub and when not to.

Recall that a message goes from the sender to the hub and from the hub to its destination. In the hub there are opportunities to do the following:

- Route the message using message type, message origin, traffic volumes, data values in the message, etc.
- Reformat the message.
- Multicast or broadcast the message (i.e., send it to more than one destination).
- Add information to the message (e.g., turn coded fields into text fields).
- Split the message, sending different parts to different destinations.
- Perform additional security checking.
- Act on workflow rules.
- Monitor the message flow.

A hub can also be used to bridge different networking or middleware technologies.

With such a large range of possible features, you will probably have guessed by now that a hub can range from little more than a router, to a hub developed using an EAI product, to a hub developed using specially written code. The access point in the middleware bus architecture can easily evolve into a hub.

From an architectural perspective, we find it useful to distinguish between hubs that are handling request-response interaction and hubs that are routing deferrable messages. These are illustrated in Figure 6-7. This is not to say that combined hubs aren't possible; it's just to say that it is worth thinking about the two scenarios separately, possibly combining them physically later. Hubs for request-response interaction have more problems. Clearly they must be fast and resilient since they stand on the critical path for end-user response times. Clearly, too, the hub must be able to route the response message back to the requester (discussed in the section on middleware interoperability in Chapter 5.)

Hubs for reformatting and routing deferrable message are far simpler. By definition there is no problem with application delays with deferrable messages, and processing deferrable messages cannot use session state, so the problems previously discussed disappear. Many EAI hub products have their origins in routing messages in a message-queuing system, and this is clearly where they are most at home.

The advantages of hub architecture lie in all the additional functionality it provides. In most cases, the alternative to a hub is to put the additional logic in the application that sends the message. For instance, instead of reformatting the message, the sender could create messages of the right format. Instead of routing in

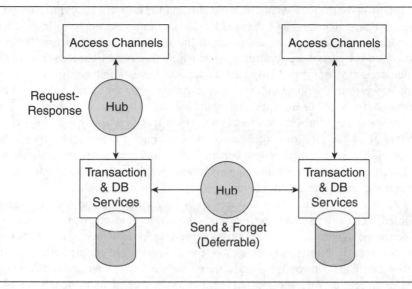

Figure 6-7 Hub architecture showing both request-response and deferrable interactions

the hub, the sender could determine where the message should go. The reason for putting this logic in the hub is to increase flexibility. For instance, suppose there is a need to route requests for product information to a number of servers. If there is only one application asking for this information, then there is little to choose between routing in a hub and routing in the sending application. But if there are many applications asking for the product information, then it makes sense to have the routing information in one place, in a hub. If the routing is very volatile— suppose the product information is moving from one server to another, product line by product line—then it makes a great deal of sense to have one place to make the changes.

Hubs are particularly useful in some scenarios, such as bridging network technologies. Networks are standardizing on TCP/IP, so this bridging is less necessary today than in days gone by but still sometimes relevant. Another case where hubs will remain important is in bridging to third-party applications where you can't adapt the application to suit your formatting and routing needs.

So if hubs help create a flexible solution, why not always put a hub into the architecture and route all messages through a hub just in case you want to change it later?

One reason is that it is another link in the chain. The hub is another thing to go wrong, another thing to administer, and another thing to pay for. You cannot cut corners in your hub configuration because the hub is a potential bottleneck. Furthermore, the hub is potentially a single point of failure, so you will probably want to have a backup hub and failsafe software.

Many organizations set out with the aim that the hub will be an infrastructure element that is managed and changed by the operations department. In practice, though, you do not need to use much of the hub functionality before the hub becomes a key part of the application. A hub may then need to become part of the systems test environment. A dispute may break out over which group—the operations group or the application development group—has the right to decide what functionality should be implemented by the hub and what part elsewhere.

In some ways, hubs are too functionally rich. It is all too easy to end up with a number of ad hoc solutions patched together by a hub. It is fine up to a point, but beyond that point the total system becomes more and more complex and increasingly difficult to understand and change. It becomes that much easier to introduce inadvertent errors and security holes.

As a generalization, middleware bus architectures can be seen as tightly coupled architectures, meaning that both the sender and receiver must use the same technology, follow the same protocol, and understand a common format for the messages. Hub architectures can be seen as less tightly coupled architectures in that their hubs can resolve many differences between sender and receiver. The next architecture, Web services architecture, is marketed as a loosely coupled architecture.

6.3.3 Web services architectures

Web service architectures use the technologies that implement the Web services standards such as SOAP, WSDL, and UDDI (as explained in Chapter 4). Looked at from a technology point of view, the technologies are just another set of middleware technologies. The reasons that these technologies make possible a new "Web services" architecture, and arguably a new way of looking at IT, are:

- Web services standards are a widely implemented, which gives you a real chance of interoperating with different vendors' implementations.
- The Web services technologies are cheap, often bundled with other technology such as the operating system (Microsoft .NET) or the Java package.
- The Web services standards are designed to work over the Internet so, for instance, they don't run into difficulties with firewalls.

In a sentence, the magic power behind Web services is the magic power that comes when the IT industry makes that rare decision that everyone wants to follow the same standard.

Most small organizations don't have a distributed systems architecture. They rely on ad hoc solutions like file transfer, a bit of COM+ or RMI perhaps, and stand-alone applications. Web services offer them a cheaper form of integration, not only because of the cost of the software but also because they don't have to invest in the specialized skills needed for many other middleware products.

This can be seen as using Web services software to implement a middleware bus architecture. Compared to traditional middleware, Web services software has the disadvantage of being slower because of the need to translate messages into XML format, but there are advantages. If the sender starts using a new message format—for instance, an extra field at the start of the message—the receiver will still accept and process the message, probably without recompilation. Another major advantage of Web services is that many third-party applications do currently, or will shortly, supply a Web services interface. The issue of integration with outside software has been a major stumbling block in past; with Web services, it might just be solved.

Larger organizations have islands of integration. One part of the organization may have a middleware bus architecture, another may have a hub, and different parts use different application and middleware software—VB here, Java there, a mainframe running CICS, and so on. Web services for them provide a means of integrating these islands, as illustrated in Figure 6-8. Why Web services and not another middleware technology? Because Web services are cheaper, integrate with more applications, and run over backbone TCP/IP networks without problems.

But there are disadvantages. One was noted earlier—using XML for message formats is slower and consumes more network bandwidth. Since the message integrity facilities are so open ended (as discussed in Chapter 5), message integrity must be analyzed in any Web services design. Web services security is an issue, but so is all security across loosely integrated distributed systems. (Security is discussed in Chapter 10.) But Web services standards and technology are evolving fast, so much of this will be resolved, and at the time you are reading this, maybe already will have been solved.

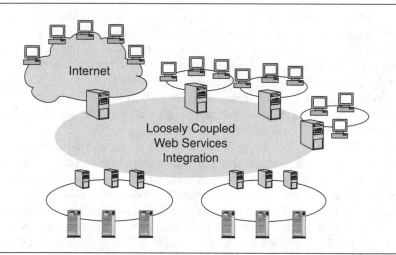

Figure 6-8   Web services architecture integrating various routing and software systems

6.3.4   Loosely coupled versus tightly coupled

The notion of "loosely coupled" distributed systems is very alluring, and the IT industry has become very excited by the prospect. In reality, though, there is a spectrum between total looseness and painful tightness, and many of the factors that dictate where you are on this spectrum have nothing to do with technology.

Coupling is about the degree to which one party to the communication must make assumptions about the other party. The more complex the assumptions, the more tightly coupled the link. The main consequence of being tightly coupled is that changes to the interface are more likely to have widespread ramifications. Note that developing a new interface or a new service need not be more difficult than in the loosely coupled case. Also, changing a tightly coupled interface does not neces- sarily mean more work on the service side, but it probably does mean more work on the caller side. One practical way of looking at it is to ask the question, how much of the configuration do I have to test to have a realistic prospect of putting the application into production without problems? With a tightly coupled configura- tion, you must test the lot—the applications, whether they are running on the right versions of the operation system, with the right versions of the middleware soft- ware, and on a configuration that bears some resemblance to the production config- uration. You might get away with leaving out some network components, and you will almost certainly be able to use a scaled-down configuration, but you still need a major testing lab. For a truly loosely coupled system, you should be able to test each component separately. This is a major advantage; indeed, for Web services between organizations across the Internet, it is essential. But just how realistic is it?

To examine this question in more detail, you can investigate the dependencies between two distributed programs. The dependencies fall into several categories:

Protocol dependency. Both sides must use the same middleware standard, and they must use the same protocol. This is achievable with Web services, and we hope it stays that way. In the past, standards, CORBA for instance, have been plagued with incompatible implementations. As new features are added to Web services, there is a chance that implementations will fall out of step. We hope new standards will be backwards-compatible. When you start using the new features, you are going to have to be careful that both ends do what they are supposed to do. Retesting the link is required.

Configuration dependency. When networks grow, inevitably there comes a time when you want to add or change service names, domain names, and network addresses. The issue is whether this will have an impact on (in the worst case) the application or the local configuration setup. The most flexible—loosely coupled— solution is for the local application to rely on a directory service somewhere to tell it the location of the named service. In Web services, a UDDI service should pro- vide this facility. We suspect most current users of SOAP don't use UDDI, so we wonder how configuration-dependent these systems really are.

Message format dependency. In middleware like MQSeries, the message is a string of bits, and it is up to the programs at each end to know how the message is formatted. (It could be formatted in XML.) Because Web services uses XML, it has a degree of format independence. There is no concern about integer or floating-point layouts (because everything is in text). The fields can be reordered. Lists can be of any length. In theory, many kinds of changes would not need a retest. In practice, it would be wise to retest every time the format changes because it is hard to remember when to test and when not to test.

Message semantic dependencies. This is important at both the field level and the message level. At the field level, numerical values should be in the same units; for example, price fields should consistently be with or without tax. At the message level, suppose some messages mean "get me the first 10 records" and "get me the next 10 records." Changing the "10" to a "20" may cause the caller application to crash. Clearly any change in the meaning of any field or message type necessitates retesting both the caller and the service.

Session state dependency. The impact of session state is that for each state the application will accept only certain kinds of messages. Session state can be implemented by the middleware or by the application. For instance, a travel reservation application may expect messages in the order "Create new reservation," "Add customer details," "Add itinerary," "Add payment details," and "Finish." Any change to the order affects both ends.

Security dependency. The applications must have a common understanding of the security policy. For instance, a service may be available only to certain end users. It could be that the front-end applications, not the back-end service, have to enforce this restriction. If this is changed, then the front-end program may need to pass the ID of the end user or other information to the back-end service so the service is capable of making a determination of end-user security level.

Business process dependencies. In the travel reservation example, suppose a loyalty card is introduced. Several services may operate a bit differently for these customers and they must interact correctly.

Business object dependencies. If two applications communicate with one another and one identifies products by style number and the other identifies products by catalogue number, there is scope for major misunderstandings. For applications to interoperate, if they contain data about the same external entity, they must identify that object the same way.

These dependencies fall into three overlapping groups. One group has a technology dimension: the protocol, the message format, the configuration, and the security dependencies. These can be either wholly or partially resolved by following the same technology standards and using standards that are inherently flexible, such as XML. The second group has an application dimension: the message format, the message semantics, and the session-state dependencies. These can be resolved only by changing the application programs themselves. No technology solution in the world will resolve these issues. The third group can be broadly characterized as wider concerns: the business process, the business object and, again, the security dependencies. To change anything in this group may require change across many applications.

"Loosely coupled" is a pretty loose concept. To really achieve loosely coupled distributed systems, you have to design your applications in a loosely coupled way. What this means is that the interaction of applications has to change only when the business changes. You need to test in a loosely coupled way. This means providing the callers of a service with a test version of the service that is sufficiently comprehensive such that you are happy to let any calling program that passes the tests loose on the production system. You must also change in a loosely coupled way. Business change is usually staggered; you run the old business processes alongside the new business processes. The IT services must do likewise.

6.4 Summary

In this chapter we set out to answer three questions: What is middleware for? How do we split application functionality among the tiers? How do we assemble applications into a wider architecture?

Key points to remember:

- From the application designer's perspective, communication among applications falls mostly into two categories: real-time or request-response, deferrable or send-and-forget.

- Communication between applications occurs in the context of support for business processes, support for collaboration, and support for business intelligence. The requirements for each are different, and this book concentrates on support for business processes.

- The notion of tiers is useful for program design. It is not always the case that tiers should be physically distributed. It is important to have a clearly defined presentation layer to support multiple external channels of communication, and this often leads to the device-handling servers being physically separate. Less clear is whether there is any need to distribute the processing logic tier and the data tier. A better way of looking at the functionality below the presentation tier is as services that are called by the presentation layer and by other services.

- The concept of tightly coupled and loosely coupled distribution has a technical dimension and an application dimension. Two applications can be loosely coupled along the technical dimension (e.g., using Web services) but tightly coupled along the application dimension (e.g., by having a complex dialogue to exchange information). The main advantage of being loosely coupled is being able to change one application without affecting the other.

- The three distributed architecture styles—a middleware bus architecture, a hub architecture, and a Web services architecture—can be combined in infinite variety. From a technology point of view, the middleware bus architecture is tightly coupled, the Web services architecture is loosely coupled, and the hub architecture is somewhere in between.

- The middleware bus has the best performance, resiliency, and security but is the most difficult to test, deploy, and change.
- Hub architectures are particularly useful when there is a need either to route service requests or multicast server requests.

In following chapters we examine distributed application design in more detail. But before we turn away from technology issues, we want to discuss how better to make a distributed design scalable, resilient, secure, and manageable. These are the topics of the next four chapters.

7

Resiliency

In this chapter and the next three, we turn away from discussing specific technology and look at the underlying principles of building resilient, scalable, and manageable distributed systems. The reason these subjects are in a book about architecture is that designing for resiliency, scalability, system management, and security may affect the high-level design of the application. Sometimes, considering these concerns leads the organization to reconsider its requirements. For instance, there may be a choice between paying a great deal of money for a highly resilient service or saving the input data in a secure location so that it can be reprocessed in the event of a disaster.

This chapter tackles resiliency. There are many aspects to resiliency. The most obvious challenges are:

- How do we reduce the number of visible stoppages?
- How do we reduce the length of time the system is down if there is a failure?

But perhaps more important than both of these questions is, how do we ensure that there is no data loss and no message loss?

There is also disaster recovery to take into account—recovery from fire, floods and earthquakes, things falling out of the sky, bombs, and other acts of God and man.

Finally, the biggest single cause of downtime in most organizations is scheduled downtime. How can we turn an application into a true 24 by 365 application?

In this chapter we concentrate on what an IT department can do, not what an IT vendor can do. Thus this chapter has little discussion on hardware resiliency, partitioning, clustering, or system software resiliency. These are all good features, but accidents happen, and this chapter is about what to do when they do and steps to avoid turning an accident into a catastrophe.

Some highly respectable authorities have expressed platform resiliency in terms of Windows providing X% uptime, UNIX providing Y%, z-OS providing Z%, and Parallel Sysplex providing P%. What they neglect to mention is that if you manage a Windows box like a mainframe, you can get outstanding reliability; and if you manage a mainframe like most people manage Windows servers, you will get appalling reliability. We are always curious how said respected authorities take this into account. If you take an application and run it on any of the major platforms, test it well, fix the problems you find, and ensure that you have good (and followed) operational procedures, you can achieve a high level of reliability. While there is a difference between the theoretical best level of resiliency you can achieve with each platform, the most important difference is in the time and effort it takes to get there.

We are going to assume that the processes required to run an application reliably on a server are known. But even if the servers are totally reliable, that does not result in a totally reliable end-user service. Hardware faults on a server typically correspond to about 20% of the total downtime. Other big factors in total downtime are planned downtime (for instance, backing up a database), application problems, and operational problems. Total server reliability is of no use in a disaster when the whole building is down. It is also of no use in a distributed environment if the network is down.

More can go wrong in a distributed application than in a centralized application, but there are new ways of tackling resiliency. In particular, take the notion of backup systems. If the system uses subsystems A, B, and C in series, it is no more reliable than the least reliable of A, B, and C. For a complex distributed environment using workstations, local servers, wide area networks, internal backbone networks, and perhaps a couple of back-end servers, there is a lot to go wrong. But if you can do processing in parallel, reliability is greatly enhanced. If one server is down on average for 1 day in every 100, then two parallel servers will both be down together on average for 1 day every 10,000 days. Two unreliable servers can theoretically give a remarkably high level of service.

Turning theory into practice is not easy, and this is largely what this chapter is about. In particular, our interest is exploring how distributed systems can be used for our advantage and what difference this makes to the application structure.

7.1   Using backup servers

The obvious way to build resiliency is to have a backup system. Consider the simple configuration shown in Figure 7-1. When the production system fails, the work is taken over by the backup system.

Recovery consists of four steps:

1. Detect the failure.

2. Clean up work in progress.

3. Activate the application on the backup system.

4. Reprocess "lost" messages.

We will take each in turn.

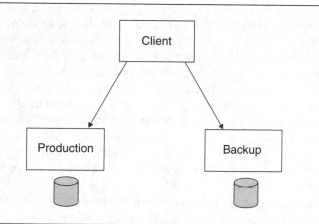

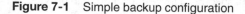

Figure 7-1 Simple backup configuration

7.1.1 Detecting failure

Many vendors offer a heartbeat feature whereby the backup system sends the primary system a message on a regular basis. The backup system says, "Are you there?" The primary system replies, "Yes I am."

There are many difficulties with heartbeats; it is a very coarse mechanism. For instance, it checks only whether the heartbeat program is running, not whether the production application is running. If the heartbeat does report a failure, the backup system can't tell whether the primary is inactive or whether there is a difficulty with heartbeats. For instance, if the network between the systems goes down, the heartbeat may report an error when in fact the production system is working fine. This problem can be overcome by using a backup network connection. If the network is fine and there definitely is an error, then the heartbeat cannot tell you whether the failure is a temporary glitch or a long stoppage.

In practice, the heartbeat must be supplemented by a range of other tests. The most important test is for the client program to give regular reports on its progress. Simple information, such as the response times of the last 10 transactions, is really helpful.

After a failure is detected, but before it is analyzed, a simple question must be posed and answered. Do we stick to the current system and fix it in place, or do we switch to the backup?

There are two alternative strategies:

Strategy 1: On any failure, switch to backup, then think.

Strategy 2: Stop, think, and switch to backup as the last resort.

Very resiliency-conscious sites, such as online stock exchanges, often take the first strategy. Most sites take the second. To be brutally frank, most organizations do not regularly test their backup switching procedures. If they are forced to switch, they run into a bunch of problems such as incorrect network configurations, incorrect software configurations or, in the worst case, a system too small to run their production load. And there are good reasons not to switch automatically to backup; many problems are not corrected by switching to backup. Many software and operational problems are not cured by a switch. Switching to backup may not cure a network problem. Disk failures may be more easily fixed locally.

The reason very resiliency-conscious sites will take a switch-first strategy is that they have already tried to eliminate all these local problems. This means anticipating all possible causes of failure and building a plan to detect and correct the failure. This is a massive effort. For instance, all operator commands should be analyzed to check whether they can cause a system stop and then procedures put into place to ensure unqualified operators don't do them. If you don't want to make the effort, don't even think about taking a switch-first strategy.

Building such plans is configuration specific. The best a vendor can provide is a stable hardware and software platform, and assistance.

For the rest of this section, we assume that the decision has been made to switch to backup.

7.1.2   Cleanup work in progress

Clearly, switching to backup requires that all the data updated on the production system is copied to the backup system. Two techniques used today are:

- Copy the database logs and apply them against a copy of the database, like a continual roll forward (this assumes non-database data is copied across some other way).
- Have the disk subsystem keep a mirror copy of the disk on the backup system by duplicating all writes on the backup system.

The second approach is easier to operate since the non-database disk is catered for. The first approach is more efficient. The network bandwidth required to send all writes to the remote backup machine might be considerable and the cost excessive. (But like disk and processor costs, network costs are coming down.)

As an aside, regular database backups should still be taken even if the data is mirrored locally and remotely. Some failures need the backup; for instance, the operator might accidentally (or deliberately) delete the database's entire disk directory.

Simply having the latest copy of the data is not sufficient; incomplete transactions must be rolled back. Doing this on the backup machine should be the same as doing it on the production machine, and the database system should handle the transaction cleanup automatically. For non-database files, you are on your own and have to synchronize the state of the file with the last completed transaction. Our recommendation would be to put all important data in the database or in secured message queues.

7.1.3   Activating the application

Once the database and any message queues are tidied up, the next task is to restart the complete running environment and put it into a state ready to accept more work. We will look at the issues of restarting the network, the batch programs, and the online programs.

After the switch, the client must send its input to the backup, rather than the primary, machine. There is a fundamental choice to be made here. Will the client be able to resume the session where it left off, or will he or she have to restart the session, possibly having to log on again?

We will consider TCP/IP networks only. Since the TCP/IP sessions for Web traffic are so short, it is rarely worth worrying about keeping browser sessions open across a switch to the backup Web server. But you may want to resume current TCP/IP sessions in other cases, such as between a Web server and a transaction server. Some techniques are:

- The backup machine can come up with the same IP address as the production machine. This is typically only possible if the production and backup machines are on the same LAN segment.
- There are intelligent routers on the market that will redirect the traffic meant for one IP address to another IP address.
- There could be special protocol written between the client and the server for the client to resume a user session over a new TCP/IP connection. Put another way, a new session is started without telling the end user.

The first two techniques will only work if the recovery is quick enough to complete before the TCP connection times out. If it does time out, the client will need to start another connection.

Once it is accepted that a new session is going to be started, then there are other options for fixing the network. For instance, the Domain Name Server can be changed to make the server name map to a new IP address. This is how it is possible to switch a Web server to backup. There are routers on the market that can give several Web servers the same domain name. This is mainly sold as a load-balancing feature (the so-called Web farms we mentioned in Chapter 3), but it can also be used as a resiliency feature.

What about restarting the programs?

Before looking at online programs, let us look at batch. Batch programs that update a database are almost always reading either an external input file or a table in the database. To restart successfully, they must reposition the input data on the next record to be processed and must rebuild any internal data, such as totals, that they are holding in memory. This can only be done by having the database system hold the program restart data, such as a count of the number of input records already processed and the current value of all total variables. This means there must be some data in the database whose only purpose is to recover a running program. Typically it will be a row in a table with a large field that the program then uses any way it sees fit. If there are no special features in the database system for restart information, then you will have to add a table into the database schema yourself.

In many ways batch recovery is more difficult than online. The first hurdle is finding out what job control deck is running and restarting that at the right place. Good mainframe operating systems do this for you. Even then there is an issue; consider the case where the job control thinks program A was running at the time of the failure and there is no restart information for program A. There are two alternatives: (1) At the time of the failure, the program was just starting and hadn't created a restart area or (2) the program was finishing and had deleted the restart area. Which one is it? There needs to be work done to synchronize the job control with the restart area and to manage the restart data itself so that, for instance, your program does not inadvertently recover from a restart point left over from a failure one month previously. (As an aside, batch job schedulers running externally to the systems executing the jobs can provide additional recovery features to help fix these problems.)

If all else fails with batch, you can reload the database (or roll it back if your database software supports that) and restart the batch processing from the beginning. This option is typically not available for online applications; the equivalent of reprocessing for them is to have end users retype all their online transactions, which is useless for customers over the Web.

In a distributed environment there are three scenarios: the client failing, the server failing, and both the client and the server failing.

If the client fails, then when it restarts it must recover itself. Suppose the client is a workstation program that is reading data from a file on the workstation and for each record it is processing a transaction on the server. This is identical to the batch case, and there must be restart information in the database. If the client is servicing a human, then it is likely that for security reasons the end user will be forced to log on again after a failure. It could be that the session will then restart where it left off, but clearly the program cannot reposition itself in the right place in the dialogue without having some restart information somewhere. In most instances that "somewhere" does not need to be the database. But remember that even if repositioning the client dialogue is desirable in the general case, there will be times where it is undesirable, such as when the client has been off-line for 24 hours and the end user can't remember what he was doing. You need therefore to design sessions that are helpful for the end user but not so rigid that they make recovery of half-completed sessions difficult.

If the server fails, it simply recovers to the last transaction. The client must now figure out which of the transactions in progress failed and which succeeded. We discuss this point in the next subsection. Also note that in most (maybe all) object middleware, the object references in the client pointing at the server are broken, which is particularly a problem if you are using stateful session beans.

Sometimes both the client and the server fail at the same time. The best solution is to ensure that there is one recovery routine in the client that handles all the scenarios—client failure, server failure, and both client and server failure. It is important not to try to be too clever in recovery code; the simplest and most effective strategy is to ensure all the state is kept in the database, and both client and server applications themselves are stateless.

7.1.4   Reprocessing "lost" messages

If you read the white papers and listen to the presentations, you would be forgiven for thinking that database recovery is enough. Look however at Figure 7-2.

Let us take the client program perspective. Suppose the client sent a message to the server and then the server failed. The client does not know whether the failure happened before the transaction was committed or after the transaction was committed. In some cases it is satisfactory to tell the end user that there is uncertainty and let the end user interrogate the database with another transaction if she thinks it is important. But many end users will simply retransmit the message when the server recovers. If the last transaction was "Debit $1,000,000 from Mr. Big's account," this might not be such a smart idea.

There are two questions to ask during a recovery:

1. How does the client know the server completed the last message input?

2. If it did complete, what was the last output message?

You can have the client emulate the sort of discovery process the end users would go through. Alternatively, you can implement a recovery protocol along the lines of the following. The client can put a sequence number in one of the fields in the message to the server. The server stores the sequence number in a special row

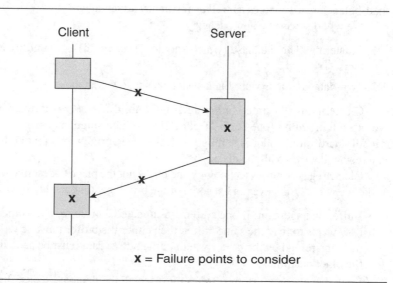

x = Failure points to consider

Figure 7-2   Lost messages

reserved for client recovery. The client increments the sequence number every transaction. On recovery the client sends a special message to interrogate the last sequence number captured. This tells the client if the last input, or the one before, was the last processed transaction.

This special recovery row can also be used to store the last output message, but it is simpler if update transactions do not return data, except errors. For instance, if you wanted to update a bank account and tell the user the new balance, it could be coded as an update transaction followed by an account enquiry transaction. This is no more code to implement because if you save the last output somewhere you still have to write code to retrieve it.

In Chapter 13 we discuss a technique called task/message diagrams that is useful for analyzing complex recovery scenarios.

7.2   Dual active

The recovery process to switch to backup has the potential for major delay. Having the backup application active and waiting for the data to start the recovery process eliminates some delay. Even better is to implement a dual active strategy by having the client logged on to both systems. This avoids the time to switch the network (the major delay of which is starting the client sessions, especially if there are thousands of them, each with a logon security check). If no delay is allowed, dual active is the only solution.

In a dual active strategy, both systems are equal, both do work. This may have load-balancing advantages as well as resiliency advantages.

We will discuss two approaches:

1. Clustering: The database (which should be mirrored) is shared by both systems.

2. Two-database approach: Each system has its own database.

Clustering is illustrated in Figure 7-3. (Note: *Clustering* is a fuzzy word and we are talking about one form of clustering, which might not be the one your friendly hardware vendor is selling you.) The basic principle is that both systems can read and write to all the disks.

Clustering is complex technology and this is not the place to describe it in detail. What we will do, however, is list some of the problems that need to be overcome:

- Buffer management: If one system has updated a buffer and the other system now wants to read the same buffer, then either the buffer must be written to disk and reread by the other system or the buffer data must be sent directly to the other machine.

- Lock management: Both systems must see all the database locks. Figure 7-3 shows the lock manager as a separate box.

- Lock manager duplication: The lock manager is potentially a single point of failure, so it must be duplicated.
- Log file: Normally databases have a single log file. Performance will be terrible if both systems are trying to write to the same file. In a clustered configuration, each system should have its own log file. You then need to implement an algorithm that ensures that during a roll forward the transactions are processed in the right order.

These problems are all solvable but at a cost of lower performance. It is impossible to predict the cost without a detailed analysis of the application. For instance, there is a considerable overhead incurred by writing lock information over a network connection. To alleviate this, one technique is to have less locking by locking out more at one time, for instance, by using block locks instead of record locks. But this increases lock contention. To make matters worse, everything takes longer because of the time taken to send messages to the other system, which increases elapsed time and therefore increases the likelihood of contention. (By the way, delay is inevitable: If the systems are 100 kilometers apart, the speed of light in fiber ensures a minimum of one millisecond to travel from one system to another and back again, which is a significant overhead for a lock.)

As an aside, you might be wondering how clustered systems improve performance like the marketing blurb insists. The answer is: It can, but only if the number of reads far exceeds the number of writes.

An alternative is the two-database approach. Each system has its own database; each transaction is processed twice, once on each database; and two-phase commit ensures the systems are kept in sync. If one of the systems is down, then the other system simply stops sending it subtransactions.

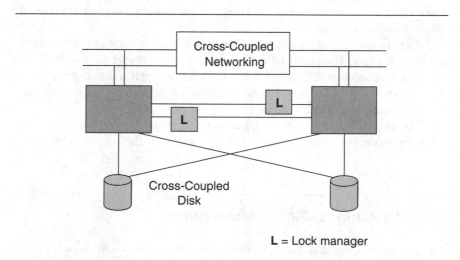

Figure 7-3   Clustered servers

It is not quite as simple as that, of course. There are two problems to overcome:

1. If a system was down and is now mended, then before it is brought online it must catch up all the missed transactions. This is more difficult than it looks. The obvious solution is to capture the information that would have been input to the subtransactions and to reprocess this information for catch-up purposes. The wrinkle, though, is that you have to reprocess the subtransactions in the same order the transactions were processed on the live system. This order is not the input order but is the order the commits were processed.

2. The system needs to handle the situation where the client connection to both systems is working just fine but the connection between the two systems is broken. This is not easy, either. A possible solution is for each system to contact a third system when it finds it can't send a message to its partner. The third system would then kill one of the systems since it is better to have one consistent system than two inconsistent systems.

What this comes down to is that you are on your own. Standard software out of the box does not have facilities such as these. (Okay, someone, somewhere is going to point to some unknown, 15-year-old software that does it all.) Actually, software has been going in the opposite direction. Coding the solution is far easier if, for each transaction, one message contains all the data necessary to do the updates in the transaction. But there is a big temptation with object software to send the update data in many small chunks by calling many methods to make one update. (If this is the case and you want to take the two-database approach, you probably need to have an expert devise a method of rolling forward one of the databases by using information from the other database's log.)

Processing the transactions on both machines incurs a considerable performance penalty. How serious this is depends again on the proportion of read-only transactions to write transactions.

The clustering solution has potentially less processor overhead than the two-database solution. The two-database solution has less networking overhead than the clustering solution. Clustering is less work for the applications developer (but more for the vendor). The two-database solution is better at handling new versions of software or the database schema.

The bottom line, however, is that both dual active solutions work well only when the volume of update transactions is low relative to the volume of reads.

7.3 Applying resiliency techniques

So far we have considered only one client and two servers. Our architecture is unlikely to be that simple. Let us consider the configuration discussed in an earlier chapter but redrawn in Figure 7-4. It consists of:

- Client Web browser
- Web server
- Transaction server with database

Maximum resiliency is a goal, but we also want to cater for disaster recovery, so we have decided that the two sites are 100 kilometers apart.

The box and network configuration is shown in Figure 7-4. The general idea is to try to push back all the tough resiliency issues to the transaction servers (since this way we solve the problem only once and don't introduce additional synchronization problems).

We noted in an earlier chapter that network routers exist to balance the Web traffic across multiple servers. The router itself is a single point of failure and there would need to be a backup router.

Ideally, since the Web servers hold mainly static data, they could be dual active (or multiple active). Thus, the more state we can take off the Web servers and put on the transaction servers, the better the dual-active strategy works. If all the session state is in the back end, it is no long necessary to worry about a clustering or a two-database strategy to implement common Web server state.

It is desirable to switch to a backup transaction server without the end user's knowing about it. This can be done by having the Web servers open connections to both transaction servers, but only using the active one. The transaction server recovery is as described in the previous section. There is no need for a heartbeat between the transaction servers since the Web servers themselves will immediately

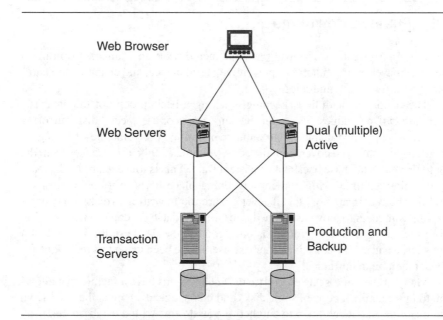

Figure 7-4   Box and network configuration for resiliency

notice if the production system goes down and can either inform the operator that something is wrong or automatically trigger the switch to backup.

It is clear that with some thought, very high levels of resiliency are possible.

7.4 System software failure

Although system software failures are alarming, they are often less dangerous than application errors simply because many are timing errors or memory leakage errors, and they can be fixed by a reboot. The worst errors are database or operating system errors that corrupt data on disk. Some of these can be corrected by doing database reorganizations such as a garbage collection or a rebuild of an index. However, they provide another reason for taking database backups and keeping a log of after-images because it may be necessary to rebuild the database using a corrected version of the database software.

You might think that there is little point in switching to a backup for system errors because the backup system should have the same software installed. But if the problem is a timing problem, there is indeed a good chance that the system will recover and continue.

7.5 Planned downtime

One of the major causes of downtime is planned downtime. Planned downtime is used for housekeeping functions, preventive maintenance, and changing the hardware and software configuration.

The major factor in housekeeping is taking a backup copy of the database. There are two techniques: Use online backup copies or use special disk-mirroring features to copy the database onto another machine. The principle of taking an online copy is that to recover from the copy, you must apply after-images from the log to bring the database back to a consistent state. This is true even if the database is not doing anything while the copy is taking place because it could still have modified buffers in memory that it never got around to writing to disk. Many organizations are loath to move to online dumps; offline database copies somehow feel more reassuring. An online dump is only good if the database log is good. But many large and safety-conscious database users have been using this technique for years, albeit on mainframes.

Many of the large-scale enterprise disk subsystems have a feature that allows you to make a mirror copy of some disks and then (logically) break the disks from one machine and attach them to another. If you do this with a database that is up and running, then the database will be in an inconsistent state just like it is after a machine stop. Taking a copy of the database in that state is the same as taking an online copy of the database—you need the log to effect a recovery of the data. It is probably operationally more useful to stop the database before breaking the mirror and giving the database copy to another machine. The copy of the database is then an offline copy, and the database can be used not only to make an offline backup copy but also for queries without having to apply any log-after images to make it consistent.

Preventive maintenance is not an issue on platforms that have features such as hot replacement and dynamic hardware partitioning. If the platform does not support these features, you can handle preventive maintenance as if it were a hardware reconfiguration.

It is possible to handle many configuration changes in hardware and software by the intelligent use of backup systems. The steps are as follows:

1. Take the backup machine offline.
2. Change the software or hardware.
3. Bring the backup machine up-to-date.
4. Switch to backup.
5. Repeat this process on the other machine.

This strategy calls for one system stop in step 4, and some organizations will want an additional system stop after step 5 to switch back to the original primary machine.

The number one reason that organizations so rarely use this technique in practice is that organizations don't have a symmetrical backup configuration and do not regularly move the load from one machine to another. They are not prepared to risk running the production load on the backup machine except in the case of a disaster.

That said, there are technical issues as well. The difficult step is the third—bringing the backup machine up-to-date. We have observed three techniques for keeping data in the backup in sync with the production system, namely, remote disk mirroring, reapplying the database log, and reprocessing transactions. The first two of these techniques do not work if the database schema is different on primary and backup. The solution therefore is to make the database schema change online on both the primary and backup simultaneously before step 1. How easy or practical this is will depend crucially on the capabilities of your favorite database product.

If you can't handle software and hardware changes as described here, it looks like you're going to have to work over Christmas.

7.6   Application software failure

In many ways, application software failure is the worst kind of error. It cannot be emphasized enough that programmers must write code that

- Prevents bad data getting to the database. Check all the input data, and if anything is awry at any stage, don't commit the transaction to the database.
- Looks for corruption in the database as it is being read.
- Displays as much information as possible about any errors detected.

They should also write policing programs that scan the database to check the data's integrity and, of course, everything should be tested thoroughly.

But in spite of everything, applications will go wrong. The best case is that the program fails. The worst case is that the program does not fail but the database is corrupted. Failing programs usually have to be fixed and restarted, although sometimes a workaround can be found. If the database is corrupted, one of two strategies can be applied: Go back to a state before the corruption and rerun the work, or fix the database in situ by writing a program that fixes the corruption.

Some database systems have a rollback facility whereby log-before images on the database can be applied, taking the database back to a state it was in earlier in the day or week. This is typically faster than reloading the database and applying log-after images until the database is in the state it was before the corruption started. (This assumes you can find the point the corruption started—as you see, we're discussing a nightmare scenario and nightmares can often get worse.) When the database is in its earlier noncorrupted state, the transactions can be reapplied. In theory, if the input data is captured, then the transactions can be replayed in exactly the same order the transactions were originally committed. (This is exactly the same point we discussed in the two-database strategy for dual active.) In practice, this kind of input audit trail was possible with traditional mainframe transactions but is virtually impossible with object middleware. The reason is that it is hard to have a log of input messages, as mainframes did, when the objects are being updated in one transaction by a large number of small operation calls. It's this kind of point that keeps some large users wedded to their home-grown middleware!

The alternative to an automated reprocessing of transactions is a manual reprocessing of transactions. Don't throw away all that paper yet!

A manual reprocessing is difficult, however, if multiple databases are involved. In theory, it is possible to roll back two databases to a point before the corruption started and roll them forward together in sync. In practice, no software exists to do this. If there is a message queue between two systems, it should be possible to roll back one database without the other and throw away the messages regenerated on the rerun. This assumes that all messages on the rerun are generated in the same order as in the original, which will only start to be possible if order-dependent messages are in the same queue.

Rollback was a really good idea for batch, but now it's hard and it's getting harder. So what about writing a program to fix the data? To do that you need to know the transaction type in error, the effect of the error (obtainable from the database before-images and after-images on the log), and the input data for that transaction, perhaps a log of the Web browser input. With that information you can work out the effects on the database the input should have had. Unfortunately, changing the database using this information does not take into account second-order effects. A program or a user could have seen the corrupt data and acted wrongly. Eventually this becomes a business decision. For instance, you've accidentally put $2,000 in someone's account and he has spent it. Do you forget it? Write him a nasty letter? Take the money out of his account without telling him? As we said, it's a business decision.

In a distributed system you must rethink your strategy for error reporting. In particular, you need the following:

- An input log of all important input transactions; you need to know who the user was, the transaction he or she was doing, and the data he or she input.
- A record in the database (or the database log) that is sufficient to tie the information captured in the input log to the transaction on the database.
- Good error reporting to display the nature of the error and enough information to be able to track back to the input log.

Of course, if you do all this, you are much less likely to have application errors in the first place because your testing will be so effective.

7.7   Developing a resiliency strategy

A line of thinking in IT is that resiliency is entirely a technical issue, that you can take any design and turn it into a resilient application. This view misses two points:

- Error recovery is a business concern.
- The designers must set the resiliency goals; adding resiliency is a cost, and you can't do a cost/benefit analysis without understanding the business benefits and risks.

Resiliency analysis requires that the designer and the implementer sit down together and discuss the business process. Let us take a simple example—submitting expenses. At the top level, this is a four-stage process:

1. Submit the expenses.
2. Sign off.
3. Pay.
4. Audit.

Each stage is a self-contained chunk of work with one or more transactions. The first two stages could be real-time, online processes and the third stage might be a batch process. Between each stage will be a delay because different people are involved.

Resiliency is clearly not the only concern (security comes to mind). Resiliency analysis is part of the wider process of implementation design.

There are three parts to resiliency analysis: data safety analysis, uptime analysis, and error-handling analysis. Data safety analysis starts early in implementation design when deciding on the data distribution structure for the application. There are numerous alternatives even for a simple process like this, such as:

- Completely distributed. The submit process could run on a workstation and send a message directly to the manager's workstation through a queue (perhaps even e-mail).
- Two central databases, one for expenses and sign off, the other for payment.
- Departmental databases.
- One database. The expense handling could be a module of the financial systems.

We started the resiliency analysis by considering the safety and integrity of the data. The main resiliency requirements are:

- Each expense claim must be captured securely, once and once only.
- There must be a reference so that the paper receipts can be tied to the payment (and the tax man or tax woman is happy).
- There must be no possibility of paying the same expense twice.

Note that data is of paramount importance; the system's being down for a few hours is a nuisance but nowhere near as important as losing important data forever. This kind of resiliency requirement is completely different from, say, an airline, where the paramount requirement is for the system to be up and running with good response times, but if a little bit of data is lost every now and then that is a real shame but not a disaster, because the business processes used by airlines have established procedures for what to do in the event of lost data. In general, passengers are more unreliable than the systems involved, which is one reason that airlines overbook.

But not every piece of data is of equal importance; for instance, the table that maps department codes to managers can be re-input from information in the personnel system.

In the expenses example, the importance of the data points us strongly in the direction of a centralized secure server with, ideally, a resilient backup. There we can ensure high data integrity. The system does not have such high uptime requirements that we have to take special precautions if the network is down. Instead of duplicating the key parts of the database, we might consider a special audit trail of expenses on either a separate database or even a non-database file that could be kept in a remote location.

The other aspect of data safety is the reliable transport of messages from stage to stage. These messages are called deferrable messages in Chapter 6. We have already noted that message queuing is ideal technology for this requirement.

After consideration of the data safety requirements, the next step is to look at uptime requirements. The impact of the system's being down is that it wastes people's time. The cost of downtime includes the cost of employees not being able to work effectively and the cost arising from loss of business through giving poor customer service. In the expenses example, it is hard to put an exact cost on downtime; the main impact of this application being down is poor perception of the IT systems (and the IT department). It is also more important for the manager's sign-off part of the application to be up and running than it is for the expense submission part of the application to be up and running. This is partly because managers have less incentive to try again since it's not their money being refunded and partly because their time is more valuable (we generalize here).

The third part of resiliency analysis is to look at error handling. This is done during the detailed part of implementation design. It is worth looking at errors caused by external factors (e.g., a department that temporarily has no manager), errors cause by IT infrastructure breakdown, errors caused by users doing the wrong thing, and even errors caused by wrong or malicious programming.

Suppose the message to the manager for sign-off uses e-mail; this is notoriously unreliable. The resiliency strategy should be to recreate the message at any time, perhaps with a message saying "This is a possible duplicate." Suppose the manager is away for 4 weeks. There should be a time limit on the sign-off and the messages sent to the next level of manager. Perhaps the next level manager signs off, but when the manager gets back, he or she rejects the expenses. A better solution would be to use e-mail as a reminder, not as a carrier of data, so the manager would actually sign off the expenses by running a program or using a Web application. Note that these are all business process issues as well as technical issues; technical designers and application designers must work together.

A good resiliency analysis has many benefits:

- Helps prevent overengineering.
- Helps prevent underengineering.
- Helps test the integrity of the business process model.

The key is a discussion of the business processes, noting that the business processes go across departments. We suggest that application designers come to the technical designers with a business process diagram (discussed in Chapter 12) and use that as the starting point for the discussions. It is easy to assume everybody knows what needs to be done; but, especially when it comes to error handling, they often don't.

7.8 Summary

Building resilient systems is largely a matter of attitude. Remember the resiliency designer's motto: "Just because I'm paranoid, it doesn't mean that they are not out to get me."

A few simple points keep on coming up again and again:

- Keep the application simple.
- Have minimal session state.
- Test programs thoroughly.
- Catch errors early and report them in full.
- Make sure the errors are traceable to end input.
- Have a backup system.
- Practice switching to the backup system.
- Anticipate errors; you're going to get them.
- Understand the business impact of different failures.

There are some obvious extra costs in building a resilient system, such as paying for backup hardware and software. Many organizations would be prepared to pay a bit extra for much better resiliency. But building resilient systems is not just a matter of cost. It needs a commitment to developing tight operational procedures, extensive testing, and a willingness to anticipate problems, even unlikely ones. Building resiliency into an existing application is usually possible (with application changes), but it is much better to design for resiliency from the beginning.

Application and technical designers must work together on a resiliency strategy for an application. We suggest a three-step process for analyzing resiliency requirements:

1. Analyze which data and which messages have special integrity requirements.

2. Analyze uptime requirements.

3. Analyze error handling.

The first two steps are important for developing a data distribution strategy for the application. The discussion should be centered around the business process diagram of the application.

Two-phase commit

The two-phase commit protocol is the most widely used protocol to ensure synchronization of transactions. The protocol is illustrated in Figure 7-5.

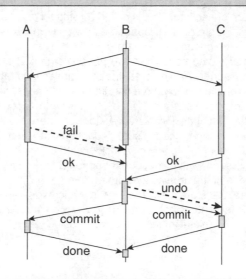

Figure 7-5 The two-phase commit

In this diagram, B is the coordinator. In the first phase, the coordinator finds out whether all subtransactions are ready to commit. In the second phase, the coordinator tells all subtransactions to either commit or abort. A commit will be done only if all subtransactions want to commit.

So what happens if one machine fails during this process? If it is in the first, or "prepare," phase, then the transaction can time out. If A or C failed, the coordinator would take the time out and abort the transaction. If B failed, A and C would take a time out and mark the transaction as aborted. The failure could be in the second, or "commit," phase of the protocol. If A and C fail after sending an "ok" message, but before processing the commit, then they must be able to interrogate B when they come back up again to see whether the transaction has to be aborted. This means the final state of the transaction must be captured somewhere in nonvolatile storage before the commit or abort messages are sent out. But what if B fails? A and C are left waiting with all their locks held. This could have a bad performance impact so some systems have a heuristic commit or heuristic abort. "Heuristic" here is computer jargon for "good guess." In this case, you might think that since many more transactions commit than abort. The good guess would be heuristic commit. But on the other hand,

(continued)

Two-phase commit (*cont.*)

since B failed, there is a good chance that the failure happened before the commit message was sent, so a heuristic abort makes more sense. Neither is very satisfactory.

A feature of the protocol is that A and C can be coordinators of their own and can have subtransactions. This is called a *transaction tree.* The total prepare phase of the protocol—propagated down all branches—must be completed before the commit phase starts.

There are performance issues with two-phase commit. There are clearly more network messages. As we noted, the subtransaction status must be captured on nonvolatile media before sending an "ok" message and again at transaction completion so there is an extra disk write. Since the commit processing takes some time, locks are held longer. There are also more opportunities for deadlock because subtransactions can become entangled. Subtransaction C could be waiting on a lock owned by another distributed transaction that itself is waiting for subtransaction B to complete. Deadlocks are handled by one of the transactions timing out.

As you can see, there are many reasons to avoid two-phase commit transactions, and in general that is precisely what you should do. Sometimes they are just so useful that they are worth using.

8

Performance
and Scalability

This chapter, the second about distributed systems principles, is about the principles that govern high performance and scalability in the context of commercial systems, especially transaction processing applications.

One of the extraordinary features of the modern IT industry is the ability of vendors to produce benchmark performance figures that seem to be in another dimension. For instance, back in 1999 a Unisys Aquanta ES2095R Intel server (eight Intel Pentium 550 MHz procs) was rated at 37,757.23 tpmC (tpmC means roughly the number of transactions per minute for the TPC-C benchmark. See www.tpc.org for a full explanation). Sustained for 5 hours, that's roughly 11 million transactions, which is enough for a major bank! And with technology developments since then, something much smaller would apparently suffice today. But banks have massive mainframe systems and gut feeling tells us that, resiliency aside, they would not be able to sustain such a throughput. Clearly, something funny is going on.

One way of looking at this is by analogy. The TPC-C benchmark is like riding a car round a racing circuit while running a commercial application is like driving a car over a ploughed field, since the benchmark is for one small application run in a unchanging environment over several hours . The fact that a Formula 1 racing car is extremely quick on a track is of little relevance on the ploughed field. This is a rhetorical argument, of course, and not very insightful. A closer analogy would be to compare computer hardware to a car engine and the software to a car's body, wheels, brakes, and all the rest that is needed to turn a power unit into something that can be used to move people. The TPC-C benchmark is a measure of the speed of the engine by looking at how effectively it performs when the vendor puts it into a racing car. What we need to understand is how to take the same engine and build the car body around it for going shopping or clambering around fields. This analogy is not bad because when vendors do TPC-Cs, they use different development tools from what all of us would use (they won't be using interpretive Visual

Basic or Java, for instance), they don't add anything for backups or fast recovery, and they have teams of experts nursing it along.

Performance keeps on catching people out. For at least 20 years, people in the IT industry have been looking at Moore's law (processor power increases by a factor of 2 every 19 months) or at disk performance projections or network performance projections and have been saying, don't worry about the performance of the software, the hardware will fix it. And for 20 years they have been wrong. What's happening? And will they be wrong for the next 20 years?

One thing that has gone wrong is encapsulated in the ancient saying, "What Intel giveth, Microsoft taketh away." Software has been getting fatter. It uses up much more memory than its predecessor 5 years ago, and it requires enormous amounts of processing power simply to keep the screen looking pretty. As 3D effects, voice processing, and natural language understanding become more common, there will be an ever-increasing requirement for power at the desktop. But the particular concern of this book is the back-end systems, so we won't concern ourselves with these front-end challenges.

8.1   The un-slippery slope

A more pertinent reason for the difference between benchmarks and reality is the hardware architecture. Look at Figure 8-1. We call this the un-slippery slope.

This diagram shows the gap between what the processor could do and what it actually does do. We call it the hardware architecture gap. The reason for the gap is simple: The processor is faster than the memory, and every now and then it must wait. Another ancient IT proverb is, "All processors wait at the same speed." Of course these days, every system has cache. But every now and then there is a cache miss—the data is not in cache and it must be fetched from main memory. Although processors now operate at 3 GHz or more and bus speeds and main memory have also increased in speed, there is still a gap. The net effect is that every cache miss means that processor cycles are wasted doing nothing. And it can get very bad. The cache might need to write old updated data to memory to make room for the new data. It might be impossible to read the data from memory for a while because another processor or some IO is writing to memory at the same time and got there first. The latest version of the data might be in the cache belonging to another processor.

There are sophisticated ways of handling these problems, sophisticated hardware architectures, in fact. Probably the least sophisticated is a simple PC using a PCI bus to memory. At the other end of the scale are machines like the Unisys CMP hardware, which has cross-bar memory interconnects, third-level cache shared by processors, separate IO processors, and other facilities. The effect of a sophisticated hardware architecture is to change the slope of the un-slippery curve, as illustrated in Figure 8-2.

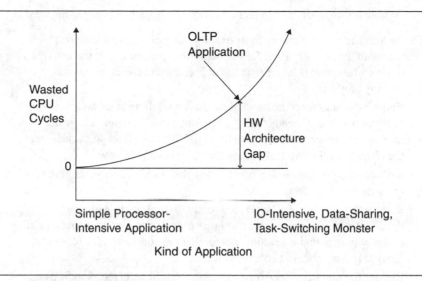

Figure 8-1   The un-slippery slope

This analysis implies that there are three ways to improve the performance:

1. Have a faster processor.

2. Improve the hardware architecture.

3. Push the application leftward, down the slope.

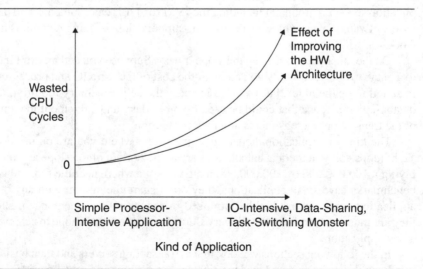

Figure 8-2   The effect of improving the hardware architecture

So how do we push the application down the slope? Here are some ways:

- Reduce the active memory footprint. By "active memory footprint" we mean the memory used for the main path processing. If the active memory footprint is larger than the cache, then cache is being continually recycled.
- Reduce the number of task switches. Task switching is slow at the best of times because it means saving away one set of register values and reloading another set. But it also has a deleterious effect on cache since the chances of the two tasks using the same data is remote.
- Reduce lock contention and other cases of multiple processors going for the same piece of data.
- Reduce the number of IOs. IOs are really disruptive. In addition to the amount of raw processing and large memory movements that can fill cache with data that is seldom reused, there is contention for locks and inevitably a number of process switches.
- Reduce the number of network messages sent or received. Sending and receiving messages has all the same overhead as doing an IO plus the additional complexities of building network messages and handling the network protocol.
- Reduce the number of memory overlays. Memory thrashing is worst of them all—practically everything is wrong.

These are all deeply techy things that your average application programmer would rather not think about. Furthermore, a number of these points are outside the programmer's control; they depend on the operating system, the application server environment including the JVM for J2EE environments, and database software. This is why we call it the un-slippery slope—going down it is hard work.

On the other hand, going up the slope is easy. Suppose you add an extra index to a database table. Not only do you incur the cost of the extra IO and processor to read and write the index, but you also increase the active memory footprint, take database buffer space that could be used by other data, and stretch out the length of the transaction, thereby increasing lock contention.

The kind of application dictates to some extent where you are on the slope. Tight loops doing numerical calculations are at the bottom of the slope and multiplying a 100,000,000 by 100,000,000 matrix is somewhere near the top. Industry benchmarks have small applications, they don't share the system with any other application, and they are highly optimized to reduce IO and memory. In short, they are much farther down the slippery slope than you can ever hope to achieve in a real application.

In the following sections we look first at transaction servers and then business intelligence data access, and we investigate some performance characteristics and what can be done to optimize the application.

8.2   Transaction processing

Let us start by looking at an optimized transaction implementation. This is illustrated in Figure 8-3.

Summarizing what we see here, we have:

- One input and one output network message,
- A number of reads and writes to the data file, and
- A write to the log file, which could be on disk or tape.

In a typical configuration the application logic takes in the order of 10% of the processor, and the network and database systems take 30% each. The remaining 30% is idle and has to be because at higher than 70% utilization (some operating systems can do better than that) queuing effects start deteriorating the response time so much that the system starts to become unusable (see the box entitled "Queuing"). This is all, of course, a gross simplification, but it gives a flavor of what is happening.

Where are the bottlenecks in this system? Let's do some "back-of-the-envelope" calculations. First, look at the network, as in Figure 8-4.

A 10-Mbit Ethernet LAN delivers considerably less than 10Mbits/sec, depending on the number of devices connected to it (unless it is switched). So we are talking about one or two 10Mbit LANs or one 100Mbit LAN. (On the other hand, if you used character-based telnet, which has a separate message for every byte, it would be a different story, and this is one of the reasons why early UNIX systems had such a problem with high-transaction throughput applications.)

What about disk throughput? Another back-of-the-envelope calculation is presented in Figure 8-5. The calculation in Figure 8-5 shows that there is no issue

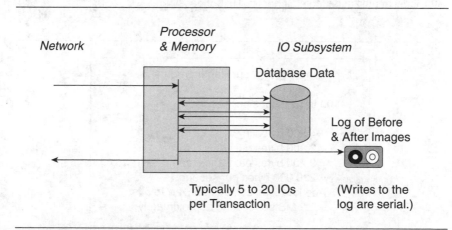

Figure 8-3   An ideal transaction implementation

Queuing

A critical queuing formula is:

Total time = service time / (1 − utilization).

In other words, if the utilization is 50%, then the total time is twice the service time. If the utilization is 70%, then the total time is a bit over 3 times the service time. This formula applies to random arrivals and a single provider. Having multiple providers on a single input queue is much better. You can see this in the real world by looking at the effects in banks, for example. Where each teller used to have a queue (or line) of waiting people, there is now one queue served by all the tellers—the next customer gets the next free teller.

What level of utilization, and hence queue length, can be tolerated? It depends on two major factors. The first is the service time. If it is short, a longer queue can be tolerated without serious overall performance deterioration. Since the key resources of processor, disk IO, and communications have different service times, different utilizations and hence queue lengths can be tolerated. (Memory adds another complication and can affect processor load and disk IO by reducing disk IO through caching in some form.) Processor service times are generally short in a transactional environment, followed by disk IO, and then communications, so different utilizations are acceptable, for example, 90% on processor, 60% on disk, and 50% on communications.

The second factor is the behavior of the operating system and other software. Some systems have been very well tuned over a long period and behave well at high processor utilization, using sophisticated throttling techniques to manage the load. Indeed, sustained operation at more than 90% processor load is possible with some operating systems. Others behave less well; in some cases, the systems simply stop working around 70% processor utilization, so a higher load is not possible.

Network Throughput Requirements

100 transactions per second

        200 bytes in
+ 2,000 bytes out
= 2,200 bytes per transaction
= 220,000 bytes per second
Add headers, etc. and convert to bits
= 2.2 MB per second approximately

Figure 8-4 Rough OLTP network calculations

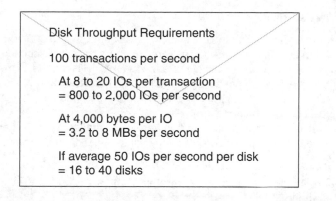

Figure 8-5   Rough OLTP disk calculations

with disk throughput since channel technology is much faster. The problem is that it implies 16 to 40 disk drives going flat out. (See the box entitled "How fast is a disk?") Since IOs will not be evenly distributed over the drives, the system would need many more disks attached, and it must be optimized to ensure that there is not an excessive number of IOs to one disk. We end up with large disk farms, large numbers of IOs per second, but low data throughput rates. Disk caching, fiber-optic channel technology, and command queuing will help greatly, but even without these features, the problem is not insurmountable so long as the database software has the ability to spread data over many disks.

But note that taking a backup copy of disk to tape has the opposite profile. Properly configured (and using enterprise-capable backup software), the limit on backups is usually the number of parallel runs where each run cannot go faster than the minimum of the serial transfer rate of the tape device, the disk device, tape channel, or disk channel.

What about memory? Here clearly there might be a problem. The operating system, networking software, and database software are big hungry systems that need lots of memory for their tables and codes. Spare memory is at a premium for the database buffer pool. A crude implementation would be to have a single copy of each application for each terminal. Since each application needs a database connection, it will be large, say, 2Mbytes. If there are 2,000 terminals, this translates to 4 gigabytes just for applications, the addressing limit of many processors. A better solution is to use a transaction monitor, and all mainframe systems have one (e.g., CICS on IBM S390, TIP and COMS on Unisys ClearPath). Systems such as Tuxedo, .NET, and J2EE application servers such as WebLogic and Web Sphere Application Server contain similar features. With a transaction monitor, programs and resources can be shared among all terminals. The number of parallel copies is then the number of active transactions rather than the number of terminals. The impact is dramatic. The active memory footprint is reduced and the memory can be used for more database buffers.

How fast is a disk?

The simple answer is that the best modern disk at the start of 2004 did about 10,000 rpm and has an average seek time of about 5 to 6 milliseconds.

This is incredibly fast—a single rotation takes 6 milliseconds. In theory it could achieve 166 IOs per second if there is no head movement or slightly fewer IOs per second if there is head movement (allowing for average seek time plus time for a half rotation).

The catch is that the processor has hardly any time to ask for a new IO. In the time between disk operations the system must do the following:

- Get control of the channel.
- Copy the data to the memory (probably with some buffering in between).
- Handle the IO finish code.
- Wait until the processor is free.
- Run application code until the next IO.
- Process the next IO code.
- Wait to get control of the disk (another IO on the disk may be in process).
- Wait to get control of the disk channel.
- Write the data across the channel to the disk cache.
- Move the disk head and do the IO.

This all takes time, and delays come in 6 millisecond chunks—the time for another rotation. Doing 30 or 40 random IOs per second and 60 or 90 serial IOs per second off one disk is doing well in a moderately busy system (rather than in a laboratory test).

Disk caching helps, of course, although clearly all the delays just outlined still apply. Reading data in a database buffer in main memory will always be quicker and incur less processing overhead than reading it from disk cache. However, disk caches are often very large, and by having battery backup to protect cached data over power faults they can save on writes as well as reads. Some activity does not benefit from caching at all. Large serial reads and writes (e.g., while copying a database to backup) do not benefit from caching (unless there are effects from reblocking—the cache subsystem reading larger blocks than the main system). Also, random reads and writes on a large file (one much greater than the cache size) are not improved. An example may be account records in a bank. The degree to which cache helps is extremely complex and hard to predict, except by a comprehensive modeling exercise.

So what is the problem? In a well-balanced system with a highly capable IO subsystem, it is processing power, which brings us back to the un-slippery slope.

Now let us consider some of technologies we discussed in earlier chapters and look at how they change this profile.

8.2.1   Object interfaces

Object interfaces normally have more network messages than a simple transaction message interface. We say "normally" because it is possible to have more or less the same number of messages by simply turning a transaction server into one large object. This is against the spirit of the object interface, so it is not usually done. Instead, one operation, such as "credit an account," will typically become two, "find the account" and "send a credit message to it," as discussed in Chapter 3.

An object interface does not necessarily imply a doubling of the network messages. Many applications do something like read an object, display it on the screen, and update the object. This could translate to find an object, get the object data, display it on the screen, and update the object. Instead of two operations between workstation and transaction server—read and write, there are three—find, get, and update.

But it could be a lot worse. Languages like Visual Basic positively encourage you to use attributes, not operations, which translates into a message to get every attribute value and a message to update every attribute value. The worst case could be something like this: Find the object, do 10 messages to get 10 attributes, display on the screen, and do 2 messages to update the object. Instead of the original 2 messages in the non-object case, we now have 13 messages. Since the overhead of message handling is so great (we assumed that the network side, which includes the transaction monitor processing, took 30% of the processing power in the original case), this implementation uses much more processing power.

The conclusion is that with object interfaces you have enough rope to hang yourself with plenty to spare. However, hanging yourself is not compulsory; you can avoid the rope as long as you look out for it. This is true for all object interfaces, such as DCOM and RMI; we strongly suspect the nuances of writing an efficient interface will exceed the performance differences among the technologies.

8.2.2   Transactional component containers

Transactional component containers have similar resource pooling to mainframe transaction monitors. Aside from being modern pieces of software, which inevitably seems to mean they use much more memory than traditional transaction monitors, they should benefit in the same way.

Assuming the object interfaces are used efficiently by the programmer as discussed, we don't see why transactional component containers should not be capable of implementing large-scale applications. And, in fact, they can. However J2EE application servers, for example, currently do not scale well vertically. Their performance increases up to about four processors, depending on the application, and then falls away. There are various technical reasons why vertical scaling does not work well; for example, objects accessed by every thread lead to contention. (The reasons are not related to the operating system being used.) Additional performance requires another application server, running in its own JVM. This has led to a design approach of horizontal scaling, typically in separate servers: If you want more performance, add another two- to four-way server with its own JVM, application server, and application, and use clustering technology and load balancing to share the work out. An alternative to adding physical servers is to run multiple copies in a single larger system, using processor affinity techniques to associate a group of processors with a particular instance.

An interesting point to consider is whether an architectural assumption of horizontal scaling led to application servers restricted to only about four processors or restrictions in the design led to the idea of horizontal scaling: Which came first? After all, it won't be the first time that implementation restrictions have led to a specific architectural approach, which then becomes accepted as the way to do things—a virtue, in other words. Quite a lot of technology seems to us to have been invented to get around problems that shouldn't exist in the first place. An example is using physically separate database servers; we discuss that elsewhere in this chapter. We believe that horizontal scaling as the best way to increase capacity is at least open to question. It should, in our opinion, be possible to scale upward as well as outward. The power of systems today should allow most transaction applications to function well in a single application server, removing a number of complications associated with horizontal scaling and clustering. Other transaction processing monitors do scale upward very well and, at least in some cases, allow horizontal scaling as well.

8.2.3   Two-phase commit

The details of how the two-phase commit protocol works is described in a box (called "Two-phase commit") in Chapter 7. What you need to know is that when you update two or more databases on different systems, there are additional network messages and disk writes. The message flow is illustrated in Figure 8-6. It shows two databases being updated, in one transaction, on two boxes. There is a network message from the master transaction to start the subtransaction in the other box. When the subtransaction has finished, it sends a reply and, finally, there are two messages for the acknowledgment phase of the commit protocol. Both systems maintain their own logs. Another source of delay is that the transaction takes longer, so database locks are held longer and there is more lock contention.

A lot depends on how many systems and databases are involved and how they are interrelated. At its simplest, everything is in one box, running under one operating system; an example is maintaining integrity between a database and message queues. Many instances that involve more than one server are just one system invoking another. Where more than two systems are involved, the method of invoking them is clearly an issue. If the invocation is in series—for example, A calls B, waits for a reply, then calls C, waits for a reply, and so on—the time is much longer. But systems can invoke a number of others in parallel, wait for all the results, and then commit (or abort) all the updates.

Although there are systems operating fairly heavy transaction loads with two-phase commit, it clearly does impose a performance penalty. For this and other

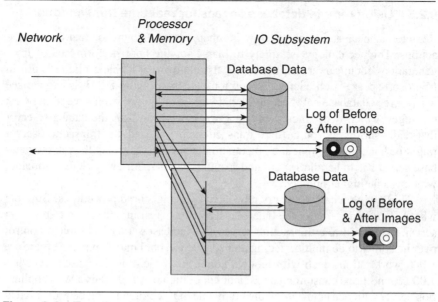

Figure 8-6 Two-phase commit

reasons (e.g., the impact on resiliency discussed in Chapter 7), a decision to use two-phase commit across multiple systems needs to be made with considerable care.

8.2.4 Message queuing

Message queues can be very efficient because they allow a number of messages to be put into one block both for transmission over the network and for writing to disk. But there is a trade-off between reducing the overhead and increasing the elapsed time to send the message. For real-time messages, elapsed time is paramount, so message blocking over the network is less likely.

The wider issue with message queuing is that you must implement your own program scheduler. For instance, if you are using message queuing for real-time processing, you may want to put all like messages into one queue. The easiest technique is to have one program empty the queue, but on high-volume systems, this will not be fast enough. The alternative is to have several programs empty the queue. But it is up to you to write the scheduler that decides how many programs run and that starts additional copies of the program if the queue is too large. An effective, and relatively simple, solution is to write a simple program to process the queue and pass the messages to a transaction monitor to schedule application components for subsequent processing. In other words, the solution uses an existing scheduling mechanism.

8.2.5 Using remote database access for real-time transactions

Remote database access technology is inherently inefficient for real-time transactions. This technology is largely to blame for the poor performance of first-generation client/server applications, also known as "thick clients" or, in Microsoft-speak, "rich clients." If you look again at Figure 8-3, it is easy to see why—every database call becomes a network message, or even several network messages, which vastly increases the network overhead. It is the database server that really suffers. If you need 20 transactions per second, the transaction server might be handling 20 input and 20 output network messages, but the remote database server has to handle 1 input and 1 output message for every SQL command, which is a far higher number.

This situation can be greatly alleviated by using stored procedures. But note what has been done here; the database server has been turned into a transaction server. Compared to a transaction server, the database server has limited control over its ability to do multithreading and connection pool management. If there are 1,000 workstations each with its own connection, then the database server has 1,000 connections consuming a vast amount of memory. If there is a Web application server with one connection, then only one SQL command can be processed at one time.

Using a transaction server (e.g., .NET Enterprise Services or Enterprise Java-Beans) solves these problems. The number of connections can easily be controlled in the transaction server. So what about using remote database access from the transaction server to a separate database server? Figure 8-7 shows a configuration that is often used in benchmarks and as long as stored procedures are widely used, it works well. It works especially well if the transaction servers are routing to several database servers, for instance, if there are several identically structured databases each handling different geographic areas. (The TPC-C benchmark is a bit like this.) But splitting databases by data range works better in benchmarks than in real life. (See Section 8.4, "Is distribution an alternative?") Vendors who publish benchmarks are prepared to put in a great deal of work optimizing these kinds of configurations, and the alarming fact is that they seem to need it.

But forcing so much into stored procedures restricts your choices of application development tools. It is true that except for enormous applications, these days you can use fast networks and powerful processors so you don't have to use stored procedures, but you should consider whether the money might be better spent running both the transaction logic and the database on one machine.

8.2.6 Conclusions about real time

The conclusion we can draw from all this discussion is that the requirements to build a high-performance transaction engine were first understood and implemented in the 1970s and 1980s and haven't changed much since. The industry has been rebuilding the same solution under different guises such as database stored

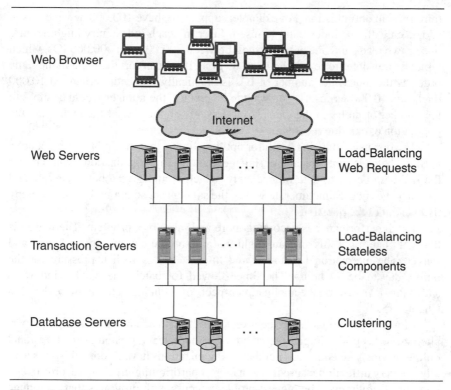

Figure 8-7   Database server benchmark configuration

procedures and transactional component managers. The main difference has been the language(s) in which we implement the transaction logic. The other conclusion is that with the massive numbers of IOs and network messages, there is no leeway. You must use software such as transaction monitors that optimize the use of resources, and you must be ready to review and optimize your disk IOs and your interface, especially if it is an object interface.

8.3   Batch

So far in this book there has been little mention of batch; the emphasis has been on new technologies and new applications where batch is less important than in the past. Batch may have a diminished role but it is still vital.

There are three basic reasons for batch. Two we have mentioned already—to support cyclical business processes (e.g., payroll and bank interest accrual) and to support housekeeping tasks (e.g., copying a database to backup). But there is a third reason: optimization. For example, suppose we have 100,000 new records to add, each with one index entry to insert. Inserting each index entry might require one or two reads and one or two writes, between 200,000 and 400,000 IOs, which typically translates to several hours of IO time. If we can sort the input in the same order as the index, the number of IOs is drastically reduced, perhaps to 10,000 reads and 10,000 writes. (If you want to be precise, the number would be close to the number of tables in the index, so it depends on the size of the tables and the population of existing records).

The downside of using batch for optimization is that the updates are not done until the batch is run, typically during the night. Many organizations would rather the database be up-to-date immediately, which would give a better service and simplify the code. Sometimes, however, the savings are so dramatic that removing them is out of the question.

Batch performance is becoming more and more of a problem. The reason is that with late-night this and late-night that, the online day has gotten longer and longer. The international nature of the Internet brings with it pressure for the online day to be 24 hours. The time allowed for batch, the batch window, is shrinking. (We discuss the application aspects of reducing batch in more detail in Chapter 15.)

From the performance perspective, the trick with batch is to have enough parallelism to keep all the processors busy (perhaps leaving enough for a residual online service). An enormous number of organizations haven't done this. It is usually not very difficult because it is a matter of partitioning the input records over a number of programs. The biggest problem occurs with programs that do a huge batch task in one transaction to simplify recovery code.

If you were designing from scratch, you could and should eliminate these problems at the source. In fact, you should write transactions to be used for both online and batch, which means ensuring that they are short. Batch program can then support parallelism from the start. On the other hand, retrofitting these changes to existing batch runs is almost certainly quicker, easier, and less risky than rewriting everything from scratch.

8.4   Is distribution an alternative?

With all these problems, wouldn't it be easier to distribute the application over several smaller systems? The answer is, regrettably, it depends.

The easiest distributed systems to implement are those where the application is inherently distributed. For instance, a warehouse control system spends most of its time processing information local to the warehouse. It needs connections to the central location to receive input data and queries, but those volumes should be low.

But how do you take a naturally centralized system like a bank database and distribute it over several machines? First, to be truly effective, you will want to distribute the data over a large number of machines. Distributing a 100-transaction-per-second application over three machines is likely to end up with machines that do 50, 30, and 20 transactions per second, respectively. The problems of managing the machine that does 50 transactions per second aren't very different from managing a machine with 100 transactions per second. To make a real difference, distribution should be over, say, 10 or 20 machines.

The first step in implementing a distributed bank would be to ensure online transactions are routed to the right machine. This could be done by having each distributed system implement a range of account numbers. You don't want all the big business accounts on one machine and all the savings accounts for children on another, so you would have to look carefully into exactly how you are allocating account numbers.

Any task that isn't based on account number—be it online update, batch report, or ad hoc query—would have to be implemented by accessing all machines. For instance, suppose the bank wants to find the list of accounts that are overdrawn; this now requires a search of all machines.

Many bank transactions not only do a debit or credit on one account but also do an update somewhere else. For instance, the system might want to keep track of how much money is in the cashier's till. So where is this data kept? If it is on a different machine, the application needs to implement a two-phase commit. However, the machine that has the cashier's till records is going to have to process a large number of transactions, so it will have to be large, unless the cashier records are distributed as well. Alternatively, the account records could split according to their owning branch, but then any account number-based operation would have to start by looking up the owning branch from the account number.

Having made the split, there are many databases that now require operating and managing, not one. Complex tasks, like handling new versions of the software and building disaster backup plans, require an additional layer of complexity.

In summary, when considering distribution, remember these four points:

1. There is a great deal of extra coding; transactions, reports, and inquiries are all more complex.

2. Evenly spread dispersal of data is hard; the largest machine is likely to be supporting much more traffic than the smallest.

3. There is considerable additional overhead, such as for two-phase commits.

4. It is much more difficult operationally; put simply, instead of having one machine to manage, you have many.

The changes are so great that unless you have built the application from the ground up to be distributed, it is very hard to change.

Many people promoting distribution are doing so to overcome a limitation in their preferred software technology. But the issues with scalability in software products often have to do with the number of attached users, not the number of transactions per second. For banks using account number ranges, the distributed solution totally fails on this score. If the bank has 10,000 users, each account-handling server must still support 10,000 users.

The conclusion is that with the increased scalability of machines, there doesn't seem to be much point in distributing a single application only for performance.

8.5   Load balancing

In white papers and press articles, the message is that scalability equals load balancing. Let us look again at Figure 8-7. There are four tiers: Web browsers, Web servers, transaction servers, and database servers. Load balancing means having any number of Web servers, any number of transaction servers all working on the same application, and any number of database servers.

Load balancing of the Web server requires a special network router that fools the outside network into thinking that there is only one Web server (i.e., only one IP address and only one name), whereas in fact, there are a number of physical Web servers. As discussed previously, such routers are available.

The other problem the Web servers must solve is ensuring that the data in all of them is the same. We describe how to do this in Chapter 7 with a dual-active scenario; the only difference here is that not only two, but many systems could be active. The best solution now, as previously, is to put all the state in the back-end database.

Scaling a single transaction service by load balancing over several physical servers is much harder. The dual-active issues apply here also if there is state (i.e., if there are EJB stateful session beans). Therefore, the number one rule is: no state. Even applying this rule, there is a further issue of balancing the work evenly across the servers. Let us suppose the implementation uses transactional component middleware with a load-balancing feature. At a minimum, this means that every time a client requests that a new object be created, the object may be located on one of several machines. This increases the overhead of object creation since the servers have to determine which of them takes the new object. This may or may not be significant depending on whether the application creates new objects often or rarely. (But the downside of creating objects only rarely is that spreading the load evenly over many machines is much harder.)

The multiple transactions servers now have to update the same database, so how about load balancing the database server across several machines? The first task is to ensure that the database connections are assigned to the different machines in such a way as to disperse the load across the database servers. If this can be done, then the multiple machines can share one database by using clustering, as discussed in Chapter 7 in the section about dual-active scenarios. Whether many clustered machines gives good performance again depends on the application. If there are many reads and only a few writes, performance can be good. When there are many writes to the same physical blocks, performance will be poor. The killer is "hot spot" data—data that all the transactions want to change.

Examples are control totals and statistics, the end of indexes (e.g., the last block in a sequential index organized on date and time), and small volatile tables. Because of locking, you single thread through the hot spots (that means one program goes through the code at a time). Since the overhead of sharing buffers on a clustered machine is greater than on a single machine, single threading of hot spot data on a clustered configuration can be even worse than on a single multiprocessor system.

All of these "it depends on the application" considerations are why vendors can show linear scalability for their products and why you can find so few examples in the real world. You have been warned.

The bottom line is that if you want your application to respond well to load balancing or other forms of distribution, then you have to design it with that in mind. For instance, if you want to eliminate an index that is a hot spot, you have to figure out which other applications need the index and find an alternative solution. This is another reason that application designers must talk to technical designers.

Our view is that the configuration illustrated in Figure 8-7 is balanced on a knife edge and it will work well on real-life applications only after a major tuning exercise. Where possible, just have a single machine holding both the transaction server and the database server (possibly with a backup) and leave complex load-balancing techniques to the organizations that are pushing the boundaries of the performance and don't have a choice. Restrictions in scaling of some products may, however, leave no option but to use horizontal scaling and load balancing.

8.6   Business intelligence systems

We use the term *business intelligence system* as a catchall for the whole range of machines from data access to decision support to data marts and data warehouses. But all these machines share two performance issues—processing ad hoc queries and data replication.

8.6.1   Ad hoc database queries

Large database queries are IO and processor intensive. The IO usage is obvious. The processor usage is from

- Checking each record against the search criteria.
- Moving data to the output message.
- Sorting.
- Parsing the query, including scanning the query text, building a processing plan, and optimizing the plan.
- Managing temporary data.
- Doing arithmetic calculations, checking for nulls.
- And doing much else besides.

Worse still, large queries will dominate the IO capacity. They also need large amounts of memory, for instance, to be used by the sort routines. They have a very disruptive impact on database buffers, filling them up with stuff no other program is at all interested in. In short, they squeeze out other work. It is hard to ensure database queries have no impact on an online transaction processing application even if they are running at low priorities. This is why organizations have been so keen to move the database to another machine where the database queries can only get in the way of each other.

On the other hand, there are more and more pressures for having up-to-date data available at any time. This is partly a reaction to the Internet where, for instance, customers or business partners can check the status of their orders. You can argue that this is no different from online inquiry transactions now, but we expect to see more of them, with larger chunks of data in each query and more flexible tailoring of the request. Of course, smaller queries aren't as disruptive as large ones, but mixed query and transaction workloads will become an increasing challenge for database vendors.

8.6.2   Data replication

While data replication helps solves the ad hoc query problem, it introduces its own set of problems.

The technology for replication is basically straightforward: Take a copy of the database and keep it up-to-date by applying the changes. It is desirable to be able to take the changes from the database log file. When you review technology that does this, you should check that it does not apply changes from transactions that were subsequently aborted.

The network load for replication is large. The good thing is that it can be a few large messages rather than many small ones. You can get an idea of how much extra network throughput is required by looking at the amount of database log data created. For instance, if your system is doing 50 transactions per second and each transaction generates 4,000 bytes of database log, then you need 200k bytes per second. A dedicated Ethernet LAN connection should do the trick.

In our experience, the significant performance problem with data replication occurs when loading the data on the target system. This can get out of hand because it is desirable that the query database have more indexes than the transaction processing application. The IO overhead of a load may not be far short of the IO load on the production machine.

So what's the solution? Having huge quantities of memory to hold as much as possible of the indexes in memory is clearly an approach. Letting the target machine get behind and catching up during the night is also a possibility. Sorting the records before loading them would also save on some IOs.

An alternative approach is to use the technology supplied by disk subsystem vendors, where additional copies of the databases can be maintained by the disk subsystem. And perhaps the database vendors could help. They could have an adjunct index for today's data, which could be merged into the main index as a background run. The index search would then have to look in both the main and the adjunct indexes. As we write this (in early 2004), we not aware of any vendor who has done something like this.

8.7   Backups and recovery

The discussion thus far leaves out arguably the most important aspect of building a large system—the performance of backup and recovery.

There is a cruel logic about large systems:

- The more users there are, the more important it is not to have a failure.
- The larger the database, the more likely it is to experience a hardware failure because there is more hardware to fail.
- The larger the database, the longer the backup copy will take.
- The more transactions there are, the larger the log.
- The larger the log, the longer reconstruction of disk data will take since it has to reload the relevant data from last backup copy and reapply the changes in the log.
- Because applying the log takes so long, backup copies must be made more frequently.

In other words, the larger the database, the longer the recovery and the longer the database housekeeping.

Let us first get a yardstick on how big the problem really is. To do this, we will take out another envelope and do a few calculations on the back; see Figure 8-8.

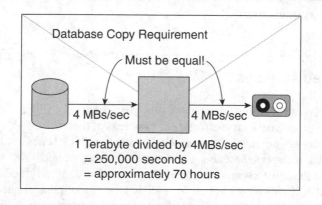

Figure 8-8   Database copy requirements

How long does it take to copy a database to backup? There are two questions: How many parallel streams can you run, and how fast is each stream? Figure 8-8 illustrates that one stream copying at 4MBs per second takes a disastrous 70 hours to copy 1 terabyte of data. In practice, it is worse than that because you might want a check phase and you never can reach maximum capacity. The conclusion is that for a large database, you need both fast backup devices and software that supports many parallel streams.

How much log is created? Say your system handles 2 million transactions per day (about the size of a medium bank). The amount of log data created for every transaction is very variable and depends on the details of the transaction, the database design, and the database implementation itself. If we assume, as before, that there are 4,000 bytes per transaction, then there are 9 gigabytes of log written each day. Within a few days the disk will be full, so the log must be copied to tape and removed.

Say there is a disk crash. The data must be copied back from the backup and the log must be applied. If there is a weekly backup copy of the database, in our example, that would mean on average working through 29 gigabytes of log (3.5 days' worth) and probably doing perhaps several million IOs to the disk unit. We hope most of the data is in disk cache or in the database buffers, but however we look at this, we are talking about many hours, maybe days, to recover the database. With the cheapness of today's disk units, the solution is to mirror the complete database. However, the organization still needs protection against catastrophe (in other words, software problems, or operations troubles) and needs the security of being able to do a complete rebuild of the database in an acceptable period of time, say, less than a day. This requirement usually means making a backup copy every day.

As in the case of data replication for business intelligence systems, the disk subsystem vendors can help. The software that supports database replication for use by business intelligence systems can also be used for recovery reasons, where a copy of the database is maintained in a backup system, either local or remote, depending on requirements.

8.8   Web services

All of the issues with online transaction processing apply equally to Web services, but Web services have some performance concerns of their own.

Web services are invoked using SOAP. Although SOAP does not have to use HTTP as the transport mechanism—no specific transport is defined in the standard—it is the most common choice. The reason usually advanced for using HTTP is that it will pass through firewalls easily for systems connected to the Internet. This in itself is questionable from a security point of view, but the concern here is performance: HTTP is far less efficient than other mechanisms, such as DCOM, RMI, and raw sockets. SOAP also uses XML, which requires parsing and interpreting, which adds to the load on processors. XML messages are human-readable and can be verbose, consuming far more network capacity than other forms of communication. A look at any XML fragment will illustrate this point; the true information content is likely to be a small fraction of the total message size. It may not matter in a LAN environment but can cause problems in the wide area because of inadequate bandwidth, either for cost reasons or lack of availability.

But in addition to bandwidth problems, there are transmission time problems associated with using the Internet. Fairly obviously, it takes time to cross a network; the farther you go, the longer it takes. The time to send a message from one place to another with an immediate response as an acknowledgment—a ping—is called the Round Trip Time (RTT). The Internet Traffic Report shows an RTT of just over 200 ms between North America and Europe, caused by a combination of intermediate nodes traversed, occasional packet loss due to congestion, and the physical transmission time of light in fiber. The effect on file transfers using FTP is well known: The effective transmission rates progressively decrease as distance increases. (This phenomenon is caused by a combination of the way TCP uses its flow control window and the time taken to transfer protocol messages.) In the context of Web services, when you add up all the time consumed for a cascaded series of requests, some of which may require several request-responses, plus the processing time in the servers involved, the response time complications become clear.

The next set of complications concerns predictability. Consider an example of a bank that offers its customers a service to display the status of all the products they hold—checking accounts, savings accounts, mortgages, insurance policies, credit cards, and so on. The service is offered to customers through the Internet via a Web browser. The service requires a customer management system (call it the CMS), which contains a list of all the products owned by the customer in its database. The CMS then invokes every application that contains information about those products, collects the status of each product (e.g., balance, last 10 transactions), formats a reply, and sends it to the customer. The product applications may all be running in one system; more likely, they would be in several different systems.

The complete enquiry is distributed over several applications, located in several servers. Within a single organization, such as the bank, the systems would probably be in the same location and interconnected by a high-speed LAN of sufficient capacity and high reliability. Coupled with the fact that the environment is predictable in the number of application invocations, the total response time would be predictable. Web services would be a suitable technology to use for intersystem communication. There is no reason to believe that any performance problems could not be easily solved.

Instead of the predictable banking environment described above, consider a full Web services application using the Internet. Predictability is far more questionable. Invoking a Web service means going over the wide area across the

Internet. The request will probably require a directory reference using UDDI to find the Web service before invoking it. Worse, the Web service may itself act as a concentration point, in turn invoking other Web services, each of which may also require a directory reference. In other words, there is an unpredictable cascade of requests. And it could be worse still. At its simplest, a Web service just requires a request and a response. However, the Web service may enter a dialogue with its requester, involving a number of request-response pairs, to complete the interaction, in addition to any cascading or directory searches involved.

So what can be done about it? Performance problems may be prevented if implementations are more specific and restricted, certainly initially while experience is gained with the technology. One approach is to use Web services technology inside an organization connected to an intranet for collaboration among applications owned by the organization, as with the banking example. Depending on the scale of the requirement, it may be possible just to use SOAP for exchange of information, thus eliminating the need for directory structures that require WSDL and UDDI. Many analysts see this approach as a good way to gain familiarity with the technology. An attraction is that the standards are widely available on many platforms, or at least committed by their suppliers, thus providing a standard means of communication within a heterogeneous environment. An additional attraction is that, at least within a data center or campus environment, the network bandwidth is sufficiently high to support the somewhat verbose structures of XML with a decent performance.

Another approach is to use Web services for intersystem connection for e-business purposes, replacing current EDI implementations with what is seen as more standard technology. The collaboration could be confined to the members of a closed group that are connected to an extranet. These restrictions remove some problems of scale in that the directories are smaller since the number of providers of services is smaller. In simple cases, directory structures may be avoided altogether. This is an area where we expect Web services to take off. After all, systems have been collaborating in the wide area for a long time now, for example, in the airline industry. The controlled and predicable environments have proved very effective. Web services technology could replace older approaches; in fact, it already has.

Realizing the full vision of Web services will take a lot of work and a willingness to be disciplined in the implementation by organizations offering Web services on the Internet. Care needs to be taken to ensure that the cascading effect is minimized and the number of invocations to use a service kept to a minimum, preferably one. It is far better to send one large request, with a single response, than to send many small ones. The alternatives are to sell the application providing the service as a product, which can be physically installed in its customers' premises for high-volume users or to accustom people to the response time consequences. This may be acceptable, given due warning. What is clear is that the unpredictable consequences of a less disciplined approach will lead to disappointment.

8.9 Design for scalability and performance

Although many of the issues we have been discussing are very technical, that is no reason to put off facing them. Performance should be considered early in design, before hardware and software products are chosen. There are three reasons:

1. The performance consequences of data distribution can be assessed.

2. The difference between deferrable transactions and real-time transactions should be noted. Using message queuing for deferrable transactions in preference to distributed transaction processing will be much faster (and more resilient, as we noted).

3. The application design model gives us the data and transaction volumes

Performance analysis is required at all levels of design and during implementation. Until we get into detailed analysis, the primary technique is for the application designers and technical designers to analyze the performance implications of the business process model. The technical designers need to see the flow of data and the data volumes; they need to know the scale of the task that faces them. Object models, class hierarchies, or entity-relationship diagrams do not give them this information.

The first step is to measure the scale of the problem. The simple expenses claim application discussed in Chapter 7 illustrates how this can be done. We know that we can reasonably expect the busiest times for submitting expense forms to be early in the week and that the maximum number of people working simultaneously on the system cannot exceed the number of employees. By analyzing the business process, we can compare the distributed and centralized solutions for the application and can estimate the load on each node and the data flow between nodes. We should exploit the fact that the data sent between the expenses system and the payment system is deferrable, not real-time.

At a more detailed level we can look at the actual expense report submission process. On one hand, we could collect all the expense report information on the workstations and send it in one message to a central server. On the other hand, we could have one transaction to the central server for each expense line item. The difference in performance will be significant but the volumes might not be high enough for us to care.

At the very detailed level, we can investigate the interfaces, code, and database usage profile to model the performance with the high-volume transactions.

Another issue in the implementation design is performance monitoring. There is a problem here. In distributed systems technology, there is very little instrumentation for measuring performance across the system rather than within a single node, a difficulty that is magnified if Web services play a significant role in the application. The chief problem is that different machines do not have exactly synchronized clocks, at least to the level of accuracy we need. It is very hard to say, for instance, that the ninth message that left box A at 2 seconds past 10:05 A.M. is the 24th message that entered box B at 5 seconds past 10:05 A.M. So, if the reply to a message was slow, it is hard to track down exactly where the delay was. For this reason, for high-performance distributed applications, it is likely that you will have to build some of your own instrumentation. We discuss this further in the next chapter.

8.10   Summary

We started this chapter by discussing the TPC-C benchmark. You should now start to understand (if you didn't before) why these benchmarks are so remote from reality. All the code for resiliency (mirror disks, restart areas, etc.) is out. All the code for system management (discussed in the next chapter) is out. There are no extra indexes for reports and no data movement to a data mart system. The price does not include the hardware for copying the database to backup. The applications are frequently written in tools not used by real application developers. The applications are optimized by experts. Sometimes the benchmarks use configurations that must be finely balanced where a better solution in real life would be more robust. The application is small and unchanging. The application has a small memory footprint, allowing cache and database buffer optimization. This does not mean that TPC-C results are not useful, but they concentrate on comparisons and not absolute figures; even then, if you change the development tools, the results might change dramatically.

We expect that many of our readers are still inclined to dismiss this chapter on the basis that hardware improvements will make it all irrelevant. The strange thing is that if we had been writing this 10 years ago, we would probably have agreed. But hardware advances seem to have been absorbed by transaction growth and inefficiencies in the software, a problem made worse by the fact that many systems require lots of software from different vendors. So performance seems to be just as crucial today as it was then. And new technologies, such as Web services, add interesting new complications.

Even assuming programmers don't write distributed applications that introduce inefficiencies such as a poorly designed object interface, hardware utilization will continue to rise. Some of the reasons are:

- Demands on the hardware will increase because of the requirement to reduce the batch window and pressure to do more database queries on the production system.
- Demand will also increase because of the use of object interfaces and two-phase commits.
- The Internet will lead to surges in demand at unexpected times, so performance will fluctuate much more than it did previously.

- New applications are being developed all the time.
- Greater hardware resources lead to a greater tolerance of poorly performing systems. In fact, a lot of very poor programming has survived only because hardware has compensated for it.

Complacency on the performance front is misplaced. If you are designing a high-volume application today you must

- Use a transaction monitor or transactional component manager.
- Ensure that your object interfaces are used efficiently.
- Model the performance of the high-volume transactions.
- Ensure that batch programs can be run in parallel and alongside online work.
- Keep transactions short (see the box entitled "Locking").
- Take great care when using Web services technology in the wide area.
- Avoid excessive use of two-phase commits.
- Control the number of indexes.
- Ensure that your chosen database vendor can support multiple disk units for one table, that the disk configuration can be changed with minimum disruption, and that logging can be mirrored and put on a different disk unit from the rest of your data.
- Ensure that your chosen platform and database vendor can support the full range of backup and recovery features, including online backup copy, multiple streams for backup copy, online reorganization, automatic management of copying logs from disk to tape (or tape logging), support for many channels and disks, and high IO throughput rates.

Design for performance is important and something that must be started early in the design cycle and continued throughout implementation and delivery. Application designers must take some responsibility for performance and not leave it all to the technical design. Even then, don't expect to get it right first time. You will need to monitor the performance and make corrections. You will also need to benchmark the high-volume transactions early to assess the performance impact.

Locking

We have ignored the effects of locking in this chapter not because it isn't important, but because by and large it can be solved.

There are two kinds of lock that will particularly affect performance—internal locks in the system software and database locks—and there is usually nothing you can do about the internal locks except use a different operating system and/or database vendor. Database locks can be record locks (also known as row locks), block locks (also known as page locks), or file locks. In most cases, you want to lock out the least amount of data, therefore, record locking is preferred. The exception is when very large numbers of record locks are needed and the overhead of managing a large lock table becomes excessive.

In online database applications, there are typically a number of hot spots—small amounts of data that are hit with great frequency, data such as accounting totals, statistics, restart data (described in Chapter 7), or even data for monitoring system activity, which was originally put in to improve performance or management. That they cause a problem becomes apparent only when the system is scaled up to production volumes. Block locks are disastrous for hot spots because there is a good chance that the records will be in the same block.

Sometimes hot spots can be eliminated. For instance, inserting many records into a table with an index on date and time will have a hot spot on the last table in the index, but putting the microsecond time as the first part of the index breaks it up. Of course, the disadvantage is that the index no longer provides a time-ordered view of the data, and there are additional IOs, so this change may be impractical.

There are several techniques for tackling locking problems. First and foremost, you must keep transactions short. Don't even think about a transaction that sends and receives a network message when locks are applied (two-phase commit excepted). Small transactions are important even for batch transactions or transactions that are emptying a message queue, otherwise you will never be able to run this work during the online day.

The second technique is to delay locking the hot spot records until late in the transaction. It seems weird to reorder your program logic for performance reasons, but that's life.

9

Systems Management

Systems management comprises many functions. One is security, which we consider to be a sufficiently important subject in its own right to merit a separate chapter—the next one. This chapter is concerned with the other aspects of systems management.

The many facets of systems management have spawned a plethora of software products, and even some hardware, and serious standardization efforts in an attempt to create order. To cover the subject exhaustively would require a book, probably several volumes long. We have therefore chosen to focus on the specific problems raised by systems management in distributed environments. Distribution raises a number of interesting problems, such as relating the failure of component parts to services affected, service-level monitoring, and the complications that can arise when several organizations are involved in delivering a service.

In order to establish a framework for discussion, the functional components, users of systems management, and their interrelationships are identified.

9.1 Functions and users

9.1.1 Functional categories

We have divided systems management into five categories; the first four are discussed in this chapter and the fifth is the subject of the next:

1. Administration

2. Operation

3. Fault tracking and resolution

4. Performance management and accounting

5. Security

The first category, administration, is concerned with all aspects of managing the configuration of a system, and therefore comprises those functions associated with changing it in any way. It includes managing the addition, relocation, and removal of hardware components, together with any associated software and database changes, and software installation, update, and removal. For example, communications circuits and workstations are typically described in configuration tables in systems associated with them, so if circuits and workstations are added to a network, the relevant tables have to be updated to include information about them. They may also require new software, or a new version of existing software, if they are of a type not currently in use.

Operation is concerned with keeping the system running and doing the work it is intended to do, a simple statement to make but which encompasses a vast range of activity. Operation divides into two parts: One is to do with the normal processes of managing the work flowing through the system and associated routine functions, such as backup of databases; the second is concerned with detecting faults or other exception conditions and taking action to correct them or at least minimize their impact on the system's capacity to do its work. The first set of functions might include starting and stopping transaction-processing applications, running sequences of batch jobs, and varying the allocation of production capacity to requirements, for example, reducing real-time transaction capacity at night to allow for batch or testing. The second set of functions is concerned with unexpected events, for example, the discovery that a group of users can no longer access an application. Some kind of immediate action will be required to determine where the failure has occurred and to try either to correct it or to find a way of avoiding it. Subsequent additional activity may be required to make a complete correction.

Fault tracking and resolution is the third category. As its name suggests, information about faults not immediately resolved must be recorded and used to trigger subsequent activity to fix them. The information about a fault includes any technical details captured at the time the fault was detected, as well as guidance on its severity and therefore urgency of resolution. This information can be updated as work is done to resolve the fault, and warnings can be raised if an urgent fault is not being resolved.

The final category is performance management and accounting. Statistical information gathered at a variety of points in a system provides the raw information for this activity, or rather set of activities. Performance information is required for technical reasons, for example, to allow a system's performance to be optimized by tuning it in various ways and to predict future capacity requirements so that action required to expand capacity can be taken in due time. It is also important for more commercial reasons, for example, to generate billing information, to tell us whether we are meeting commitments to service levels and whether others are meeting their service-level commitments to us.

9.1.2 Interrelationships and organization

The functional categories, although distinct, are interrelated, as shown in Figure 9-1.

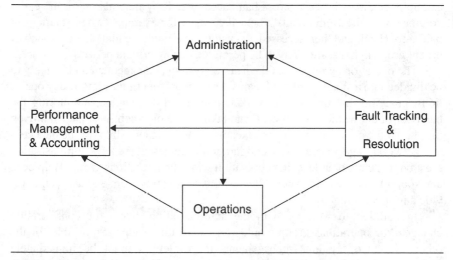

Figure 9-1   Relationships of systems management functional groups

In any organization other than the smallest, different groups perform and are responsible for the different functions and have, or certainly should have, well-defined relationships with one another. Depending on the size of the organization, each group may have a number of teams to handle different sets of functions. Consider how the organizational structure for the various systems management functions within a typical medium to large enterprise could be set up, starting with administration.

The primary function of a systems administration group is to ensure that changes to the configuration—what is running—are made in a secure and orderly fashion. This is not a trivial task because most organizations are changing all the time. Requests for configuration changes come from many sources, resulting in changes that vary from the very simple to the decidedly complex. Typical examples include business units requesting the addition of new users, at one end of the complexity spectrum, and the installation of major new applications with associated hardware and software, at the other end. In addition, requests for changes may come from other systems management groups, specifically performance management, and fault tracking and resolution.

All requests for changes to the configuration would be received by an administration group, reviewed and verified with the requester, and would prompt suitable updates for the affected systems. An important control element enters at this stage in that in many cases changes cannot be made at any time; they must be made when operational conditions are right. Administration normally entails a change management function that defines when changes can be made and issues the ultimate approval for making them. Many organizations have regular critical times (e.g., month-, quarter-, or year-end) when special activities take place, for example, crediting interest across bank accounts. They may also have increased volumes of traffic from clients at specific times, for example, when salaries are paid into a bank and then accessed by customers. Only essential changes, such as urgent problem fixes, are likely to be permitted during critical periods.

The operations group sits at the heart of systems management and is likely to be divided into a small number of teams. Its primary function is day-to-day operations, ensuring that the normal work is completed as planned, monitoring the behavior of the whole environment, and taking care of exceptions. Depending on the size of the organization, separate teams could be responsible for the data center, networks, and end users. Configuration changes agreed by administration must be made by, or at least in cooperation with, the operations group. Help desk and support teams would handle all questions originating from end users and provide any support required.

In addition to working with the administration group for configuration changes, the operations group would work with the groups responsible for the other aspects of systems management. If problems cannot be immediately resolved and closed, operations must work with the fault tracking and resolution group, which will take responsibility for the problems and ensure they are resolved in due course. And operations works with the performance management group, ensuring that the necessary statistical data are supplied.

The fault tracking and resolution group records all faults not immediately resolved by operations (or elsewhere), ensuring that the relevant information about a fault is captured and that corrective action is taken. This requires contact with those able to help in this process, including internal applications and software support groups, and external product or service suppliers. When a problem is finally closed, the administration group implements any configuration changes required, for example, inserting software corrections. And a record of faults tracked and resolved provides useful statistical data for performance management.

The performance management group is likely to contain teams responsible for short-term performance monitoring and longer-term capacity planning. The group receives the needed raw information primarily from operational statistics but also from fault resolution and tracking. This group has a strong relationship with administration for the planning and implementation of configuration changes to meet new requirements. For example, a critical transaction system may be subject to deteriorating response times. Statistical analysis by a performance group should identify the resource bottleneck (e.g., processing power, memory, I/O or network capacity, or some combination), which should lead to configuration changes to correct it. And even if there are no current problems, capacity planning should highlight potential problems based on a projection of current performance and expected traffic trends.

For any large organization, such as a bank, an airline, or a government department, systems management requires significant resources if it is to be effective. These resources cannot be just people; technology is essential, not only to manage costs but, more important in our opinion, to ensure the highest levels of performance and availability. Large-scale environments cannot rely on too many manual processes; they are too error prone. Integrated technology, involving high levels of automation, is essential for successful systems management, with human interactions reserved for the kind of complex decisions best made by people. This is true for relatively self-contained systems; distributed environments compound systems management problems, making automation even more critical.

Consider now the problems associated with managing distributed environments.

9.2   From silos to distributed environments

A useful starting point is to look at systems management for a relatively simple, isolated system—a silo system—and then consider the complications introduced by distributed environments, where applications are distributed over several systems. A further complication is distributed ownership of infrastructure; increasingly the systems are located in different companies. Many organizations have evolved through these stages, with at least some of what were isolated systems integrated into new distributed environments.

Figure 9-2 shows a simple, isolated system environment. This is typical of how many organizations would have started in the 1960s, 1970s, and 1980s. The hardware platform was a mainframe, with disk and tape subsystems, as well as printers and other equipment. The network consisted of leased circuits, managed by the owner of the system, with end users equipped with dumb terminals. A communications processor of some kind, with associated software, controlled the network. The mainframe contained an operating system, under which ran transaction and batch applications, file and database managers. The transaction applications used some form of transaction monitor, sometimes home grown, which provided scheduling, resource pooling, transaction management, and other services. In the earlier days, a new application could have required another similar environment, complete with a parallel network.

Software and networking developments during the 1970s and onward greatly increased the sophistication of these environments. Packet-switched technology allowed a single network to be connected to multiple application systems, with end users able to switch among applications, allowing applications in different systems to share one network. However, the applications were still essentially silo systems, generally with little interaction apart perhaps from transferring files.

In many ways, the management problem was relatively simple, in that the owner of the system managed everything, including the network. And only a handful of systems contained software. However, although the environments were simple by today's standards, the limited tools available at the time meant that systems management was labor-intensive. System operation involved a great deal of console interaction, mounting tapes and so on. Similar levels of manual action

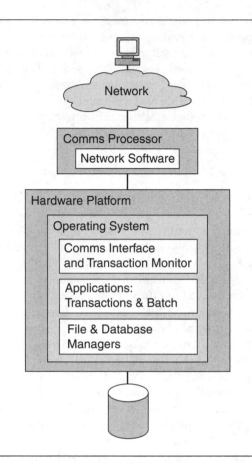

Figure 9-2   Isolated (silo) system

were required by the other groups, as was the interaction between them. Some mainframe-based applications were developed to help, such as fault tracking applications, but much relied on the vigilance of human operators and other management staff.

Starting in the early 1980s, the microprocessor revolution, developments in telecommunications, notably fiber optics, and the Internet explosion following the invention of the WWW and the Web browser, together with many software developments, have changed the face of IT environments. Figure 9-3 represents a typical IT environment in a medium to large organization today. The figure shows a number of applications servers, typically containing a mixture of applications of various ages. Some are mainframes, running applications that may have been in use for some years, and others contain applications running under various flavors of UNIX, Windows, and Linux. The servers run in a data center environment and are physically connected with a LAN. The applications provide services to a variety of users. They do this either individually or in collaboration. For the purposes of this discussion, assume that they have all been kept up to date and are able to communicate with one another and with external systems using middleware of some kind.

External users are connected to the application servers by various networks. The first, labeled Internal Network in Figure 9-3, comprises a mixture of IP routers and switches, with some legacy network technology. User equipment includes workstations, browsers, and possibly some remaining terminals. It may also include some connections to other organizations using legacy protocols. The second is an outsourced IP network, managed by a network provider, which assumes responsibility for the network up to the connection into the data center and agrees to meet defined service levels. End-user devices would typically be workstations and browsers and perhaps some application systems. Finally, the Internet supports direct customer access from browsers and other devices, such as mobile phones. In the example, assume also that there are Web services connections to other systems operated by business partners. These networks are connected to the application servers, via an internal LAN, through a number of servers, as shown in the figure. These servers could be as simple as routers or communications processors, or much more sophisticated systems such as portals.

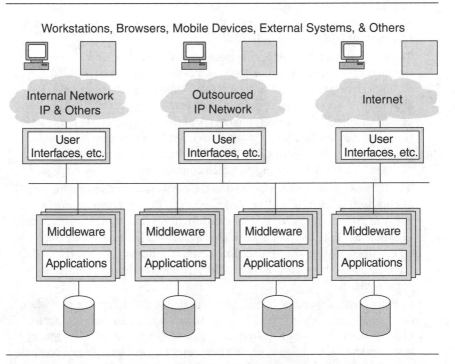

Figure 9-3   Simplified schematic of medium to large enterprise IT environment

To make this clearer, suppose the organization concerned is a bank. There would be applications to handle products such as checking accounts, savings accounts, mortgages, investments, insurance, and customer management. Services would be delivered either by a single application or with some cooperation among the applications. For example, a service to request the balance of a checking account would probably require access to only one system. A service to provide the status of all products owned by a customer would require access to the customer management application to find out what they are, followed by requests to each product system to get the current status. Internal networks might connect the bank's main offices and call centers to the applications. The outsourced IP network could connect all the branches to the data center, while the Internet would allow clients direct access to services and also connect to external service partners, such as companies that provide products not directly supplied by the bank (e.g., insurance products).

A number of important attributes of this environment have a significant effect on systems management.

- The environment is much more complicated than that shown in Figure 9-2; it contains many different components comprising hardware, software, and applications. The number of systems containing software of some form—servers, PCs, and so on—may well run into the thousands or tens of thousands. Each needs some form of management on its own, for administration, operation, and other functions. Even establishing an inventory of what is there is difficult.

- The large number of components means that there are potentially huge numbers of different conditions being reported. How is it possible to distinguish between what is important and what is relatively trivial? How are priorities set? How is it possible to prevent being overwhelmed by repeated instances of the same problem? And the components do not exist in isolation; they are variously involved in end-to-end services: If one fails in some way, which services will it affect? If one is changed, which others are affected? If a service is changed, which components should be changed?

- The IP network is an important part of the environment; its behavior clearly affects the quality of overall service provided. But it is outsourced to a network provider, which could lead to difficulties in determining the source of problems. Take the banking example again. A teller in a branch may call a Help desk, saying that the checking account system cannot be reached. Is the IP network the source of the problems, or is it in the data center, or somewhere else?

- Some services depend on accessing external application service providers, for example, as Web services. These application services are in someone else's system, over which the requester has no direct control. How much management information is needed to ensure that problems in performance and availability can be tracked?

It is clear that effective management of such an environment requires sophisticated management tools. And as might be expected, systems management technology has not stood still in the face of these challenges.

9.3   Systems management technology

The arrival of microsystems in the 1980s, and their phenomenal improvements in cost and performance since then, has enabled the development of a wide variety of systems management products using the cheap hardware that became available. The same microsystem technology has also been widely used to add intelligence to a variety of storage and other subsystems, making them not only far more functional but also much easier to manage. Disk and tape subsystems, for example, have been revolutionized, apart from other developments in the technology of the media—storage density and so on. For example, disk subsystem backup and replication of data, usage optimization, capacity management, and more are greatly simplified, often without a need to involve any of the systems using the mass storage.

Operational systems management software can be divided into two elements. The first, call it Monitor and Control, interacts directly with the rest of the system—operating system, database manager, middleware, applications, and so on. It monitors what is going on by gathering information from the software, for example, about the failure of an external connection. It can also cause the system to do things, for example, start or terminate a program. The second element is concerned with activities such as processing and recording information, instructing the other part to take action, and displaying information for operators. Call this part Process and Manage.

Mainframes, minis, and UNIX systems all started and continued for some time with both elements in a single system, using an unintelligent console terminal for the operator interface. The arrival of low-cost microsystems allowed the possibility of moving some of the management intelligence out of the system being managed. The Monitor and Control element would have to remain, but parts, or all, of the Process and Manage element could be moved. A simple example is the use of a PC as a console to provide increasing levels of operational automation; programs in the PC could respond to system questions and initiate activities, based on time, for example. They also provided a graphical operator interface for information and command input.

But much more is possible and indeed desirable. All of the Process and Manage element can be moved out of the managed system and into a separate platform. An attraction of this approach is that the manager can now manage more than one system. Another is that increasingly sophisticated processing can be carried out without consuming the power of the system being managed. A good example is analyzing large quantities of information, to sort out what matters from what does not, and to reduce the problem of duplication, such as when the same event is reported many times.

This approach can be abstracted into the well-known model shown in Figure 9-4. In this model, the Manager contains the Process and Manage element of systems management, while the Managed Object contains the Monitor and Control element, in the form of the Agent. The managed object may be anything that might need management: an application program, a database system, a card in router, and so on. The ubiquity of microprocessors has opened up a world of possible managed objects. The Manager may also contain an agent, allowing it to communicate with higher-level managers in a hierarchical structure where a manager of managers sits at the top.

The Rules Engine is something like a scripting language for preprocessing the incoming data, filtering out what is irrelevant and highlighting what is very relevant. It may also consolidate many errors into one and send back commands to the agent for corrective action. Without the rules engine, system management is little more than remote operation. With the rules engine, tasks can be automated and information can be more focused; this is where the real savings are made. The Information Base stores all the information collected from the agents. It can be as primitive as a few simple text files or as complex as a full-grown object database. The Protocol defines the way the manager communicates with the agent, while the Message Formats define the attributes and values of the managed objects. These two components have been the subject of standards; the best known is the Simple Network Management Protocol (SNMP). Protocols allow attribute values to be

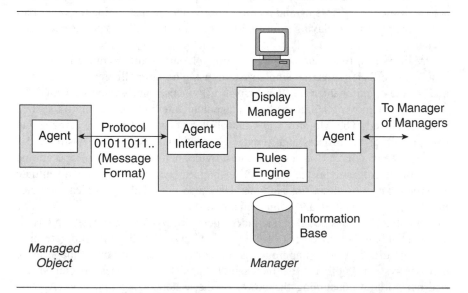

Figure 9-4   Systems management model

retrieved by manager (e.g., SNMP GET), sent as unsolicited messages (e.g., SNMP TRAP), and changed (e.g., SNMP SET).

Although SNMP started as a network management standard, it is now widely used elsewhere. This is possible because it allows devices from one vendor to be managed by any manager. SNMP defines the attributes of the managed objects in a Management Information Base (MIB). A MIB is a formal description of a set of network objects that can be managed using SNMP; its format is defined as part of SNMP. All other MIBs are extensions of this basic MIB. MIB I refers to the initial MIB definition, later extended to MIB II. SNMPv2 includes MIB II and adds some new objects. There are MIB extensions for each set of related network entities that can be managed. For example, there are MIB definitions specified in RFCs for Domain Name Services and various LAN and other interfaces. Product developers can create and register new MIB extensions, which many companies have done. They have also provided applications to run in the manager, presenting the information in graphic form for ease of understanding.

SNMP is very effective at managing network components, such as routers and switches, as well as the communications-related components in servers. It is less effective at managing system software and applications, mainly because the MIB extensions have not been defined to the necessary level of detail to make them effective. A full set of standard MIB extensions is nearly impossible because of the variety of platforms and applications.

Given the increasing complexity of systems management, the continued focus to develop standards beyond SNMP is not surprising. Two developments are Web-Based Enterprise Management (WBEM) and the Common Information Model (CIM), which are both under the control of the Distributed Management Task Force, Inc. (DMTF). The DMTF is the industry organization leading the development, adoption, and interoperability of management standards and initiatives for enterprise and Internet environments. Its members include major IT and telecommunications corporations and academic institutions.

Web-Based Enterprise Management is a set of management and Internet standard technologies to unify the management of enterprise environments. The DMTF has developed a core set of standards that make up WBEM, which include the Common Information Model standard; an encoding specification using XML; and a transport mechanism, CIM Operations over HTTP. CIM is equivalent to the MIB, and there are ways of mapping SNMP MIBs to CIM classes, so it is possible for one device to support both. A device that supports WBEM can typically be managed from a Web browser.

There are further alternatives. Unisys has a product called Single Point Operations (SPO), which picks up the console text streams that have been used to manage most computers for many years. A scripting facility (the rules engine in Figure 9-4) allows SPO to parse the input messages and then take defined actions, which may be as simple as logging the event or as complex as taking automatic action across several systems and activating external alarms. It also allows operators to open a console window into any system connected to it. The advantage of this approach is that it can accommodate any device that produces a serial message output; it is not confined to the traditional console. And it does not exclude other protocols; SPO, for example, accepts SNMP TRAPs.

Operational management also includes routine operations, for example, batch job scheduling. Clearly, batch jobs can be initiated from a console or triggered by time. Batch jobs can also schedule additional jobs on completion, using the Job Control Language (JCL) facilities of the system concerned. However, in today's more complex world, batch job scheduling may need to take place across several systems in a structured workflow. Products such Opcon/XPS from SMA provide facilities for doing this. The manager contains definitions of the complete workflow across multiple systems and communicates with an agent in each system to start specific jobs, monitor their progress, inform operators of progress, and take corrective action if needed.

What about the other aspects of systems management—administration, performance management, fault tracking, and resolution? Some administrative functions can be carried out using the operational tools, for example, adding or deleting configured entities dynamically. Examples are adding users, deleting users, and changing user privileges. Significant configuration changes, such as new versions of applications, require a more structured approach. The advent of distributed applications makes this more complicated because new or changed components may be distributed across many systems that comprise multiple servers and possibly large numbers of clients.

Exactly how this works depends on the specific development tools and the capabilities of the run-time environments. Application development and generation tools have to cope with managing distributed applications with potentially large numbers of run-time components spread over multiple systems: mainframes, other large and small servers, end-user workstations, or combinations of all of them. Systems to support such environments typically manage source code and provide version control, configuration management, and many other functions, built around a repository. They generate the appropriate run-time versions (object code, Java byte code, etc.) and load the generated components into the target systems, with agents of some kind to handle the process of getting the run-time code into appropriate files and so on.

Performance management and accounting consists of extracting the required information (statistics, etc.) from the target system and then processing it to produce a variety of displays and reports, both displayed graphically and incorporated in written reports. Systems have always had some facilities, which are usually a combination of tools provided by the system's vendor and local extensions made by the owners of the system. Typically, the information was stored in files and processed by batch runs, which produced reports. In addition, there would be some simple enquiry tools, plus facilities for turning on and off specific information gathering.

Performance management tools require an agent, which runs in the system being measured, and contains configurable "hooks," or probes, into the software elements to collect the required information. The collected data are then reported to a manager, which contains a variety of display and reporting tools. Since the manager is external to the system being managed, it can correlate information from a variety of systems, for example, to enable redistribution of loads. The gathered information can also be recorded for long-term analysis to help with capacity planning. Typical products are able to manage a wide variety of platforms by providing appropriate agents for each one.

The final element of management to consider is fault tracking and resolution. Before off-the-shelf products were available, many organizations developed their own applications to record and track faults. Today, powerful products are available to manage the complete cycle from fault reporting through to resolution, including escalation procedures, which raise the priority of faults and brings them to management's attention if they are not resolved within acceptable limits. While such products can be used more or less independently, they can integrate with operational products, for example, to allow information about faults to be captured automatically.

As has already been pointed out, there is a daunting range of products on the market covering all aspects of systems management. They can be divided broadly into two groups: so-called point products, which perform a specific aspect of management, sometimes confined to a single platform or group of platforms; and suites, which aim to provide a more or less complete set of systems management capabilities. The two are not mutually exclusive. Suites usually allow specific point products to be integrated with them, and point products provide external interfaces that allow them to feed other products and receive feeds from them. Some organizations have constructed effective management environments by integrating point products, and others have adopted suites as the basis of management, perhaps supplemented by one or two point products integrated into the suite. It is not clear which of the two approaches is best. Success depends more on the starting point and, particularly, the implementation approach.

Finally, automation is a critical attribute of many aspects of systems management. It can be applied from external management systems, such as Unisys SPO, that can respond to system events or questions automatically. Another example is batch job scheduling across multiple platforms. The whole workflow is set up, then managed by a suitable product without needing operators to start and stop things. Many other management functions can be, and have been, automated in the same way. The increased sophistication of products such as disk and tape library subsystems greatly helps reduce manual intervention as well.

But automation can also be applied within systems, that is, within the managed objects. In most cases, automation in the form of self-correction has been available for a long time, provided by the operating system and other software; some operating systems are very good at it. But current thinking goes beyond this: There is much interest in self-management within systems, referred to as autonomic management. The aim is to allow systems to be self-healing, detecting and correcting problems and reporting the events for the record and perhaps requesting repairs or other corrections later. Today's storage subsystems already provide a lot of self-management features. Exactly how far this can extend is still open.

Self-management is not confined to error recovery; in large-scale environments, administration can be a big burden. It is therefore highly desirable to have systems generate the configuration they need, and otherwise adapt themselves when connected into the environment. A simple example is DHCP, which allows devices, typically PCs, to acquire an IP address when connected to the network. In the large environments of today, and with people moving around different locations with laptops, the problems associated with having to configure IP addresses manually would be overwhelming.

9.4   Putting it together

So how should an environment such as that shown in Figure 9-3 be managed? An important point is that the system environment will have been created over many years, which of course also applies to the systems management infrastructure and supporting organization. It is a question of enhancing what is already there, not starting from scratch. Ensuring continued effective systems management is a never-ending process. Applying new technology or making better use of technology already in place can always improve management. The possibilities are likely to vary widely, depending on the technology already installed and the processes followed by the systems management organization. There are, however, a number of principles, or guidelines, that can be followed to help move in the right direction.

The first principle concerns the *scope* of the different management functions, where "scope" means the amount of the environment over which the management functions apply. Clearly, all management functions (e.g., administration, operations, etc.) could apply over the whole environment and be controlled from a central location. Given the complexity involved, and the fact that parts of the environment shown in Figure 9-3 are not owned by the organization itself, this is not possible. It is possible, however, to establish a workable approach by dividing management into those functions that change an environment in some way, either administrative or through operational commands, and those that do not change it but collect information about its status and behavior. To understand what is going on, and to facilitate any corrective action, it is important that a view of the status of the whole environment be maintained. In the environment shown in Figure 9-3, for example, the outsourced IP network is a critical element to overall performance of the system; it could be a bank's branch network. It is therefore essential that those responsible for application systems operation know what is happening in the network and be able to extract additional information from it, which can then be correlated with the operational status of the applications systems. Such information enables corrective action to be taken proactively, ideally before any loss of service. It also allows help desks to respond to questions from remote users, who may for some reason not be able to access key applications.

This universal monitoring principle can be organized to cover what may be thought of as horizontal "slices" across the environment. Take middleware, for example. The applications servers shown in Figure 9-3 contain middleware, which is used for various kinds of communication among them, using message queuing, procedure calls of various kinds, and perhaps some Web services technology such as SOAP. This collection of middleware is a distributed infrastructure, which has to function in its entirety. It requires careful monitoring because failure or other malfunction in one system could have a ripple effect on the whole environment. Operations staff need to be able to see the status of this whole layer of software to ensure that the applications continue to function and deliver the required services. And they need to be able to start and stop the middleware in a controlled manner, ensuring that all the pieces come in production in the right order. In some ways, this problem is analogous to managing batch applications across many systems. In fact, batch job schedulers have been used with some success to manage the startup of middleware spread across several systems.

The other side of this principle is that administrative and any other changes to the environment should be carefully managed, with the whole environment divided into autonomous domains of some sort. For example, the outsourced IP network will already have a management group able to make changes; no other group should be allowed to do this. But that does not prevent others from having visibility to its status, both for immediate operational reasons and for performance monitoring, for example, to decide if service-level agreements are being met. The principle of restricted change but wide visibility extends to other external parts of the environment, such as application services provided by partners on the Internet. The same principle could also be used within the organization by dividing it into autonomous domains subject to restricted change but with wide status visibility.

The organization of the Internet itself illustrates that a loose coupling of domains can be very effective. There is an authority that defines the basic network standards, assigns IP address spaces, and gives out domain names, but much depends on ISPs managing their own local networks and various country organizations managing their part of the backbone network. It is less clear at present that adequate visibility as to status is available to those who need it.

Automation is a second principle. A high level of automation is essential to reduce costs and improve overall quality. Automation allows separation of what matters from what is of minor importance, given that a veritable tsunami of events could be reported in distributed environments. It also makes it possible to reduce manual intervention greatly, which many studies have shown to be very error-prone—a major cause of failure, in fact. In the increasingly complex distributed environments, the scope for error increases. In a high proportion of cases, the manual actions (e.g., simple responses to console questions) can be automated. The goal should be to leave human decisions to what is handled best by people and cannot be automated because they require human-level policy decisions.

Automation can be a combination of externally applied automation and internal, or autonomic, automation. The combination depends on the capabilities of the servers and other components in the environment. Automated functions should, of course, be consistent with the scope principle. For example, an operations group managing the applications in our example may receive notification of errors from the outsourced IP network. Any automated responses should not make changes to the network in any way, but they may cause other changes in the applications servers and also cause warnings to be sent to the IP network management control center.

A third principle concerns *end-to-end service provision,* which could be called vertical management. The environment comprises a large number of different components, managed objects in the terminology of the model. Each of these reports status and status changes and is subject to administrative and other externally applied changes. However, these components do not exist in isolation; collectively, they deliver services to users. It is therefore essential to know the impact on services of any component failure and to identify the potential impact on services if a component is changed.

There are various approaches to gaining a better picture of end-to-end service status. One simple way is to execute test transactions from a number of places into critical applications and to measure the results. Such tests can be run using a test driver following a script; some systems management products also support this kind of function. The results of the tests (e.g., success rates, failure rates, and associated statistics, such as response time) can be used for performance analysis. They can also be fed into operational systems, allowing alerts to be raised for further attention, for example, if no response is received.

There are other ways to address end-to-end service status. There are products on the market that allow components in an environment to be related to the services that depend on them, for example, NetCool, from MicroMuse. And the DMTF aims to address the problem in its standards.

A fourth principle is that *applications can contribute to systems management,* enhancing the overall manageability of the environment in various ways. One way is to ensure that applications are able to log what is going on. Consider performance monitoring, for example. To get a complete picture of performance requires measuring the performance of every step in the message flow. All the message performance measurements could be put into the message. Alternatively, a unique message identifier (e.g., user identifier plus a sequence number) could be inserted in each message so that performance logs from different servers could be pulled together to trace the performance of individual messages. Another example is fault detection. If an error is detected somewhere, knowing who the end user was and what the input message was when the error happened (and maybe was the cause) is valuable information. A good input logging system, along with the user identifier in the message, provides this information. The application itself may still need to take corrective actions. For example, a timeout on a synchronous procedure call could result in sending a message via a queue or aborting the request, depending on the context, as well as logging the event through systems management.

In short, logging is a general requirement. The log should always include user identifier; role identifier; message identifier; timestamp; error code; and often the input message data as well, unless that can be retrieved from a separate log using the message identifier. Ideally error information is reported as soon as it is detected, and reported once only to avoid flooding the system with error messages. A general point about logs is to keep them as small as possible. Applications can be provided with libraries of common services that allow them to log and report events easily. The services could also extract additional information to supplement that provided by the application.

The final principle is to do with the way we should go about enhancing a systems management environment. Our view is that an *evolutionary approach* is essential. We stress throughout this book that new technology in development and run-time environments should be integrated with what is in place already; it is not practical to throw out everything and start again. The same is true for systems management. New technology can be applied with great benefit, but it should be introduced incrementally. The introduction of some of the systems management suites provides useful lessons. In some cases, there were attempts to introduce these products in big projects, effecting radical changes in systems management structures. The results were disappointing in that the projects frequently overran and incurred much higher costs than expected. Where systems management suites have been introduced gradually, the results have been much better.

The reason for incrementally introducing new systems management tools is that it is not possible to anticipate the effects of introducing new technologies, for example, exactly how to automate using a new tool. The systems currently in place are important because interesting technologies may not be easily applicable; for example, there are no agents available on some systems. And, in addition to the technologies, organizational procedures and processes are part of the in-place infrastructure; they may need to be changed if new technology is introduced, which would require considerable care. By building the systems management environment gradually, experience can be gained as to what is possible and desirable, and what is not. Much better results can be achieved more quickly and with lower risk of disruption through a series of small sets of enhancements that are reviewed regularly by management teams before moving onto the next set. Experience is needed to decide what is best at each stage. Even in the unlikely case where the entire environment is created from scratch, an incremental introduction of systems management technology still pays off, for the same reasons.

9.5   Summary

Systems management is a critical piece of infrastructure in today's complex, distributed environments, which pose many management challenges. Just as these environments, in most cases, have grown up over a long period, so the systems management infrastructure has similarly developed. This applies not just to the technology and tools used, but also to the organizations using them. The concern is therefore with enhancing what is in place today, rather than building a new infrastructure to manage the environment.

Key points to remember:

- Enhancing an existing environment depends to a fair extent on what is currently in place. Improvements can always be made, and a lot of new technology and standards are in development. But they have to be applied carefully. Follow a controlled, evolutionary approach. It is more conducive to success than implementing large-scale changes to the way systems management works.

- Pay careful attention to the scope of the different functions. For monitoring, it is important to have a view of the whole environment, including those parts supplied by others so that, for example, problems in different areas can be correlated, and proactive action taken to correct them. But monitoring is read-only; it does not change anything. Administrative and other functions that change the environment, on the other hand, need to be carefully constrained, for example, by restricting their scope to specific parts of the environment (domains).

- Try to automate as much as possible, for cost reasons but, more important, to improve the quality of operation.

- Take an end-to-end view. Delivering services involves many components; understanding the effect of any component failure on end-to-end services is important.

- Pay attention to applications, not just the infrastructure. The way applications use the environment has systems management ramifications. It is important that failures are notified through systems management, as well as the application taking corrective action itself.

10

Security

Security is a hot topic, thanks largely to the Internet. Security is also an enormous subject and growing daily. We can't do the subject justice in such a small space, so we will concentrate on discussing how to incorporate security concerns into the architecture.

But first, let us ensure that we are using the same terminology. Major security concerns are authentication, access control, protection, and security management.

Authentication is about identifying the users; it is about checking that people are who they say they are. An analogous situation occurs at the front desk in an office block. Before entering beyond the lobby, everyone must either prove his or her identity by showing a pass or register as a visitor at the front desk.

Access control, also called *authorization,* is about giving users the authority to use a resource in a specified way. An analogous situation is using your pass to open doors in the building. Resources can be big things such as servers and databases, or small things such as database commands, or even attributes in selected rows of selected tables in a specific database.

Protection is about stopping unauthorized access to resources. In our analogy, it's about making sure the back door is locked. *Protection* is our word. Security experts don't talk about protection; instead they divide the subject according to categories of threat. An incomplete list of protection concerns is:

- Confidentiality—protection against disclosure
- Integrity—protection against tampering
- Nonrepudiation—protection against one kind of fraud
- Denial of service—protection against malicious service blockage
- Physical protection—protection against unauthorized people walking up to the computer and doing their worst

Security management is about how security is administered and how security breaches are reported.

Security technology discussions tend to focus on two areas, network and server security. For the purpose of writing a fairly short book, we are going to assume that you—or someone in your organization or some outside expert at your beck and call—know how to do this; in other words, you or they understand the technology and its purpose. In this chapter we discuss putting this knowledge into an architectural context. More specifically, we cover:

- How to decide what security is needed
- How to build a secure distributed system using secure networks and servers
- How security design affects the architecture

10.1   What security is needed

The first step in designing a security architecture is deciding what security is needed. The details change as a project progresses, but you do want to think about security concerns early because security design often influences the architecture, sometimes dramatically. We recommend drawing up a list of security requirements before designing the implementation architecture.

We suggest you start by looking at the data. Consider the major data elements and decide what categories of person needs to see them. For product information, you might end up with a list like this:

- Product information, concept phase: product management, engineering, marketing
- Product information, development phase: engineering, product management
- Product information, released: everybody

All the different kinds of people correspond to roles. You should expect to find the following for each type of data:

- One or a few people who are intimately concerned with a few data objects. These people are either responsible for managing that part of the business or they are the subject of the data (the data is about them).
- A few managers who have a watch, brief over a larger amount of data and might need to be involved in unusual transactions.
- Some others who need reports.

In other words, the number of roles concerned with any type of data is small. If they are not, something is probably wrong. A common mistake is to convert job descriptions into roles. A security role is a category of access rights to data; it is not part of a job description. It's rare that any employee does not have multiple roles. If two roles have the same access rights, then they should normally be merged. This is especially important at the early design stage because with a large numbers of roles it is hard to understand the security requirements. It is always possible to make a design more complex, but it is much more difficult to make it simpler.

It is interesting to note that the notion of a person having special access privileges to a small number of objects (e.g., to a few products or to their personal data) is not rare. In fact, it is the norm, a very common security pattern.

When the application is complete, the security administrator assigns access rights to each role. At the early stage of design, you don't know what operations the system will support, so this can't be done. Instead we suggest you record for each role a statement of intent that covers the following:

- Information needed: What read or write access to major data elements do they require?
- Data constraints: Do special privileges apply to a subset of the data (e.g., the products they are responsible for)?
- Location and channel dependency: Can this role be used anywhere or is it restricted to people in certain locations?

Compiling this list should be relatively straightforward and quick. Three difficult questions are worthy of discussion in the early design stage (up to the point that you have an approach for tackling the issues and not to the point where there is a detailed design). The three questions are:

1. How do you assign roles?
2. How is duplicate data protected?
3. What strategy is there to guard against the enemy within?

Assigning roles is a difficult issue because you need to strike a balance between ease of use and protecting your assets. All too often, changing your access rights is made so hard that people look for, and probably find, alternatives. For instance, people give their user codes and passwords to others, or data is loaded in spreadsheets and mailed around the world.

In most organizations, some data is replicated. There is no point to ensuring the data is highly secure in one place only to have to it completely visible to everyone somewhere else. If data is replicated, you need to think about how to keep the access control synchronized and consistent across all copies.

Protecting against the enemy within is a key issue. Many major frauds had inside help. If you look at examples of organizations trying to prevent internal corruption, you will see three techniques used:

1. Have two or more people give permission for something to be done. For instance, have two people sign a large check.
2. Build fast detection systems that look for suspicious activity.
3. Assume violation is possible and build in recovery procedures.

You can build these kinds of checks into your application. For instance, very secure operations can be logged and messages sent to the security administrator. Applications can be changed so security for access to vital operations requires two steps: one step to initiate the operation and another to approve it, or sign off on it.

Special care can be taken to recover sensitive data. Access to sensitive data can be monitored and reports sent to a supervisor.

This discussion highlights another security need—the need to audit security. The questions that must be answered are, what security-sensitive actions need to be audited, and who is going to look at the audits?

10.2 Traditional distributed system security

It is intuitively obvious that assembling a number of secure servers together, using a secure network, will create a secure system. Unfortunately, it is untrue.

We shall discuss this in the context of what we call the "onion model" because this is the simplest model for distributed system security. The onion model is illustrated in Figure 10-1. In this model, each concentric ring represents a protective screen. Each ring contains one or more resources. The rectangles represent access points. Each access point makes a number of services available to the outside world. A service may be provided by a resource within the layer or may be

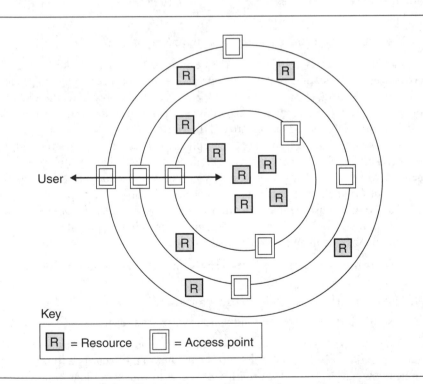

Figure 10-1 The onion model

provided by calling an access point in the inner layer. Thus, for the user's request to be processed on an innermost resource, the input message must go through one access point for each layer of the onion. An access point can be implemented by a firewall, middleware, server system software, or user-written code. The access point may also do authentication. For instance, for Internet access to a bank account, the request may go through a firewall to get to the Web server application. It is then authenticated by the Web server application and passed through another firewall to the server that has the account details. In practice, there are almost always additional layers. For instance, it is common to have a demilitarized zone (DMZ), which is essentially a layer in the onion without local services—in other words, a layer whose only purpose is security.

The onion model has a nice secure look to it, largely because it has some resemblance to the many walls of a castle. Recall that a castle has many walls so that if one wall was broken, the defending forces could retreat behind another wall inside it. The equivalent in the onion model is that if one layer is broken into, the inner layers still provide security. Thus, the most secure data can go into the center of the onion while the least secure data can be placed in an outer layer. But arguably, the onion model is less safe than it looks.

One reason is authentication. Authentication depends on the end user's device; authenticating someone over the phone is different from authenticating someone over the Web. Authentication must therefore be done in a server toward the outside of the onion. If a hostile force can break into the authenticating server, it can assume the identity of any other user, so in a sense security is only as strong as the authenticating function is secure. Let us take an example. Suppose a bank allows customers access to their account information over the Web. Authentication in this scenario is done by the Web server at the start of each session. If anyone can break into the Web server and assume another identity, anyone can read that other person's account. There are protective measures to lessen the risk. Besides the obvious—the authenticating server must be put in a physically secure location and all the software must be kept current to eliminate known threats—there are more architectural solutions. Assume that a hostile person has found a way of gaining administrator privileges on a Web server; it is still possible to make it difficult for him or her to compromise the security of the whole system. One action is to ensure that all security-sensitive data is not on the Web server. That means no important application data, such as the bank account in our example, and no user security information. This can be done by putting the software that checks the password and other information from the Web on another server and making this server a single-application, highly secure server. The hostile force with the privileged user code would then have to read the application's memory to gain this information, which is a much more formidable technical challenge, although not impossible on many operating systems.

Most system-provided access security works with "roles." When users log on, they are given one or more roles and access privileges are assigned to the roles. The rationale for this approach is that it is much easier to manage the access rights of a few roles than the access rights of many individual users. An onion model that relies entirely on roles is vulnerable as soon as any user can break into a layer that allocates the roles.

Security in the onion model can be greatly enhanced by using some form of location security in which messages of a particular type are restricted to come from a particular location. Thus, account access information can come from the Web server. Audit information can come from a server located in the audit department. System administration changes can come only from the operational consoles. The Web server can't ask for an audit report, the audit server can't update an account, and no one outside the computer department can change the configuration. Location security is particularly important if one layer in the onion includes office systems. Suppose you have an internal network used for e-mail, intranet, and low-security departmental applications. Without location security, it is possible for anyone on that network who has knowledge of user codes and roles to send requests to the account server.

A direct implementation of location security is a firewall. In extremely high-security environments you might want to implement location security as far as possible by having distinct separate networks.

Sometimes you need to have the application access control cognizant of the location. Suppose your organization has many branches. You might want to allow the branch to access accounts that belong to that branch and no others. Sometimes you want to assign different privilege levels to the same user when the user accesses via different end-user channels. Suppose you want to allow Web users to update their accounts but allow mobile phone users access only to their account balances. In both scenarios, access control goes beyond simple user codes and roles.

In some cases, access control is sensitive to a combination of user identity and data; for instance, a specific user is allowed access only to a specific account and not to all accounts. Usually data-sensitive access control can be implemented only by user-written code.

Most organizations haven't and couldn't implement an onion security model. Instead they have what we call the "boiling lava model" (think of documentary films about volcanoes where you see the lava lakes slowly going plop, plop). This is illustrated in Figure 10-2.

The boiling lava model is so prevalent because different security management regimes are being applied to different parts of the system. This is partly a historical accident, partly a result of each silo development looking after its own security requirements, and partly a result of using many technologies that implement security in different ways. It is also often a result of a deliberate policy of having departments look after their own security needs. Changing from the boiling lava model to the onion model is always difficult, and in large organizations some degree of local autonomy is probably desirable. It's not simply a case of onions good, boiling lava bad.

The boiling lava model introduces additional threats. The biggest threat is simply that the end user is likely required to have different log-on sequences to

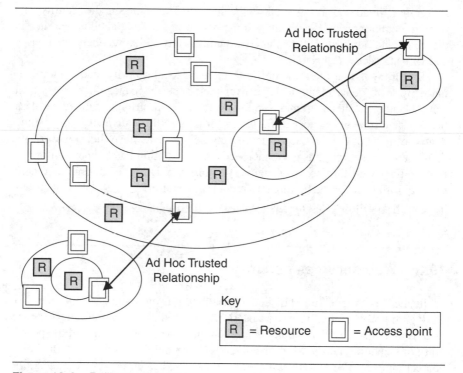

Figure 10-2   Boiling lava model

access different services. Before long an end user ends up with five, ten, or more user codes and passwords. Users can't remember them all, so they write them down. Very soon people become blasé. They give their user codes and passwords to colleagues, put them in notes stuck to the computer, or forget them and harass the security administrator to reinstate the password. The proliferation of security regimes means that when an employee leaves or just changes jobs within the organization, there is an increased likelihood that not all their security rights (to do the old job) will be rescinded.

These issues can be tackled by using single sign-on software. The user logs on once and the system does the local logons. Single sign-on also manages the access rights to different services centrally so that when the user leaves, all his or her access rights can be rescinded with one command. An alternative solution is to use security technology like Kerberos (see the box entitled "Kerberos" on page 197), which is inherently single sign-on. Unfortunately, using Kerberos might mean making changes to the servers so it cannot be implemented overnight.

With the boiling lava model, it is very difficult to have confidence that the system is secure. In a large organization there are bound to be some bad practices somewhere, and a bad practice can be as simple as too casually giving out new passwords. Because there is a need to send data from one application to another, it is common for ad hoc arrangements to be devised. Thus, holes in the security cordon are commonplace. Finally, it is in the nature of silo applications that data is dispersed and duplicated. It becomes difficult simply to know where the data is and who has access rights to it.

The irony is that often the desire to increase local security leads to a reluctance by local departments to hand over their security management roles to a central authority. It's extremely annoying to have to struggle with a faceless bureaucracy somewhere to get the security rights to do your own job, so some degree of local autonomy is justified. Many departments have their own private data. Human resources has personnel records. Accounting has financial information. A tight well-knit security regime for this data is highly desirable. Where security suffers under the boiling lava model is in enterprise-wide data (e.g., product data and customer data), which is used by many departments.

10.3   Web services security

While the onion model might be fine internally within an organization, it does not work on the Web. Here services are peers, not layered like an onion. The arrangement is more like a crate of apples than an onion. Furthermore, there is little possibility of location security. More specifically, if you publish a service on the Web, you certainly aren't going to assume another server has done correct authentication without having very, very good reasons. Since the boiling lava model is made up of a number of onions, similar problems apply.

Many Web sites these days have a sign-on sequence that runs under Secure Sockets Layer (SSL), which asks you for user codes and pass words. (See the box entitled "Secure Sockets Layer" if you want a very brief background to SSL.) It would be possible for Web services to be used in a similar way. The requester program could open an SSL connection to the Web service and the first few messages could exchange user codes, passwords, and any additional security information that was requested. This is not difficult programming. It may even be more secure than manual logon since the program could keep security information in an encrypted file, whereas today most people just write down their user codes and passwords. So what is wrong with using standard Web site security for Web services security?

One reason is stateless Web services. Most traditional security is based on the idea of a session. You log on at the beginning of the session and establish your user credentials, you do your work, and you log off. A stateless Web service can be perceived as one in which sessions consist of one input message only. Using session logon and logoff for one working message is very inefficient. Also, as we have noted time and time again, sessions introduce all kinds of problems for performance, reliability, and design, so it is a bad idea to revert to longer sessions; it's better to have an alternative form of security.

Secure Sockets Layer

The Secure Sockets Layer (SSL) was originally designed by Netscape to allow any user to send secure messages over the Internet, for instance, to send credit card details. It is now being standardized by the Internet Engineering Task Force (the Internet standardization body), which has developed the standard further under the name of the Transport Layer Security (TLS). SSL allows you to send and receive messages over a TCP/IP connection. You can tell that a Web session is using SSL rather than normal sockets because the address will start the letters "https:" rather than the normal "http:". Since for the programmer the interface to SSL is more or less the same as the interface to standard sockets, it is easy to implement on any product using TCP/IP.

SSL uses both symmetric and asymmetric encryption (see the box entitled "Encryption and hashing"). It uses asymmetric encryption when the session opens. The client asks the server for its public key. From this it generates a further key and sends this to the server, using the server's public key to encrypt the message. Both sides now generate an identical key that is used for symmetrical encryption for the rest of the session. Thus, while the start of the session is considerably longer than a simple TCP/IP session, the data flow thereafter is nearly the same.

Note that SSL does not have password criteria. It does, however, optionally support certificates for both the server and the client. In the credit card number transfer over the Web, the server may supply a certification but the client probably wouldn't. If you were using SSL as a secure connection to an existing application, you might want to open an SSL session and then have a user code/password dialog to complete the logon.

In spite of not having sessions at the application level, we expect that SSL will still be commonly used for secure transport of messages, especially over the Web. There are alternatives. Inside an organization Kerberos or IPSec may be used. There is also a standard called XML-encryption that has the data portion of the XML message encrypted, which may provide an adequate solution on the Web.

The solution for stateless Web services is to have the user's identity embedded in the message. These embedded items are called *security tokens*. A security token is a bit like an electronic version of the pass most organizations insist you wear around your neck or attached to your collar. The token is a piece of data that identifies the user and maybe has additional information such as the date and time and the user's privileges. The simplest form of security token is a username, but the problem with usernames is that they can be faked easily. Kerberos tickets are security tokens, as are X.509 certificates. These are sometimes called *signed security tokens* because the receiver can verify their correctness. For instance, the

Encryption and hashing

Someone sitting with a network monitor on the same LAN as you are will see your password. If sufficiently expert, she or he can spoof your dialog, sending messages as if they were from you. The solution to this problem is encryption.

Encryption is weak or strong depending on how easy it is to break. As hardware gets more powerful, what is strong today will be weak tomorrow. The strength of the encryption depends largely on the size of the key. Even weak (e.g., 40-bit) encryption, however, takes a concerted effort to break unless you happen to have specialized encryption-breaking hardware, so you must really want to break the message to even bother trying. Weak encryption is enough to prevent casual snooping but not the professional spy.

There are two forms of encryption: asymmetrical, or public key; and symmetrical, or private key.

Asymmetric encryption uses a different key to encrypt than to decrypt. The great advantage of asymmetric encryption is that you can publish your key and anyone can send you secret messages. The disadvantage is that asymmetric algorithms are slow. The best known asymmetric algorithm is probably RSA.

Symmetric encryption uses the same key to encrypt and decrypt the message. Symmetric encryption is fast. The most widely used symmetric encryption algorithm is probably DES.

Cryptography is used for not only encryption. It is also used for digital signatures. Digital signatures use asymmetric encryption, the private key to create the signature and the public key to check it. The total message is hashed before the encryption is done, which ensures not only that the signature links the signature with a person but also that the document contents are the same as when the signature was created. Clever, isn't it?

security token might have a digit signature to prove that users are who they say they are and a hash to prove that the token has not been tampered with.

A standard, WS-Security, has been developed, which covers the encryption of Web services messages and the addition of security tokens into SOAP headers. Note the task of acquiring security tokens has been taken away from the application service calls. Another standard, WS-Trust, describes (among other things) how to acquire a security token. Using a secure Web service is a two-stage process. First, have a conversation with a Security Token Services using WS-Trust, which creates for you a security token, and then use the security token to access any number of application Web services using WS-Security. This is illustrated in Figure 10-3.

Security tokens may also play a part in improving the security when a service calls a service. Assume there is a configuration in which a requester calls Service A and Service A calls Service B. There are two basic kinds of security

Kerberos

Kerberos is the probably the best known ticketing security infrastructure. A ticket is attached to every message and identifies the user and either gives to or withholds from that user the authority to use the service. Acquiring a ticket is a two-step process:

1. Log on to the Key Distribution Center (KDC) using a user code and password to get a Ticket Granting Ticket (TGT).
2. Use the TGT to get a ticket for a particular service.

This two-step process gives you a single sign-on facility because with one TGT you can get any number of service tickets. So that no one hangs on to a ticket indefinitely, all tickets expire and the user must log on again.

In Kerberos the KDC must be completely secure because it contains all the keys. The KDC is a potential bottleneck, especially over a WAN, although it can be duplicated.

As an aside, an interesting aspect of Kerberos is that it does not require a session. (It was designed for a UNIX environment with a lot of UDP traffic, for instance, to NFS file servers.)

While Kerberos is more functional than SSL, it cannot support a secure dialogue with a completely new user, unknown to the KDC, and therefore cannot support a credit card payment over the Web from any person on the Web. Kerberos performance is excellent because it uses symmetrical encryption throughout. A downside is that for an application to use Kerberos, both the client and the server programs must be programmatically modified (unless the Kerberos code is hidden by the middleware).

Many organizations use both SSL and Kerberos. The likely scenario is SSL over the Web and Kerberos in-house.

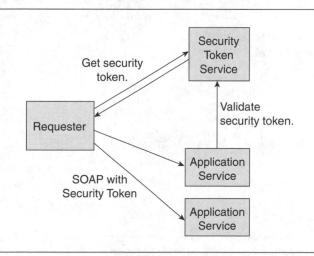

Figure 10-3   Security token service

configuration, which are illustrated in Figure 10-4. The top part of this figure shows two security contexts. In the top left, the requester has a security token that allows them to talk to Service A. In the top right, Service A itself has a security token that allows it to talk to Service B. In this scenario Service B does not know the identity of the original requester (unless Service A has put it in the message data). Also, the requester may not be able to access Service B directly because it does not have a valid security token for B. You can think of multiple security contexts much like a Web equivalent of location security. Service B does not trust the requester directly, but it does trust indirect access through Service A.

The bottom part of the Figure 10-4 shows a single security context. Here Service B is passed the same token passed to Service A. In fact, Service A may do no security checks at all. If both Service A and Service B are on the Internet, there is nothing stopping the requester from accessing Service B directly.

Up until now we have been looking at security from the service perspective, asking ourselves whether the services should trust the requesters. But what

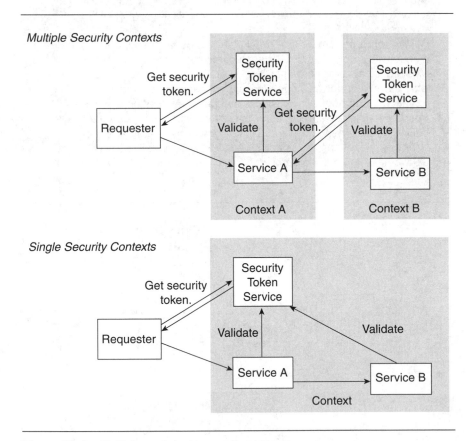

Figure 10-4   Multiple and single security contexts

about the other way around—should the requesters trust the services? In general, requesters have no choice; they must trust the service. In the single security context model, requesters must trust all downstream service providers, even if they don't know who they are. Although secure communications (e.g., using SSL) stops snoopers from acquiring your security token, there is no technical reason that the service provider cannot store your security token and reuse it later for its own nefarious purposes. If this is a concern, you should consider timeouts on the security token (e.g., it expires 8 hours after it was acquired) or, in extreme circumstances, one-off security tokens (i.e., security tokens that are used once and then eliminated). Even if there were one worldwide security token service, we expect that people would ensure they have several security tokens, for instance, one they use for really trusted services and one they use for less trusted services.

Note that you cannot assume two requests using the same token are from the same person because the token may be set up by an intermediary service that itself serves multiple people. Also, you cannot assume that two requests using different tokens are from different people.

On the Web there is a concern that the requester may not be certain that service providers are who they say they are. Certificates are meant to answer that concern. You use the certificate to check with a third-party that what is written on the certificate is true. You cannot do any security without trusting someone or something, somewhere. Managing trust is an important subject but outside the scope of this book.

So far we have described security at the user level. We noted earlier that it is more practical for an access control list to specify the privileges for roles rather than for users. But in general it is hard to see common security roles being defined across the Internet, so the mapping between user and role is left up to the service itself. However, a standard called XML Access Control Markup Language (XACML) is being developed to provide a common way of expressing access rights in an XML message.

Web services security is new and largely untested in challenging environments. There is no shortage of standards; in fact, there is a rather alarming proliferation of standards although most of them have not yet (as of early 2004) been ratified. But there should be few concerns about using Web services securely over an intranet because there is good integration with well-established technologies such as Kerberos. Also XML firewalls now exist, which should make configuring a secure Web services solution that much easier. Over the Internet, the picture is less clear. Business-to-business (B2B) communication can survive using bilaterally arranged SSL connections. But consumer-to-business (C2B) or the use of portals that call external Web services on your behalf would certainly work best if all the standards were ready, implemented, and stable. One can envisage a future in which your bank might provide security tokens that you can use to book your vacation, and the tokens are passed from booking agent to hotel or airline. Even if that were the case, the big uncertainty would be the question of trust.

10.4   Architecture and security

When the needs of security have been defined, albeit roughly, the design can be modified to take them into account. There are five main implementation questions to answer:

1. Which applications belong in which security context?

2. Where is authorization going to take place?

3. Where is access control going to take place?

4. Where is security management going to take place?

5. What threats exist and what are the countermeasures?

When these questions are answered, we find it useful to take a network diagram and overlay the security by indicating where the access control, authorization, and security management are to be done. In practice you might want to use a subset of the full network diagram or a simplified version of the network diagram. An example is shown in Figure 10-5.

The question of security context is particularly pertinent when there is a requirement to integrate with an existing system. An existing application will have its own security management and probably its own unique set of user codes and

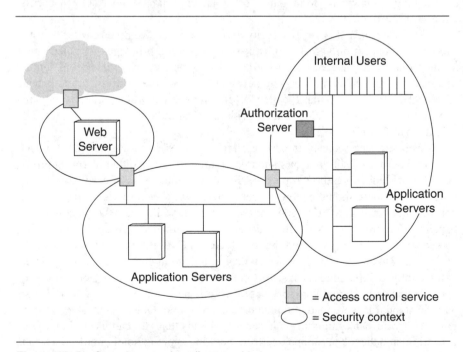

Figure 10-5   Security overview diagram

passwords. If the new system is going to use the same security context, then it needs to work with the same set of user codes and passwords and link with the existing security manager. If the new system will have its own security context, then there needs to be a decision on how the old application will view the new application from a security perspective. In other words, when a message comes from the new system to the old, what user code, if any, applies to that message? Clearly, since integration opens up a new way of accessing an existing system, it also opens up a new avenue for security attack.

In most cases, this decision is made for you by a company policy to move in a certain direction, for instance, you are putting all new systems under Kerberos. It is more difficult if a new application needs to integrate with several existing systems, each with its own security contexts. At some stage, it may become reasonable to merge security contexts. This is best done when introducing a new channel to an existing application. If, for instance, you are changing an old application to use a new Web interface, this may be the time to rationalize and simplify the security management.

Another major design question is, where will access control take place? The obvious place is at the server, but in some cases it is desirable to have a separate access control service that sits in front of a number of application services. This is illustrated in Figure 10-6.

The time to introduce an access control layer is when the security is (a) complex and (b) common across several services. For instance, suppose you are giving

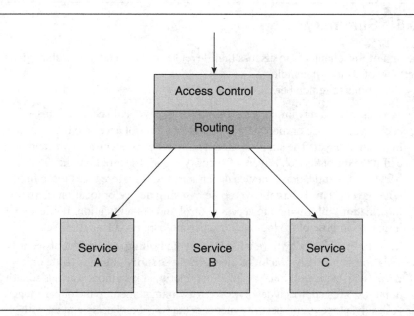

Figure 10-6 An access control layer

customers direct access to their accounts. The check between customer and account number could be done in one place before the message is passed on to the relevant service. A common access control layer is also useful when you want a gradual migration from one service to another. Without a common access control layer, the requesters might have to handle two kinds of security regime, one old and one new. With an access control layer you can implement the new security regime and have the access control layer software do the bridging to the old security context. The requesters can then be updated to the new security regime before migrating the back-end services. We expect this technique to become more important if a wholesale migration to Web services takes place.

When the architectural design has been done, it should be analyzed for resiliency to security threats. Look again at Figure 10-5. We have drawn a line around each security context. At every point where a network crosses the security context boundary, there should be an access control point. The main check is whether it is possible to let the people who fulfill the roles access the application and to prevent the people who don't fulfill the roles accessing the application. The final configuration may be different from the configuration you anticipate during the design phase so when security is implemented, all the assumptions in your design need to be rechecked. While designing the architecture, you do not need to put all the detail on the security design, but you need to be sure (as near as you can be) that it is practical to build a secure system with your proposed design.

10.5   Summary

The aim of this chapter is to discuss high-level security design rather than give an overview of security technology.

Key points to remember:

- Most security today implements the notion of layers of security, where each layer has one or more access points that control access to the resources in the inner layer. The simplest model consists of concentric layers and we call it the onion model. Layers of security are less secure than they look because authentication is device dependent and therefore takes place in the outer layers. This is largely overcome by using device or location (network information) information in access control and authentication. For instance, it may be impossible to log on with a certain user code from the Web.

- Most large users today have what we call the boiling lava model of security. This consists largely of a lot of independent security domains (little onions, if you will) with additional ad hoc trust relationships among various security domains. This approach devolves security management to the departments. A disadvantage of this security model is that most end users end up with many user codes and passwords, and it can be hard to know who has what privileges.

- Many existing techniques—sessions, using location information, having layers of security—don't work on Web services. Instead, Web services use security tokens. A security token is supplied and validated by a security token service. All the services controlled by one security token service is called a security context. However, given the unbreakable nature of most encryption these days (in practice, if not in theory), Web services can be highly secure.

- A high-level security architecture identifies which servers go into which security context and within each security context establishes the security roles and the criteria for trust.

- By overlaying the security contexts on a network diagram, you can analyze the security to ensure that there are no backdoor entries to the services.

This is the last chapter on technology principles; there are some important conclusions common to all these chapters.

You still have to be prepared to put code into your applications for handling facilities like multiple versions, security, error logging, performance monitoring, and error recovery, including switching to backup. This is a major reason why the notion that you can press a button on your design model and a fully working system will spring to life is premature.

A second important conclusion is that not only do technical design decisions affect these areas, but application design decisions do also. This is partly because the implementation designer needs to know in detail the precise performance, resiliency, and security requirements. There are trade-offs everywhere. For instance, a very security-sensitive application may need to log all messages, which clearly would have a detrimental impact on performance.

A final conclusion is that there are real opportunities for code reuse, especially in the areas of logging and error reporting. These opportunities should be grasped. There often seems to be a rather cruel 80:20 rule that applies to programming that goes along the lines that 80% of the functionality is implemented in 20% of the time. A good part of the additional 80% of the time goes into implementing infrastructure code for performance monitoring, resiliency, systems management, and security.

The upside of implementing comprehensive infrastructure code is that if you attack it early, it enormously aids testing and debugging new application development.

11

Application Design and IT Architecture

This chapter is a linking chapter, linking the technology discussions of the previous chapters to the design discussions of the following chapters.

During our discussions so far, many design questions have been left unanswered. At what point is the decision made to use a middleware bus architecture, a hub architecture, or a Web services architecture? If the decision is too early, there may not be enough information to make a good decision. If the decision is too late, there is a danger of being forced to rewrite much of the application. At what point is the functionality assigned to tiers, and how is this done? In this chapter we present an outline of how we tackle these problems. In the following chapters we focus in more detail on some of the major design activities.

Before carrying on, let us make clear something we don't want to discuss. We don't want to discuss how to gather requirements, design, code, test, and project manage stand-alone, or silo, applications. We are assuming that you or your organization knows how to do that. The purpose of these chapters is to discuss the architectural design of integrated applications.

Much of what we propose should be done before the application project is under way; it is about IT planning. In other words, design precedes the scoping exercise of a typical project. Only when this design is finished do you have some idea of the size and cost of the proposed development.

This chapter has three main sections. The first discusses the problems with application development as it is practiced today and attempts to explain why architecture and system integration design is often poorly handled. The second discusses what we call "levels of design" and presents a way of thinking about design that resolves the problems discussed in the first section. Finally, we discuss the issue of reconciling different approaches to design.

11.1   Problems with today's design approaches

Application development today is mired in controversy. An inspection of the archives of some Web discussion groups will reveal contradictory views expressed with quasi-religious fervor. In this section we examine in a calm and collected manner where fault lines between the entrenched positions lie.

11.1.1   Design up front or as needed?

When people first started to program, they didn't realize there was much of a problem with application design. For instance, COBOL was designed to read like English, and the hope was that business people could quickly grasp what was going on. What wasn't understood was the huge gap between the few lines that an end user would need to describe an application and the thousands of lines of actual programming code. When people did grasp the enormity of the problem and the sheer proneness to error in programming, two ideas came to the fore: structured programming and waterfall development. The rationale for waterfall development was (and is) that problems are easy to fix in the requirements gathering stage, less easy to fix in the design stage, and hard to fix in the program. Therefore, it makes sense to take time to study the requirements and make sure the design is right before starting programming. The rest of the history of application development can be seen as a series of attempts either to shore up the requirements-design-implementation structure or to break it down.

The notion of requirements-design-implementation in waterfall is so intuitively correct, what can possibly be wrong with it? In practice there are three main problems. First, end users and the business don't know their requirements, are unable to express their requirements with sufficient rigor, or even worse, have contradictory requirements. Introducing a new IT application is changing people's jobs. People have difficulty visualizing what's needed for the new system to work. Departments may have different views on who does what. Some in the organization may have vested interest in the new system not working at all. Introducing change is always difficult. A consequence of these problems is that requirements change during the implementation phase or later.

The second problem is that it is difficult to express the design in a way that is understandable and usable both to the programmer charged with implementation and to the business sponsors charged with ensuring the design meets their requirements. Misunderstanding is rife.

The third problem is that the division among requirements, design, and implementation leads to overengineering. This is particularly true in large bureaucracies where one group is specifying the requirements and another group is designing and implementing. The requirements group is petrified of leaving something out because they know they will never get the budget to add it back in. Also, the easiest way to achieve compromise is to throw in everybody's ideas. As an aside, this is the same problem standards committees have and the reason that standards too are often overengineered. Furthermore, if design and implementation has been outsourced to an external systems integration company, they have a vested interest in making the project as big as possible.

Practically every book and article on application design over the last 15 or more years has criticized waterfall development. But waterfall projects are still commonplace. They work well when the requirements are easily grasped and seldom change. Unfortunately, the pace of business change dictates that such cases are rarer and rarer. In many cases, the contractual agreements and "quality assurance" processes that have been put in place to enforce the contract keep the waterfall process in place. And in many of these cases, the project is a large, costly disaster.

All alternatives to waterfall have iterative development. Classic iterative development is really a series of waterfall projects, often overlapping. Each iteration produces a workable application that can be released for testing by the end users. This gives an opportunity for requirements for downstream iterations to be modified to reflect feedback and business changes. As a further refinement, there may be some upfront requirements gathering and design for the whole project before the iterations start. This is important for architectural design, as we shall see.

But what we have called "classic iterative development" does not question the requirements-design-implementation life cycle steps. Indeed they have been strengthened. Design has been made more visual by using modeling tools to express data structure and process flows diagrammatically. Repositories have been used to keep requirements and design information and to track the impact of change across the design and implementation.

Other design approaches do question the requirements-design-implementation life cycle. The first of these was probably Rapid Application Development (RAD), which came to prominence in the 1980s. This was a full frontal attack on the requirements gathering problem. The idea was that with a few minimal requirements you could create a prototype application. You would then elicit detailed requirements by showing your user interface to the end users, changing the application or adding new functionality as requested, and then repeating the process many times. The idea is that end users get exactly what they want, quicker and with less chance of overengineering than would be done by either waterfall or classic iterative development. So by the mid 1980s the battle lines were drawn and, to be honest, they haven't moved much since.

That is not to say that the weapons and the strategies of the opposing camps haven't changed. Since the 1980s, classic iterative development has taken on an object-oriented flavor and has standardized on Unified Modeling Language (UML, from the Object Management Group, OMG). UML has been through several versions and now has a large number of diagram types with their underpinning data definitions. More recently Model Driven Architecture (MDA, also from OMG) has been announced and some MDA products are reaching the marketplace. The idea of MDA is to lessen, perhaps eventually eliminate, the implementation step by generating the implementation directly from the design. It's sufficiently different from early classic iterative development that we will give it a new name, model-based development.

RAD projects continue to be done but today the most vocal opposition to classic iterative development has been taken over by the agile movement. The agile movement started (in its present form at least) by the advent of extreme programming (often shortened to XP). Later the Agile Alliance was formed (see www.agilealliance.org), which published the agile alliance manifesto. This manifesto is short enough for us to quote in full:

> We are uncovering better ways of developing software by doing it and helping others do it. Through this work we have come to value:
>
> - Individuals and interactions over processes and tools
> - Working software over comprehensive documentation
> - Customer collaboration over contract negotiation
> - Responding to change over following a plan
>
> That is, while there is value in the items on the right, we value the items on the left more.

The manifesto is backed up by a series of principles.

It is hard to disagree with the manifesto, although it is true that many projects are managed in a way that contravenes it. More and more methodologies claim to be agile (see the Agile Alliance Web site for a list) and practically any methodology could be made "agile," including model-based development.

But while the agile movement has a soft friendly outer shell, it has a hard inner core, and that inner core is best exemplified by XP itself. It is not too unfair to say that the core belief of XP is that XP programmers don't need designers and systems analysts. But XP is not programmers run loose; it is a highly disciplined process. It is not the purpose of this book to describe XP in detail, but we do want to focus on one point. XP can be characterized as "design as needed," in contrast to model-based development, which can be characterized as "design up front." Note that "design as needed" does not mean no design at all. XP has what are called architectural spikes for making architecture decisions, but XP programmers try to make the minimal architecture to meet the requirements rather than anticipate future requirements. Some XP programmers draw model diagrams but then throw them away. The only design artifact that matters is the code.

Recall that the waterfall was invented because the cost of change is much less during requirements gathering and design than during implementation. How does XP solve this problem? The technical ways they attack this problem are first by test-driven development and second by refactoring. Test-driven development is about building the tests before building the functional code. A consequence of test-driven development is that a large library of tests is built, which allows the XP programmers to make radical changes to the application with confidence. Refactoring is about making many small adjustments to the code, not to add functionality but to keep up the quality of the design. With test-driven development and refactoring in place, XP projects can make changes more easily than traditional projects.

The argument between design up front and design as needed goes on, and there are few signs of an early resolution.

11.1.2   The role of business rules

It has long been a dream to specify an application in a manner that the non-IT manager can understand. If that could be done, then the next step would be to generate the application directly from the specification, cutting the programmer out of the loop. The current incantation for materializing this dream is "Business rules."

What is a business rule? Information in a database is facts about the real world. Business rules define the structure of those facts and define how those facts can be processed. This makes it sound as if the business rules are little more than a database schema with additional processing rules, and that is indeed how one school of business rules sees it. This school is headed by Chris Date and Hugh Darwen, and where possible they have tried to express business rules as database integrity rules. Another school takes as its starting point the UML model and is seeking to add rules to the model to beef it up to a comprehensive description of the application. Tony Morgan in his book in this series, *Business Rules and Information Systems,** takes this route. He describes five rule patterns:

1. *Constraints,* for example, "An urgent order must be accepted if the order value is less than $30." Note the subject of the constraint does not have to be a data element. It could be a role or a process. The subject would be described either in the model or by another rule.

2. *List constraints,* for example, "A customer can be raised from bronze to silver status if (a) his or her account has been positive for 12 months, and (b) the average account balance exceeds $500." A list of constraints applies to one subject.

3. *Classification,* for example, "An order is urgent if the delivery must be done in less than 3 hours."

4. *Computation,* for example, "Ratio = price/earnings."

5. *Enumeration,* for example, "Customer standing can be gold, silver or bronze."

Note that although the examples express the rules as easily understood English commands, they are underpinned by formal logic. When are the rules triggered? The model defines the business events, and some clever piece of software needs to analyze the events to figure out which rules to check.

---

*Morgan, Tony. *Business Rules and Information Systems: Aligning IT with Businesss Goals.* Boston: Addison-Wesley, 2002.

Another school of business rules takes as its starting point inference engines originally developed for AI applications. The rules in rules engines are normally if . . . then . . . statements: *If* a condition exists, *then* do action. This is in contrast to the other schools of thought where rules are statements that must always be true. In practice, inference engines are useful when a chain of reasoning is required, such as in processing an insurance claim. We see that these schools are converging to some extent. People are seeing advantages in different approaches in different scenarios.

There are many uncertainties with this work. The OMG is looking to create some business rules standard, but others (e.g., proponents of the relational data model) believe that UML itself is not a firm foundation for this work. There are other difficulties. For instance, take a rule like "All urgent orders must be delivered by 9:00 P.M." This is more a good intention than a logical imperative because it is possible to envisage a set of circumstances where it can't be done. Many rules in business are not absolute; they really are not like physical laws or mathematical theorems. Furthermore, business rules are about expressing constraints on business processes, and business processes have a non–IT component, typically people following instructions. There is always the question of whether the rule should be implemented by the IT application at all, and if it is done by people, what happens if they forget to obey it? You can also use rules as a reminder mechanism to give guidance rather than orders. It can also be used as checking system, for instance, checking which urgent orders haven't been delivered by 8:00 P.M. and 9:00 P.M.

In spite of the uncertainties, there are business rules products in the marketplace. They are typically a rules engine plugged on in front of a database.

There is a long way before the dream of eliminating programming is realized. Take the example of a Web application that displays product information. There is a tremendous amount of programming here: the user interface, the database access, the scrolling, and the selection logic. But there are no business rules. There is no reason why programming applications such as displaying product details should not be automated; in fact, in the past it has been automated. The problem that these application generators have always come against is that the technology-du jour has always changed from underneath them and they have had difficulties keeping up. Many organizations have always rejected such software on the basis that "it runs on a mainframe," "it doesn't use my favorite database," "it does not use Java," "it does use Java," "I can't put my company logo on the screen," and so on. Until IT starts thinking more about business benefit and less about technology, it is hard to see this changing. The OMG in its MDA program has a plan to stop this, which is to decouple the logical specification of the system (the Platform Independent Model, PIM) from the physical specification of the system (the Platform Specific Model, PSM). We can only wish them success.

11.1.3   Existing systems

Engrained in IT is the notion that there are two classes of programmers: the lowly maintenance programmer and the superior new application development programmer. This attitude has been partially responsible for the fact that so many organizations have an enormous number of stand-alone applications. It is clear that this attitude must change as the requirement for organizations to have a more integrated IT system grows. Almost every project larger than the trivial has an element of systems integration in it, and systems integration programming is largely about changing existing production applications.

Almost every application development methodology in existence completely forgets to mention existing systems. The notion of an orderly advance from requirements to design to implementation breaks down when there are existing systems. People do talk about reverse engineering to discover and document the requirements and design of existing systems, but this is a huge amount of work, much of which is likely to be unnecessary. Furthermore, if you then alter the requirements or design, you must forward engineer to create a new version of the existing application. Since many of the existing systems are old mainframe applications that implement complex business functionality and have exacting recovery and performance requirements, there is a good chance the newly created forward-engineered application will be unacceptable.

We describe in Chapter 15 some techniques for modernizing existing applications. The only point we want to make here is that there is a choice between developing a new application, interfacing to an existing application with minimal changes, and modifying the existing application to support new functionality better. Application development methodologies give little or no guidance on how to make this choice.

Many organizations make these decisions on technological grounds. If the technology is old, they try to leave the application unchanged as much as possible. The irony is that making the existing application more modular and more flexible is often the best way to cut the old application up and get rid of it piece by piece.

And of course, all these concerns about application development integrated with existing systems apply equally to applications written recently with the latest technology. Developing good design strategies for integration with existing systems is a vital development skill that will only become more important.

11.1.4   Reuse

When objected-oriented (OO) technology became popular, its primary selling point was reuse. This marketplace in reusable class libraries never took off.

When components became popular their primary selling point was reuse. The market place in reusable components never took off. Why?

For component reuse to become commonplace, development must be broken down into three roles:

1. The programmer who writes reusable components

2. The assembler who writes scripts that call the components

3. The administrator who writes the deployment descriptors and configures the production system

The model is illustrated in Figure 11-1.

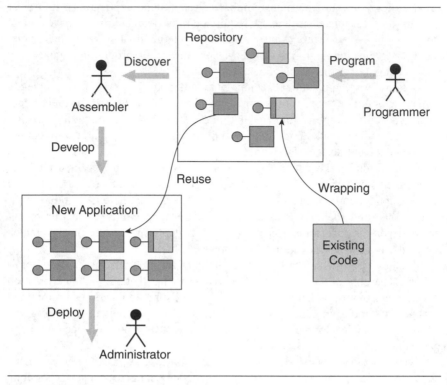

Figure 11-1   Serendipitous reuse

The assembler creates the applications. The programmer writes the components and places them in the repository where the assembler can find them. The administrator sets up the new application in its run-time environment. The difference between this thinking and earlier approaches is the split between component programmer and assembler; previously they were combined into the single function of programmer. The logic behind the split is twofold:

1. The system can respond quickly to business change by changing the script or by modifying the deployment parameters.

2. Components can be reused. Reusable components should be more battle-hardened (better tested, better performance) than components used only once. A market should develop for buying reusable components.

The fundamental question is, is this model realistic? If so, is it always realistic, or is it only realistic within a certain set of conditions?

Component reuse is often presented as identifying a functional gap and finding a component that implements the required functionality. Our name for this lucky process is *serendipitous reuse*. It relies on luck because in practice there are many reasons why a component is unsuitable, for instance:

- The component does not do everything you need. The question then becomes whether you can live with the shortfall, change the component, or fill in the missing functionality with another component.
- The component might do too much. For instance, the component might be doing some printing but might have an unwanted FAX interface that is inappropriate for your end users.
- The technology is inappropriate (e.g., you want a Java bean and the component is a COM component).
- The component is too slow.
- The component might not interface with your security or system management routines.
- The component might make an assumption about the database design that isn't true.
- The component might use a different database vendor's technology.

Finding an exact fit is hard. Therefore, to make serendipitous reuse work you need a large library of well-documented components, many implementing the same or similar functionality. Given the size of the library, you are also likely to need a specialized search tool.

In a large project finding a component that fits is even harder. In Figure 11-2 there are two applications illustrated. One is a simple application of script and component. The other is a more realistic complex application.

Simple configuration—serendipitous reuse is practical.

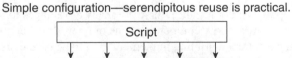

Larger, More Realistic, Configuration

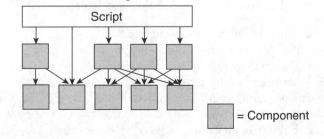

Figure 11-2   Component dependencies

Whereas serendipitous reuse may be good for the simple application, it is unlikely to be effective for the complex application because components use other components. Components supporting business objects are likely to need to call other components that control access to common data (the customer and product data), common infrastructure (security, system management, printing, e-mail interfaces, etc.), and standard routines (interest rate calculations, data manipulation, etc.). Find two components over the Web, for instance, and it is unlikely that they will call the same system management error reporting interface or the same customer information retrieval interface. Businesses have problems agreeing on standards for business-to-business communication, and software vendors are not famous for their cooperative approach to standards development; hence, component vendors are unlikely to agree on consistent interfaces. There is a domino effect; choose one component and you find yourself being forced to use others.

The alternative to serendipitous reuse is *architectural reuse.* You can think of serendipitous reuse as bottom-up reuse. It is analogous to building a house by looking around for suitable building material. If you find something you like, you change the design to fit it in. Architectural reuse is top-down reuse in the sense that the architecture is paramount, and you work on reuse opportunities while defining the architecture. Reuse happens because you design it in; it is analogous to designing a house from standard components—standard bricks, standard door sizes, and standard window frames. The key practical difference is that with architectural reuse you start by defining the interfaces and then look for components that implement the interfaces, rather than looking at the component and living with whatever interface comes with it. Components that are most likely to be reused by architectural reuse are:

- Horizontal components: For instance, there are many advantages to enforcing one or a few security components, one or a few error reporting components, and a common printing implementation to be used consistently across many applications.

- Interface to common data: For instance, customer and product data is likely to be used by many applications. This is discussed further in Chapter 14.

- Interface to common routines. Examples are routines for interest calculation, data manipulation, string manipulation, and so on.

Architectural reuse enforces the architecture.

This subsection concentrates on component reuse, but this is not the whole story. The range of reuse opportunities is illustrated in Figure 11-3.

Reuse has been used for screen layouts, screen format parts, design patterns, documentation, testing routines, symbolic code (program source), practically everywhere in fact. When you copy an example from a text book, this is reuse. Encouraging reuse is important in every IT department. Programming groups should build a "pattern book" of code that works. Reuse of the screen formats is particularly important because it can enforce a common look-and-feel over many

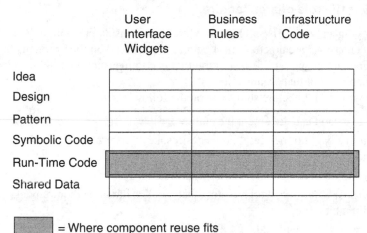

= Where component reuse fits

All others are different reuse opportunities.

Figure 11-3   The range of reuse possibilities

screens and can ensure that when the same kind of data (e.g., an address) is displayed, it is always displayed in the same way.

There have actually been many successful examples of organizations using reuse, but in our experience it is enforced reuse from the top that works, not bottom-up reuse from broad-minded, cooperative programmers. In short, we already know that architectural reuse works.

11.1.5   Silo and monolithic development

As noted in Chapter 1, a major problem with development over the last few decades has been silo development—applications developed in isolation with consequent uncontrolled duplication of data. Silo applications did not come about because there were bad application developers. Arguably, the chief cause was having the wrong project boundaries.

In organizations where there are not many silo applications, there is typically the opposite extreme—a large monolithic application that is hard to understand and hard to change. It seems that if we widen the project boundaries we automatically, without thinking, create one monstrous application. We seem to be bad at looking over a large number of requirements and splitting them into logical chunks that can be implemented as a number of integrated applications.

11.1.6   The role of architecture

Developing an "enterprise architecture" can be a consultant's delight. Our view is that an enterprise architecture must be directly focused on the problems faced by the organization and outline a solution that is commensurate with the budget and the capabilities of that organization.

A typical architecture study will do the following:

- Understand and document the current system.
- Build a list of principles, biases, desires, key performance indicators, and so on.
- Identify and compare technology options.
- Propose a new target architecture that handles the same requirements or a little bit more.
- Compare new with old.
- Document possible projects to turn old into new.

You need to multiply this by the different kinds of architecture. There are infrastructure architectures (e.g., network, security, system management, disaster recovery) and there are application architectures (e.g., database architectures, business intelligence architecture, and so on). A fully comprehensive enterprise architecture provides enough consultancy work for an army for years.

The most common failing with this approach is that by allowing yourself a free rein when devising the new target architecture, you end up with a new target architecture that is so different from what exists today that it implies a complete rewrite of the whole system. If the organization has an unlimited budget and could survive without new IT functionality for a few years, that might be the best option. We just don't know of any organizations in that lucky position.

Organizations are always looking for:

- Faster development
- Cost reduction
- Better security, reliability, and performance

Enterprise architecture should help on all these points: faster development through being able to combine existing services rather than writing new services; cost reduction through supporting fewer technologies; and better security, reliability, and performance through solving the infrastructure problem once and applying the solution to many services. But architecture is a means to an end, not an end in itself. An important part of an architectural study is to investigate why development is slow, why systems are costly, and why there are deficiencies in the security, reliability, or performance of the systems. The long-term vision is then derived by melding the proposals from each study and ironing out inconsistencies.

A long-term architectural vision is a good idea as long as it is short and easily understood and staff can understand how the architecture delivers the benefits for faster development, cost reduction, and better security, reliability, and performance. Developments can then be judged on whether they take the organization toward the architecture or away from it. But just as important as a long-term architecture are short-term goals for the IT department, such as:

- Have consistent security management across core applications.
- Reduce the number of customer databases to one.
- Have a shared presentation layer for key core applications.

Ultimately, it is only application development and infrastructure development projects that make the vision happen. If the vision does not have an impact on the choice or direction of the projects, it is useless.

11.2   Levels of design

In this section, we question some basic assumptions that underlie so much of the work on IT design processes and methodologies.

At the start of the twentieth century, people said that science was done by scientists looking at all the evidence, accessing and analyzing the evidence, and deducing a scientific law. Then along came Karl Popper who pointed out that it isn't like that. What happens is that someone has an idea, a hypothesis, and then tries to shoot it down. The good hypotheses are the survivors. This section is an attempt to introduce a Popperian view into the world of application design.

In practice, design outside of IT works something like this:

- Understand. Learn a bit about the background and gather a few important requirements.
- Brainstorm. Develop a few alternative strawman solutions.
- Clarify. Select one of the solutions and put some more detail on it.
- Analysis. Analyze the solution, seeking to find and fix faults in it.
- Repeat clarification and analysis until cooked. If you find an unfixable fault (or the fixes make the solution too ugly), you find an alternative solution and try again.
- Go down a level of detail and find or design the components. If this is too hard, revisit the upper-level design.

Take an example outside of IT; suppose we are to design a new passenger plane. We find out the required specifications such as how many passengers, range, and target cost. We think up a few alternatives: jets or propellers, two engines or four, wing joined to the top of the fuselage or the bottom. We take our preferred solution, or perhaps a couple of our preferred solutions, and analyze them to figure out the maximum allowed weights of the parts and the required thrust of the engines. If the analysis doesn't work out well, we play around with some options until we have a preferred design. We then divide the design into components and turn over the component design to detailed design teams. The detailed design teams go through the same kind of process, looking for alternatives and analyzing them. They may even go a level further. For instance, the fuselage designers may turn to specialists to design the doors. It could be that during this process a specialist group runs into a problem and has to say it can't be done (or it can't be done for an appropriate cost). The higher-level design must then be reviewed and altered to give a less demanding specification for the component.

Not only airplanes are designed this way. The architect for a house does not usually design the dining room furniture. The bridge designer does not design the details of the column before deciding whether the bridge will be an arch bridge or a suspension bridge. Levels of design are illustrated in Figure 11-4.

Observe how different this is from the classic IT notion of requirements, design, and implementation. The most striking difference is that the design has levels—it forms a hierarchy. The requirements from lower down the hierarchy come from (a) the sponsors and (b) the higher-level design. For example, the engine design may have a requirement from the sponsor that the engine noise cannot exceed X decibels, but the required thrust comes from calculations done on the higher-level design. The second large difference is the role of analysis. It is not an analysis of the requirements, but an analysis of the solution to see whether it meets the requirements.

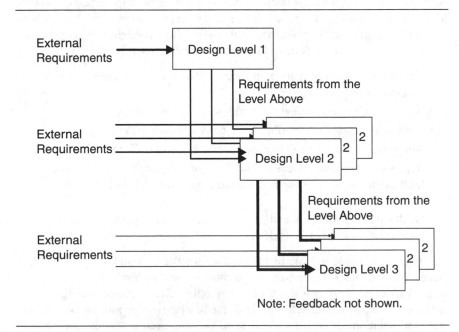

Figure 11-4   Levels of design

So why is the design of IT applications uniquely different from every other kind of design known to humans? We have a simple explanation—it isn't. The main difficulty in applying these ideas to IT is that the levels in IT design are not as obvious as they are on a plane design.

We will start defining the levels at the top. The first point to make clear is that application development is part of a wider picture. The overall business goal of the top layer is therefore not to design an IT application. The goal is to design a new or amended business process or service, supported by IT. We call the top layer the *business process level;* what goes on here in terms of design is not classic IT application design but is better described as IT planning or high-level architecture design. The main decisions that need to be made here are:

- Write a new program or extend an existing program?
- Have one centralized database or several databases?
- What data must flow between applications?
- Implement a middleware bus, hub, or Web services architecture (as described in Chapter 6)?
- Use what technology for the applications?

The main benefit of business process level design is that it prevents silo development. Doing business process level design is described in the Chapter 12.

Business processes (or services) break down into tasks in which one person is doing one job at one time. From an IT perspective, the task is a dialogue. In classic IT design, a task corresponds to a use case. We call the level below the business process level, the *task level.* Some dialogues are trivial, some are complex. The purpose of the task level is to understand how the end-user tasks align with underpinning data flow between applications. In practice, task-level design is usually about designing generic dialogue patterns that are reused over and over again. Most applications have a few patterns that apply to many dialogues and that means a single pattern can be applied to many tasks.

Designing the dialogue is just one element of task-level design. Task-level design also includes:

- Database logical design
- Security logical design
- System management logical design
- Business rules definition (if you are using business rules)

By "logical design" we mean the specification of what needs to be done and when and where it is executed. It excludes the details of how it is done.

The reason all these elements are considered together in this one level is because they interact with one another.

Task-level design is described in Chapter 13.

At the bottom level is detailed design and implementation. We call this the *transaction level.* At this point, all the input and output messages should be known from the task-level design. The task-level design, along with the database design and the business rules, should be enough information to build components and write code. Note, however, that end-user requirements are still needed because this level is where the detailed screen layouts are designed and implemented.

Some may want to split one or more of these design levels into multiple sub-levels, for instance, split the transaction level into a detailed design level and a coding level. The focus of this book is architecture and system integration design, and for this purpose we will stop with three levels.

11.3   Reconciling design approaches

If you accept the level view of design just outlined, how should your design methodology change?

First, recall that business process level design is about avoiding the opposite sins of silo development and monolithic development. Existing methodologies have little to say on this subject; they start from the assumption that the project boundaries are well set. We suggest that business process level design is done first, because the outcome from business process level design may be more than one development project.

In Rational Unified Process (RUP) there is a phase at the beginning called Inception. This is usually described as defining the project boundaries, doing esti-mates, identifying benefits, and assessing risk. It is hard to do this rigorously with-out having done business process design, so we suggest that business process design be done before the rest of the Inception phase. For instance, there is often an enormous difference in the estimate for extending an existing application and the estimate for replacing an existing application; these are the kinds of decision that come from the business process level design.

A use case description is a description of a task, so the implication of our approach for model-driven development is that you organize your iterations so that each iteration completes one or more tasks. In other words, each iteration does some task design and its associated transaction design and implementation.

If you are following an XP process, then we would still advise doing the busi-ness process design up front. In theory, you could use "design as needed" here, but once there is agreement among business management on the business process design, high-level architecture design should not be a long process (only one or a few days for each business process), and the downstream savings on having a basic implementation design outline are considerable.

XP implementers will want to do task-level design by taking a simple description of the task, programming a solution, and then molding the solution as it comes under intensive scrutiny by an end-user representative. If the task design is very simple, this is not a problem. If the task design is complex and requires a great deal of systems integration, then the success of the XP is completely reliant on the expertise of the programmers. As noted, there may be many tasks, but there are probably only a few patterns. The XP project should ensure that the first time each pattern is implemented it is done by the best programmers and fully discussed by the whole team.

It is very often the case in a large-scale system integration project that there are separate teams working with different technologies. For instance, putting a Web front end onto an existing mainframe application may have separate teams developing the Web application and making the changes to the mainframe application. The two teams need not follow the same methodology at the transaction level. As long as the integration design has been done at the process and task levels, the teams only work with each other during systems test and deployment. However, each team should create a test bed for the other team. In our example, the Web application team should write a driver for testing the mainframe application, and the mainframe team should write a service interface that mimics the mainframe application.

11.4 Summary

In this chapter we cast a quick eye over the many, many issues of application development.

Key points to remember:

- There are two main schools of thought on design, which we characterized as design up front and design as needed.
- We prefer a third approach—design in levels. Here design is completed at a high level. Lower-level design takes a part of the higher-level design and develops it in more detail, and so on until the level of detail is the implementation. It is always possible, though we hope rare, that the lower levels of design find flaws in the higher levels.
- Design in any level is a process of understanding the problem, brainstorming some solutions, clarifying one or more solutions (i.e., working out the detail), and analyzing the solution. The purpose of the analysis is to fix flaws in the design. If fixing is too hard, it is time to look for an alternative solution.
- The three levels we identified are business process, task, and transaction levels. That does not mean there are not more levels.

The tasks in these three levels of design are summarized in Table 11-1.

The next two chapters describe the business process level and the task level in more detail.

Table 11-1 Levels of design and related responsibilities

Level	IT Design Responsibility	Business/Requirements Responsibility
Business Process	Large-scale architecture Add/Change/Delete applications Choice of technology	Business process design Data accuracy requirements
Task	Message flow between applications Session/user dialogue design Database logical design Security design	User dialogue assessment Nonfunctional requirements Business rules definition
Transaction	Component design Database physical design	Assessment of user interface usability

12

Implementing
Business Processes

Understanding business processes is key to implementation design. This chapter explains why. We expect most readers of this book will have either a technical background or an application design background. Earlier chapters probably cover a lot of material that is familiar to the techies; this chapter will in part be familiar to the application modelers.

Business process modeling was late coming into the mainstream of IT application design. Until recently, functional analysis was much more common (see the box entitled "Function versus process" at the end of this chapter). In the mid 1990s and earlier, few design methods paid more than lip service to business process modeling. It was only when the Hammer and Champy wrote their book *Reengineering the Corporation* in 1993, which made business process reengineering fashionable, that the IT industry sat up and took notice of business processes at all.

Today, business process analysis is widely used during analysis. It is less often used for input to architecture design; we hope to show you the degree to which technical decisions should be made on the basis of understanding the business processes. Also, although not explored further in this book, technology creates business opportunities, and the way to take these opportunities forward is for the technologists to sit down with the business planners and discuss business processes.

IT applications need to be integrated because business processes are integrated. If business processes were stand-alone things that had an impact on only one small section of a company, there would be little need for IT to be integrated (and life would be much easier).

Business processes are integrated in several ways, for instance:

- Business processes can be subprocesses of larger business processes.
- Business processes can initiate other business processes.
- Business processes share information.

Consider a car rental process. There are many business processes: handling new rentals, handling returns, checking and cleaning cars, moving cars between offices, handling accident reports, and so on. They are all connected. Traditionally, application developers implemented systems like this without really thinking about business processes at all. They implemented a series of discrete transactions against a car rental database and maybe had a separate application and database for maintenance. The application designer would have seen what needed to be done and turned it into a sequence of screen formats, and the database designer would have identified the major tables. The programmer would have taken it from there and probably discovered errors in the design and work a way around them.

Now what happens to this system when a gold/silver/platinum/blue/premium/ etc. card is introduced? The original application for handling new rentals is irrelevant to customers because all they need do is make a phone call and the car is waiting for them. Looks like a new application, so a new application is written. Then comes the messy bit, the integration with the original rental system. Perhaps the card system pretends to be a terminal on the rental system. (Perhaps it prints the information and someone retypes it into the original system.)

If we take a business process perspective, we see that there is one long process—the car rental process, of which handling new rentals is only a part. The original handling new rentals process and the card member's rental process are alternative subprocesses in this central car rental process. If the original system was written with a clean break between subprocesses, the new subprocess could be slotted in with a minimum of disruption, and the result would be a much cleaner design—easier to change, easier to maintain, and probably faster and more resilient as well.

By analyzing the business processes, we can understand a great deal about the possible implementation, in particular:

- The fault lines for change
- The constraints for data distribution
- The requirements for performance
- The requirements for data resiliency

The fault lines for change fall between business processes or between a master business process and its subordinates; it was illustrated by our previous example. Put simply, the unit of change in the business is the business process or subprocess. By aligning the implementation components along business process lines, we reduce the number of components that need to be changed.

On the data distribution front, clearly all the data could be centralized. But if it isn't, we need to locate the data near the business processes and again split it along business process boundaries. Not only should this be more efficient and responsive to change, it is potentially more resilient as well. What if the network to the central system breaks down? Using the business process analysis, we can determine what objects are required to carry on processing locally. A solution to maximize resiliency would be to keep local and global copies of various pieces of data. The business process analysis tells us when we can make the copy and when it must be synchronized. For instance, a copy of the new rental information needs to be available to other rental offices within the time it takes to drive to a new return location.

In this chapter we first describe a business process and then discuss business process-level design.

12.1   What is a process?

At this point, some of you may be wondering where we draw the line between business processes and all the other things an organizations does. We take the view that almost everything a business does can be described as a business process, but some processes are better defined than others. Business process analysis has its roots in improving manufacturing, which is obviously regimented and repetitive. One of the insights from the business processing reengineering revolution is that the notion of processes is much wider than that and some of the same thinking can be applied outside the factory.

A process is a series of activities that delivers something, be it concrete or abstract, a solid thing or information. Examples of processes are cooking a meal, opening a bank account, ordering a pizza, delivering a pizza, and buying a car. Some processes can be well defined, meaning that they can be repeated consistently time and time again. Some processes are by their very nature not well defined at all. Design and research are examples of processes that are impossible to define, at least in detail. Even the IT department has processes. There are application development processes, system operational processes, and budget planning processes, to name but three. Quality improvement is largely about examining the processes and improving them.

We will explore the notion of processes by looking at an example outside of IT—building a house.

A well-defined process breaks down into an ordered sequence of activities; in our example, building foundations, building walls, and building the roof. Some activities can run in parallel—wiring and plumbing, perhaps—and some are repeated. In most cases there is a wait between one activity ending and the next starting, for instance, calling the plumber and the plumber arriving. A good deal of process improvement comes from analyzing the waiting period. For instance, a building contractor will try to ensure the builders are busy and not waiting for bricks or concrete to turn up.

An activity can itself be a process; wiring a house is a process in its own right. It's a question of what level of detail you want to analyze the process. The lowest level of detail—the activity that is not subdivided—we call a *task*. A task is usually done by one person in one place at one time and requires the application of some skill or resource. Tasks are discrete; they are taken to completion or undone completely. In our example, laying a single brick is a task.

These processes are shown diagrammatically in Figure 12-1.

Not every process flow is a simple set of sequential or parallel activities. In most real-world processes there are alternative routes. For instance, building a house in concrete is somewhat different from building it with bricks. The more you look at the details of a process, the more alternatives you find. In many real-world processes there are loops; laying a wall with bricks is clearly a repetitive process. Sometimes it is the whole process that loops back on itself; put another way, the process is ongoing. The process of checking whether a nuclear reactor is at a safe temperature is, we hope, ongoing. (We say processes have deliverables, so what is delivered from a looping process? In this case, a safe reactor.)

We have seen that processes can be subprocesses of larger processes, but this is not the only relationship between processes. Many processes trigger off another process—what we can call "send and forget." For instance, while building a house, bills are incurred and payment processes are started. If the company is lax about paying its bills, it does not immediately stop the house being built; so from the point of view of the house-building team, the payment process is not their responsibility. In no way could one say that the payment process is a subprocess

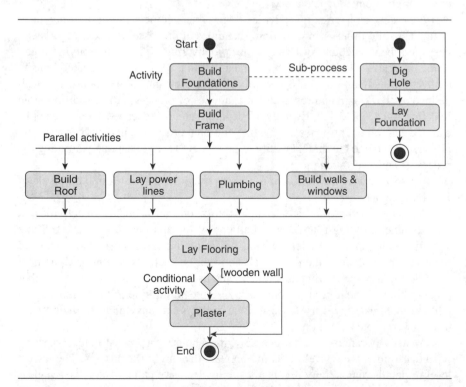

Figure 12-1 Parallel activities and subprocesses

of the house-building process even though the house-building process made the order that triggered the payment.

What we have described so far is a very prescriptive way of viewing processes; the process is a rigid series of activities. We like to think of this as the military approach because of the propensity of the military to drum process steps into raw recruits by insisting they "do it by numbers," that is, shout out numbers for every step of the way. The opposite extreme is not specifying any order or alternative routes, but laying down some rules.

Prescriptive processes can be shown diagrammatically or documented by a series of numbered steps. You can even use structured English (English written using programming language conventions such as indented if statements.)

Rule-based processes are typically documented in normal English (e.g., the rule book in board games, the policies and procedures manual in business), but they could be documented in a formal rules language.

There is a good reason behind the military approach; they "do it by numbers" for efficiency. A prescriptive approach is fast and repeatable, and the process can be followed without thinking. It is hard to be prescriptive for some processes, such as sales, although we've certainly been visited by salesmen at home who have clearly been following rigid rules. Sometimes prescriptive processes turn out to be less prescriptive on closer inspection. At least that seems to be the case when one tries to assemble some flat-pack furniture.

Another alternative is to follow a plan. Builders cannot be prescriptive about all the detailed steps in building any house. They are following a plan. What you then need is a process for converting the plan into a one-off process definition.

Organizations need to analyze processes to improve their efficiency. Having a process diagram, like Figure 12-1, is a useful first step. Analysis may be on error rates, costs, or resource utilization. For the latter, the focus of the analysis is not so much on the activities as on the lines between them because the lines usually represent delays or queues for resources. For instance, when looking at the "building a house" process, the analyst might be interested in ensuring there is no delay waiting for bricks; the analyst might also be looking for a way to ensure the bricks are not delivered before they are needed. Alternatively, the analysis might highlight resource constraints. Suppose there are a limited number of electricians whose task is to wire a number of houses being built at around the same time. The process analysis might try to optimize their usage.

On the other hand, the end result of process analysis may not be small incremental change but massive change. In our house-building example, this could mean changing to use factory-built walls and roofs.

Let us summarize these points:

- A process delivers something, usually some goods or a service.
- A process follows a plan that defines the order of the activities.
- Activities can sometimes be processed in parallel.
- Activities can be conditional, that is, process plans can have path choices.

- An activity can be a process in its own right or it can be a task. A task is an activity that cannot be subdivided and cannot be half done (i.e., if there is a problem, it must be undone). A task is typically done by one person, in one place, at one time.
- A process can start another process (send and forget).
- A process may be ongoing, meaning that it loops back on itself.
- There are two extremes of plans: At one extreme the plan is very prescriptive and defines the steps in detail (the military approach). At the other extreme is a plan that defines the rules that must be obeyed (e.g., build the walls before the roof) but gives maximum flexibility within the rules.
- In practice, process execution may deviate from the plan, especially if something goes wrong.
- An organization will have many processes going on at any one time. The processes are likely to be competing for resources.

12.2 Business processes

Since a business exists to deliver something, be it goods or services, processes are the essence of business. The fundamental activities of every business can be described as processes. All a business does is operate processes, manage processes, sell and market process deliverables, and plan how to change processes in the future. Almost every part of a business can be described in process terms. An example of a high-level planning process is an annual budgeting process. The deliverable is the budget plan.

Typical processes in a manufacturing business include:

- Buying from suppliers
- Controlling goods into and out of warehouses
- Manufacturing
- Delivering
- Processing orders
- Billing

Typical processes for a bank include:

- Opening an account
- Closing an account
- Processing debits and credits
- Handling overdrawn accounts
- Processing requests for information (e.g., in support of a mortgage request)
- Paying interest
- Clearing checks

Typical processes in every business include:

- Paying employees
- Processing expense claims
- Taking on a new employee
- Paying taxes
- Generating annual accounts

Nonbusiness organizations, such as government departments, can also be described in process terms. Processes might deliver health care, a trained army, or a successful election.

12.3   Information and processes

Information in business has little meaning outside of the context of processes. The vast majority of data is either part of the process (e.g., an electronic copy of an order), supports the process (e.g., customer information), or is telling management how processes are going. Without understanding how the data relates to the processes it supports, the data is meaningless.

Most information used in business computer systems falls into one of four categories:

1. Plan objects: Information about the process plans (e.g., an airline timetable or a work schedule)
2. Tracking objects: Information about where an individual process has got to in its execution (e.g., where an order is in the manufacturing/delivery cycle)
3. Resource objects: Information needed by the process, usually information about resources or information external to the business (e.g., customer data, product details)
4. Result objects: Information that is itself a process deliverable. (e.g., a delivery note)

Diagrammatically the relationship between processes and information is illustrated in Figure 12-2.

For every active business process (e.g., for every order being processed), we normally have one tracking object. For order processing, this object is the record of the order. For manufacturing, this object keeps a record of where, in the manufacturing process, the thing is being built. Note that it is an object, not a row, in a relational table; it could be complex. If you are building an aircraft, the manufacturing object would be extremely complex and probably distributed over many systems.

The result of one process might be a resource for another, for instance, a process for introducing a new product creates the product information used by many other processes. One would anticipate that all resource objects have associated

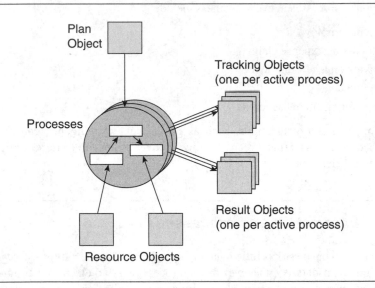

Plan Object

Tracking Objects
(one per active process)

Processes

Result Objects
(one per active process)

Resource Objects

Figure 12-2 Processes and data

business processes that create, maintain, and delete them. This is illustrated in Figure 12-3.

Typically, in implementation terms it is very common to merge the result object with the tracking object, for instance, in order processing—the half finished order tracks how the order processing has progressed, and the completed order is the result.

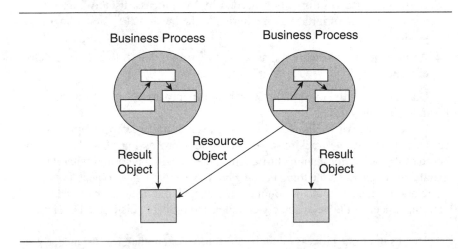

Business Process

Business Process

Result
Object

Resource
Object

Result
Object

Figure 12-3 Business processes for resource objects

12.4   Architecture process patterns

The key decision in business process design is choosing an architecture pattern to follow. There are four basic patterns that can be mixed in various ways, which creates a large number of possible combinations. The four patterns are:

1. Single centralized application

2. Tracking Multiple centralized application

3. Pass through

4. Copy out/copy in

The first two of these are illustrated in Figure 12-4.

Let us take airlines as an example. The Single Centralized solution would be to have one application and one database for all reservations, payment and ticketing, check-in, and boarding processes. A Multiple Centralized solution would be to have multiple applications, possibly physically distributed (e.g., one in each country), but each application would handle all reservations, payment and ticketing, check-in, and boarding processes. The advantage of both these patterns is that the information would need to be stored in the database only once and thereafter not have to be moved anywhere. A second advantage is that high levels of security and reliability can be achieved in centralized data centers. The disadvantage is that

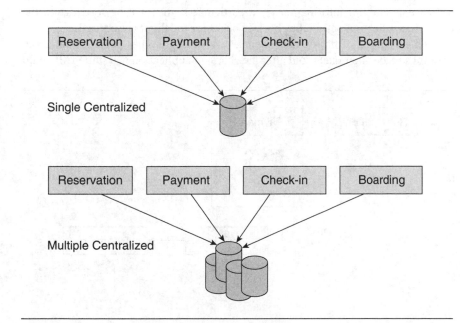

Figure 12-4   Single or Multiple Centralized application

it relies on the network from airports and other places for the data center to be reliable, although this is not usually a problem.

The Multiple Centralized solution works fine if the process-tracking data distributes easily. In the reservation example, it does not. The tracking data consists of two kinds of object—a reservation object (called a Passenger Name Record, PNR, in the industry) and a flight object that records how many seats are taken on this flight on this day. While it would not matter if the PNRs were distributed geographically (e.g., stored in the country the booking is made) or if the flight objects were distributed geographically (e.g., stored in the country the flight starts from), it would help a great deal if the two geographical distributions were aligned. In other words, having to cater for a PNR in one country and flight information in another would make the application considerably more complex.

The third architectural pattern is Pass Through, illustrated in Figure 12-5. Here each application does its job and passes the data to the next application, probably using a deferrable message. The advantage of Pass Through is that each application can be implemented with its own technology, possibly using an off-the-shelf package. A further advantage of Pass Through is that the database can be restructured to look nothing like the database in the sender. It needs only data that is relevant to tracking its internal subprocess, which may be more data or less data than is held for the previous subprocess. Pass Through also allows some efficient and resilient implementations. For instance, in our airline example, the check-in and boarding applications can run at the airport where the flight will depart. The disadvantage of Pass Through is that there may be timing dependencies. In our airline example, all information for a particular flight must be loaded into the check-in application before the check-in desks for the flight are opened.

This example of timing dependencies illustrates another point—what about bookings made and tickets sold after the check-in application has started? It could

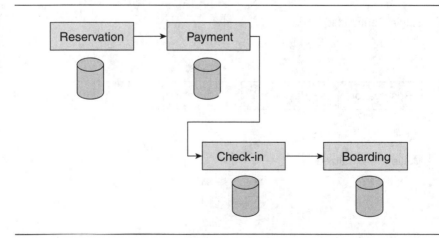

Figure 12-5   Pass Through process

be that in practice the check-in application happily accepts passengers who have tickets it knows nothing about; after all, airlines take reservations for more seats than the plane physically holds. This illustrates another point. When things go wrong or the process deviates from the norm, it's quite common for human intervention to sort out the mess. When you are designing at the process level you must never forget that the IT application is only part of the total picture, and you must be clear what is and is not the responsibility of the application.

The fourth architectural pattern is called Copy out/Copy in, illustrated in Figure 12-6. This starts like a Pass Through—one application sends data to another application, which implements the subprocess. But at the end of the subprocess the data is sent back, probably updated in some form. Many advantages of Pass Through apply equally to Copy out/Copy in. The tracking data can be restructured for the subprocess, and the subprocess can proceed without a connection to the central database. The specific advantage of Copy out/Copy in is that a centralized database has an overall view of what is happening to this process. For instance, a Copy out/Copy in pattern could be used for the airline boarding application. The application could run in a local server at the departure gate. The passenger details could be sent in a flood by the check-in application when the departure application is started and other passenger information could come in dribbles thereafter (message queuing will do this nicely). When the flight has left, the information could be sent back to some centralized application, perhaps for further transmission to the destination airport. The disadvantage of the Copy out/Copy in pattern versus Pass Through is that it is more complicated.

There is a variant of Copy out/Copy in that is a lot more complicated—when there is a requirement to Copy out the same information multiple times. This is the kind of problem that IT configuration management repositories face because more than one programmer wants to work on the same code at the same time. In theory,

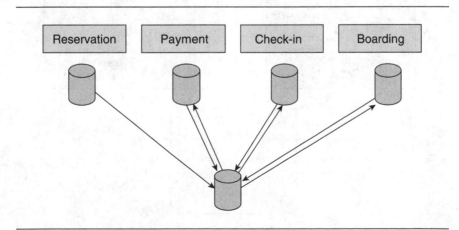

Figure 12-6   Copy out/Copy in process

this problem could be faced in commercial application development. For instance, in an insurance company, several people may want to look at an insurance claim at the same time. The simplest solution though is to revert to a centralized application, and in most cases that suffices.

12.5 Clarification and analysis

In Chapter 11 we discuss design being a process of understanding, brainstorming, clarification, and analysis. Understanding in process-level design is simply understanding the existing or proposed business process. Brainstorming is about looking at the different architectural patterns discussed previously and seeing which one is most appropriate for this process. As noted earlier, the patterns can be combined to use different patterns for different subprocesses.

We normally start clarification by drawing a process implementation diagram. An example process implementation diagram is illustrated in Figure 12-7.

As an aside, many airlines have a centralized solution for reservation, payment, and check-in. Other airlines have a separate check-in application, and in

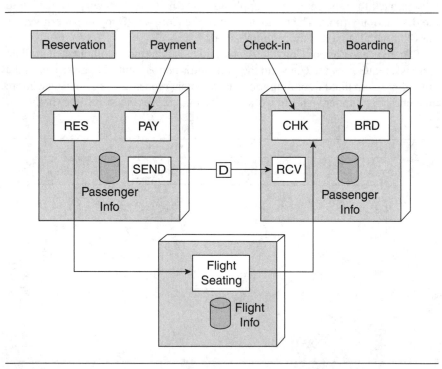

Figure 12-7 Process implementation diagram

some airports check-in to flights is done not by the airlines but by some other organization. The boarding application is often run in a PC at the departure gate.

The purpose of the process implementation diagram is twofold. On the one hand, it shows how process activities and tasks are supported by IT applications. The process activities and task are on the top of the diagram, and the IT applications and services are in the middle. On the other hand, it shows how services depend on other services and data. The dependency on other services is shown by lines for real-time and deferrable messages. Deferrable messages are distinguished from real-time messages by the box with a D in it on the line. The databases are on the bottom of the diagram. The idea is to show how it all hangs together.

There is an art to drawing process implementation diagrams. It's rather tempting to go into a great deal of detail, especially when the business process itself is tortuous and long. First, don't go into any more detail than the task—one person doing one thing at one time. Second, if several tasks are closely related and follow each other and all use the same application and database, then group them together into one box. What we are trying to capture here is the relationship of the process to the implementation. If you need to do process redesign, then you might want a more detailed activity diagram. But trying to put the process activity diagram along with all the implementation information makes the diagram too busy. Third, at the database level, only mention the major tracking and resource objects; don't try and mention everything. Fourth, represent a batch step as a single application. More detail will be needed eventually but that is the job for detailed design. Finally, don't mention any technology; for instance, describe the message flow as real-time or deferrable, not as message queuing. The reason is that you are likely to need help from the business side to understand the process flow, and you don't want to divert the discussion into technology pros and cons.

Sometimes you might want to add further information on the process implementation chart such as the end-user presentation device used or the geographic location of the servers. Only do this if it is particularly important. The primary purpose of the diagram is to focus discussion. It may also serve to document the design, but for that the diagram must be backed up with an explanation so detail can be always left for the text. We would in any event recommend building a list of points for the implementers because ideas and issues will come up that could later be forgotten.

It is important in process implementation design to identify which applications are packages and which applications exist already. It is the job of the next design level, system integration design, to figure out how deep to make the changes. The system integration designers could discover that it is too hard to alter the behavior of these applications, in which case the process-level design will need to be revisited.

If during process-level design you come across an important question you can't answer, it may be worth suspending process-level design and doing a study to explore the issue in more detail. For instance, if the question is a technical one, the study might take the form of a technology proof of concept.

Finally, during clarification you should identify cases where a common process structure can or must be applied. An example of this is a call center that is handling orders and inquiries for many types of product. The processes in place in the call center may impose restrictions on your business process design or on your proposed implementation.

Once the process-level design is clarified, the next step is to analyze it. The idea is simply to pick holes in the design. There are (at least) seven areas for analysis:

1. Performance
2. Resiliency
3. Error handling
4. Data accuracy
5. Timing constraints
6. Migration
7. Flexibility

You will find that when you are selecting the architecture pattern, the discussion will largely be focused on performance and resiliency issues. IT designers in our experience naturally gravitate to these subjects. For the rest of this section we will concentrate on the others, except data accuracy, which has a chapter to itself.

12.5.1 Error Handling

Processes are made up of activities. Activities can be subprocesses in their own right or tasks. Remember that a task is one action being done by one person at one time. If a task or an activity fails, there are two things to worry about:

- What happens to the data that was updated before the failure?
- Who or what receives the error report?

Broadly speaking, there are three approaches.

1. Fix what needs to be fixed and try again.
2. Leave the whole problem for manual reconciliation later.
3. Revert to another process (e.g., manual process).

Each has its own set of problems. For example, suppose a computer fails in the middle of airport check-in. At first the check-in agents might wait for the computer to recover. If it becomes apparent that isn't going to happen anytime soon, then the agents will revert to manual procedures. There are several questions, such as:

- At the departure gate, how do they know who checked in before the failure?
- If the application comes back, how does the application know who has been manually checked-in?

- If the application comes back, what happens to the partially processed check-in data for the person who was in the midst of check-in when the failure occurred?

Error-recovery strategies should be discussed during process-level design because they can alter the functionality of the application.

12.5.2   Timing

We have seen an example of timing issues already in the need for reservation information to be sent to the airline check-in application before check-in commences. In any process implementation where data is sent from application to application, timing may be a problem.

When you look at a process activity diagram, always ask what controls the flow from activity to activity. Sometimes it is the system controlling the flow but often it is something external. In the airline example, the time between when check-in ends and the departure starts is controlled by how long it takes the passenger to walk from the check-in desk to the departure gate. That defines the time window within which the system must send the check-in information to the departure application.

The other consideration for timing is that organizations may have goals that something is done in a certain time duration. For instance, there may be a rule that "urgent packages are delivered by 9:00 P.M. the same day."

12.5.3   Migration

In most cases a new business process replaces an existing business process. Change from one to the other can be sudden or gradual. If done gradually, it can be done subprocess by subprocess or unit by unit; for instance, a new order entry system may switch in for new products only. In the process-level design you must consider how to support the intermediate stages when old and new run together.

12.5.4   Flexibility

There is a huge danger in process-level design. Because you are likely to be laying requirements on what end users will do, there is the possibility that they or their management might refuse to do it or may demand to do something slightly different. Put another way, the team doing the process-level design may not have the authority to make all the changes; you may have to sell the changes rather than impose them.

It helps the smooth running of the project if you can indicate the areas most likely to change. You may be able to alter the design to minimize the impact of change. For instance, if you know they are considering using a mobile device as an interface to an application, then you may want to ensure that the business logic is in one central location.

Another form of flexibility to consider is building the application to handle many kinds of products or many kinds of bank accounts and allowing new products or new bank accounts to be easily added to the application. From the application programmer's point of view, this is the difference between a table-driven application and a hard-coded application. Indications of such flexibility are important and provide valuable information for the implementer.

12.6   Summary

A business process perspective helps in many ways, such as:

- It provides a tool for improving the quality of data by letting you understand where the data comes from, how it is used, and how it affects the business.
- It provides the fault lines where the system will change, which has a direct bearing on deciding how to split an application into components.
- It defines which message flows between processes are deferrable and which must be in real time. This is essential information for building a good middleware implementation.
- It provides the rationale for resiliency requirements.
- It provides the rationale for performance criteria.
- It provides the underlying basis for the discussion about security requirements, especially if we are seeking to protect against internal threats.
- It provides the underlying basis for the discussion about data distribution.

The chapter also discusses process-level design or how to take a business process and decide how to implement the IT applications to support that process. Key points to remember:

- Business processes should be understood by the technical designers.
- Four basic patterns can be used to implement business processes: Single Centralized, Multiple Centralized, Pass Through, Copy out/Copy in. These patterns can be mixed in any combination.
- Using the Pass Through pattern creates smaller, easier-to-develop applications. The data is localized, which has performance advantages but it may have system management disadvantages.
- The Copy out/Copy in pattern has applications that are similar in size to Pass Through but it has an additional application in the center, which increases the complexity but allows for closely tracking the state of the business process.
- Centralization is a better pattern if the data needs to accessed from numerous locations.

- Once a design has been chosen and clarified, it can analyzed by investigating performance, resiliency, error handling, data accuracy, timing constraints, migration, and flexibility.

In summary, most process-level design is about deciding what applications to build and setting the high-level requirements for those applications. It is the major technique for counteracting the tendency to build either silo applications or monolithic monsters.

Function versus process

The distinction between function and process is a subtle but important one for designers. Functions are about what happens, in other words, the end result. Processes are about how it works. There is a hierarchy; you can take a function and describe the process that implements the function. But the process description will be an interacting set of functions. You can then take each of these more detailed functions and describe the process that implements it. This is illustrated in Figure 12-8.

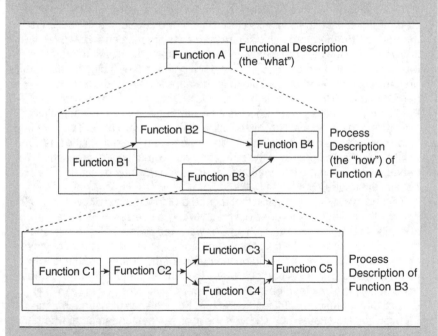

Figure 12-8 Functions and processes

However, you can make a functional hierarchical decomposition that bears no resemblance to the process structure. In fact, this is exactly what most organizations do; it's called an organization chart.

(continued)

Function versus process (*cont.*)

Many design approaches have taken a strongly functional view. Data flow diagrams are about functional composition, not process decomposition, because they show only how information flows between the functions, not the flow of work—that is, the order in which things are done to achieve a result. Use cases focus on a single task, so they lose the business process context.

Clearly, the functional approach often works. Many business processes are straightforward and so well understood by everybody that explicitly highlighting the process flow does not tell anyone anything they didn't know already. A functional approach is also good at automating what people are doing already, like turning paper-based processes into equivalent computer-based processes. Again, it works because the processes are clearly understood.

But functional analysis is a primary reason why IT departments have built silo applications.

The first danger is that the functional approach is departmentally driven. To be fair, it is very difficult to break out of the departmental straightjacket. Departments make the business case, pay for the development, and judge the results. (Furthermore, departments are social groups and have been known to put their own prosperity above that of the organization.) Many business processes cross departmental boundaries; they include order processing, customer relationship management (CRM), and billing, to name but a few. Data quality in particular is a cross-departmental concern. For instance, a sales person submits an order for several items and enters the total price on the first line; all the other lines have zero price. The people in the sales department don't care. Their only concern is reducing the hassle of filling orders. But people in the marketing department are distressed because they need the information to analyze the revenue by-product, not just the total.

Second, functional analysis is not a good tool for analyzing how to change the business. This does not mean that it is useless. Functional analysis does deliver good insight into how systems work now; people can mull over the model and think of other solutions. However, the focus on any process improvement should be on the output of the process, and this is lost in the functional model. A particular case in point is that functional analysis does not tell you whether the traditional order of activities is a trivial historical accident or fundamental to the process. For instance, it is fundamental that you build the house frame before the roof, but not fundamental whether the plumbing or the wiring is done first. Flexible IT applications should not force an arbitrary order to a series of actions because when you come to put a new interface on the old system, the old order will only get in the way.

13

Integration Design

Integration design is a major element of task-level design. It covers the design of two related topics:

- The interaction application to application, and application and end user
- The integrity of the task

More formally, integration design can be seen as the design of protocols, the protocol between application and application, and the protocol between application and end user. Integration design may be complex and difficult, or it may be trivially easy. But even when it is hard it does not take very long, so it's well worth taking the time and effort to put the implementation on the right track.

13.1   The context for integration design

At the beginning of integration design, the following information should be provided from the process-level design:

- An identification of which applications need to be written from scratch or modified
- A list and a (very short) description of the tasks these applications support
- A list of which databases need to be designed or modified and which tasks use which database
- An identification of the data that needs to be sent from one application to another

In all of this information, the level of detail is very low. For instance, the process design may refer to "order forms or order objects" but say very little about what data is in the order form. Process-level design almost certainly has produced a list of design suggestions, ideas, assumptions, and perhaps some business rules. All of this sets the context for integration design.

The information from process-level design is not sufficient; requirements must be obtained from the business representatives to fill out the detail of the task. The way this is handled depends on the processes and methodology of the development teams. Some teams have a systems analyst complete a use case description for every task. (This is well documented in many books, so we don't cover it here.) An eXtreme Programming (XP) team, on the other hand, will probably start from a very simple description of the task and then modify the design as they code the system and discuss the issues with an end user representative. This is fine as long as the programmer or the programming pairs have all the knowledge to do intuitively what we describe in this chapter. Some do, but many don't. If they don't, then we suggest kicking off each task implementation by convening a small group and doing a short integration design exercise.

In addition to a description of the task from the end user's perspective, the integration design group needs to be told the nonfunctional requirements for this task, such as:

- Does the task have critical performance goals?
- Does the task have up time and recovery time goals?
- Does the task have special security requirements?

Parallel with integration design is database design. Most database designers think they should design the database directly from the business rules. Most programmers think the database should be designed to meet their requirements. There is truth on both sides. Since the database supports many tasks, taking the perspective of a single task is dangerous and likely to lead to designs that are incorrect for the business as a whole. Furthermore, there are data-gathering requirements and data integrity requirements that should be enforced for a particular task for the good of the business as a whole, whereas it may be that the end users of the task in question take a more cavalier attitude to the data. (This is discussed in more detail in the Chapter 14.) But database designers should not be oblivious to the needs of the programmer. The database may need to store data that does not support any business rule, for instance, session recovery data and statistics. The conflict between programmers and database designers is a much discussed topic in Internet discussion groups. To alleviate the tension, we suggest that the database designer participate in integration design.

The output from integration design is not program design or even component design. It is simply a description of the input and output messages the program must implement and any session state needed to control the protocols. The integration design taken together with the database design should give the program designer all the information necessary to complete the job with one exception—the layout of the end-user displays. Some processes and methodologies call for further detailed design post task-level design and before coding. This is not the topic of this book.

In large systems, many integration designs follow a similar pattern. If a task follows a pattern that has already been designed, then integration design for that task becomes little more than a discussion with the end-user representative about the dialogue and a check with the database designer that there are no additional data requirements.

At the other extreme, there may be a few tasks that are particularly troublesome, in the worst case leading to reevaluation of the process-level design. The recommendation, as always, is to address the most difficult ones first.

13.2   **Recovery and long transactions**

Before going into the detail on integration design, we discuss the important issue of dialogue recovery.

We noted earlier that business processes typically have tracking objects in the database that keep tabs on how the process is proceeding. The tracking object could be, for instance, an order object in an order processing system or the insurance claim in a claims processing system. When a user is doing a task in a business process, he or she typically has a session with the application. In theory, having a session is unnecessary; however, that would mean, for instance, when processing an insurance claim the user would have to identify the insurance claim with every input to the application. When the insurance clerk has finished one claim, he or she starts working on another, in other words, switches to another instance of the business process and works on that. This is all done in the context of a single security logon to the system, and it is illustrated in Figure 13-1.

Within a task dialogue there may be a series of updates against the database, mostly against the tracking object. But what if there is a failure? Take an airline check-in example; suppose the check-in agent has allocated a seat and printed a

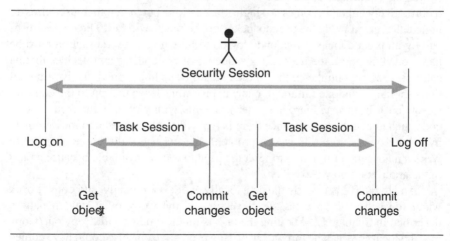

Figure 13-1   Long transactions

baggage tag but then the customer gets frightened, grabs the bag, and runs out of the terminal. Clearly the application should then undo or invalidate all the updates made against the database for this passenger.

In many ways, the whole task dialogue looks like a single transaction. It is atomic—either all the updates need to be made or none of them. It is isolated—when one person is working against a tracking object, that person needs exclusive access. Note that it may not be strictly isolated; for instance, the airline check-in agent needs exclusive access to a passenger's records but not exclusive access to the flight's seating plan. The task needs also to be consistent, meaning that all business rules should be obeyed. And the task updates should be durable. Since the dialogue follows all the transactional ACID properties, albeit in a less strict way, we say that the task is implemented by a long transaction.

Long transactions have always been a thorn in the flesh. For performance reasons, transactions should be short. Even worse, in a long transaction, there is nothing stopping the end user from going away in the middle to have lunch or going home for the evening. If standard transaction facilities are used for long transactions, there is the possibility that a database lock could be held for hours, almost certainly eventually grinding the application to a complete stop.

There are several ways to solve these problems. If the task has one or more reads but only one update, then a simple detection scheme is probably appropriate. The object read contains a counter or a timestamp that indicates when it was last updated. If the counter or timestamp hasn't changed between the time of the first retrieval and the update, then no one else has updated the object in the interim. If the counter or timestamp has changed, someone has been working on the same object at the same time, and the update must be aborted.

For longer tasks, or ones with multiple updates, a "pseudo lock" (a lock enforced by application code) may be appropriate. A pseudo lock is implemented by adding an attribute to the record, which identifies the user who is updating the record. Every input becomes a single transaction, but if another user tries to update the record while the pseudo lock is on, he or she will fail. The biggest difficulty with pseudo locks is that undo logic for the whole long transaction must be hard coded. Suppose the user is in a sequence of ten updates and decides that he can't proceed beyond the sixth. All the updates done in the previous five transactions should be undone (although many applications leave that up to the end user to sort out). In theory, there are other problems with writing your own locking code such as deadlocks; but since there is typically only one pseudo lock grabbed by a long transaction, this isn't a problem. You probably do, however, need to write a management function to reset the pseudo lock to available because a fault in the application may leave it on.

An alternative is to copy the data locally, work on it locally, and copy it back when finished. This is a task-level version of the Copy out/Copy in pattern described in Chapter 12. Aborting the task is much simpler with Copy out/Copy in—the local copy can be thrown away. However, someone else could have copied out the same object at the same time. When he or she copies it in, it overwrites the earlier update! Both the techniques discussed earlier can be applied. If a counter or timestamp is used, the second copy in fails. If a pseudo lock is used, then the second person is not allowed to copy the object out in the first place.

In a sense, during a long transaction, the user "owns" the process tracking object. It is worth investigating whether there are additional long-term ownership issues. Processing an insurance claim is an example. There are a number of actions against the claim, which correspond to short transactions, but there is a longer period during which one person has ownership of managing the claim. It could even be that that person keeps a local copy of the claim on his or her work-station and every now and then copies in the latest updates. The interesting busi-ness point about ownership is that ownership can be moved. It is possible, for instance, to copy out data to one user and move the copied data to another user, and for the second user to copy in the modified data.

A similar set of issues can exist in an application-to-application interaction, especially if one of the applications is little more than a thin shell over an old end-user interface. An important skill in integration design is knowing how deep to cut away old code to form a base on which to build a new interface. This subject is discussed in Chapter 15.

13.3   How to do integration design

As discussed in earlier chapters, we see design as a process of understanding, brainstorming, clarifying, and analyzing. Integration design is no different. Under-standing and brainstorming are, we think, self-explanatory. In this section we want to discuss clarification and analysis.

We do clarification in integration design by using a task/message flow dia-gram. It's our invention, so you won't find this documented anywhere else. It works fine for us, but if you have a better alternative, that's fine too. An example is shown in Figure 13-2. This shows the message/task diagram for an order entry application.

A task/message flow diagram is rather like a UML sequence diagram. Time flows down the page, and the diagram shows messages being sent from the user on the left side of the diagram to applications in the middle of the diagram. But message/task diagrams differ from sequence diagrams in several important ways. First, people, or end users, are allowed into the diagram. Second, rectangles with light grey lines indicate the scope of a task. In each task, people interact with the system in a task dialogue. In Figure 13-2 two tasks are shown; one to become a member of an organization and another to order goods from the organization. The line connecting the stick figures indicates one person is doing both tasks. Third, the grey vertical slabs aren't objects; they are applications doing some processing on behalf of the task. The applications could be the latest up-to-date Web services, or they could be an online transaction system developed 20 years ago. The point

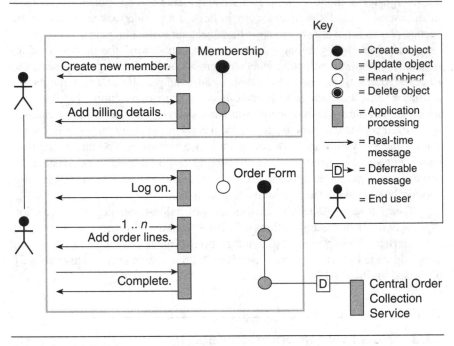

Figure 13-2   Task/message diagram

is, there is a need to capture the fact that something is processing the message. We don't have to worry what that something is.

Fourth, a task/message diagram documents read/writes to persistent data. In Figure 13-2, the little circles are all order form objects or membership objects. The lines between the circles indicate that the same object is being used at different points. The black circle represents object creation; the grey circles represent object updates. We also use a white circle to represent objects being read, and a black circle with a white circle around it to represent object deletion, but they aren't shown on the example diagram. The data could be in a database, a simple data file, or even a special system-provided log. The important point is that the data is persistent because persistency is crucial to recovering the task if something goes wrong.

Sometimes the diagram would be too cluttered if all the state updates were added, so you may need to be selective. The two main criteria for selectivity are:

1. The data is important in the follow-up analysis.

2. The data helps clarify the purpose of the task.

The fifth difference between a task/message diagram and a UML sequence diagram is that task/message diagrams record whether the messages are real-time or deferrable. By default, messages are real-time; but a D in a box on the line (as in the line in the bottom right-hand corner) indicates that the message is deferrable.

In a nutshell, a task/message diagram is about expressing the integration requirements in a manner that is as technology neutral as possible. The reason for technological neutrality is to identify the essence of a proposal without being distracted by arguments about technology. The idea is to clarify the integration proposal, figure out the chain of messages between the applications, and make sure we understand the purpose of each application in the total delivery of the service.

In practice, people often have strong opinions about technology; therefore, holding off discussion and selection of the technology while you draw the task/message diagrams is sometimes close to impossible. You can't hold them off for too long, so the next step is to select the technology. When this is done, it can be recorded by overlaying boxes on the task/message diagram, as in Figure 13-3. (We've used a different example because the order entry application would be rather boring here.)

This ends the clarification stage. The real meat of integration design comes in the analysis, and the task/message diagram is the central artifact here also.

Analysis is broken down into eight areas:

1. Scalability and performance
2. End-to-end data integrity
3. Security
4. System management

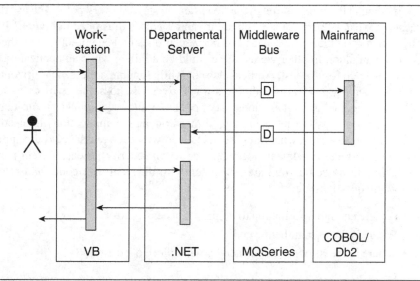

Figure 13-3   Technology choice

5. Enterprise data consistency

6. Ease of implementation

7. Flexibility for change

8. IT strategy compliance

The output from all these analysis tasks is the same. First, there may be modifications to the task/message flow. Second, there will be a list of points to consider in the detailed design. As the analysis phase progresses, this list grows longer and longer. Third, various "problem scenarios" can be identified. These are usage patterns that will put the system under particular stress for one reason or another. Identifying problem scenarios not only helps build test scripts, it also helps other project members understand the design.

At any stage during the analysis, if the changes are too radical, you should revisit the earlier analysis areas to check whether the assumptions and the conclusions still hold. We now describe the analysis tasks in more detail.

Scalability and performance analysis starts by taking the data volumes for each task and calculating the numbers of messages. From this you should be able to identify possible network bottlenecks. You might be able to make a rough estimate of the elapsed time of each process and from there calculate the number of concurrent processes required. Much more difficult is to estimate the IO, but you might be able to calculate an order of magnitude estimate of this as well, taking into account that the implementation will probably introduce many additional IO operations. For actual sizing, it is always best to estimate the size by projecting from similar systems of similar complexity rather than try to calculate from first principles.

End-to-end data integrity analysis is done by taking a task/message diagram and methodically tracing through the flow, step by step. At every point, you ask the question, what happens if there is a failure here? This is illustrated in Figure 13-4. The X marks on the vertical slabs and horizontal lines indicate points where there might be a failure. In other words, there could be a failure while an application is executing code for this task (vertical slab) or while sending a message (horizontal line). Data integrity analysis almost always gives rise to some changes to the task/message flow, as well as a long list of points for the programmer to consider.

Security analysis has a technology dimension and an application dimension. The central question is, what roles are associated with each message? If the application spans security contexts (see Chapter 10 on security), then different parts of the task/message diagram are associated with different user codes and roles. Follow-up questions are:

- Is there enough information to do proper access control?
- Where is the user authenticated?
- Where is access control done and by what piece of software?

In the overview of design given in Chapter 11, we indicate that security logical design should proceed parallel with dialogue design. This means that before you

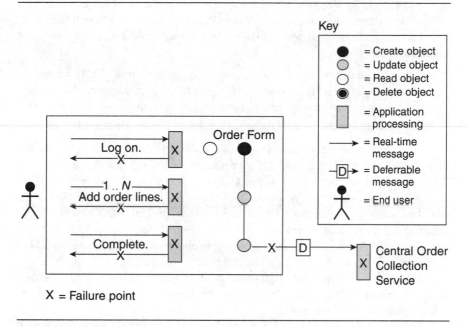

X = Failure point

Figure 13-4   Failure points

can answer these three questions, you need to have developed a strawman security design. (This is discussed in Chapter 11.) Sometimes it is worth creating a few task/message diagrams to illustrate different scenarios before considering security design in detail. Subsequent task/message flows will be handled easily (unless a flaw is found in the security design).

System management analysis can also become very technical, so for high-level design you try to identify the main issues and to think about them sufficiently to see if there are any show stoppers. The two main concerns are monitoring and configuration/version control. As mentioned previously, during the analysis you should be building a list of problem scenarios. For system management analysis, you want to look at each scenario and ask the question, how can this scenario be monitored sufficiently to detect problems before the end users notice? This analysis will focus on the following areas:

- How to trap key events early
- How to report them accurately without being flooded with information
- And, possibly, how to fix them automatically

Configuration and version control should consider not only how to distribute changes but also how to detect a version mismatch.

As with security analysis, the first time through system management analysis may trigger the logical design of system management. The earlier comment applies here too; it is sometimes worth delaying the system management design until a few task/message diagrams have been drawn to illustrate different scenarios.

Enterprise data consistency analysis is a tricky area. There are two main questions:

- Is this design dependent on the accuracy and completeness of data from another application? If so, is the data currently accurate and complete? If not, what needs to be done to make it accurate and complete?
- Does this design duplicate data held elsewhere? If so, does it matter?

The questions are easy enough to pose. Answering them can be difficult, and this is when having the database designer present pays dividends. A wider issue is that these questions have a horrible propensity for "opening a can of worms." Data across large organizations is notoriously inconsistent. There is also the chance that your budget won't stretch to fix all the problems you find, in which case the application scope must be redefined or, in the worst case, the application canceled.

Ease of implementation analysis is largely about answering the question, has your organization done something like this before? If it hasn't, then you should do a short proof of concept study before the main project gets under way. The purpose is to try out the technology and build some confidence that your organization (plus helpers) can make it work.

Ease of implementation is not only about familiarity with the technology. It is also about how tight the coupling is between requester and provider. A tightly coupled interface is more likely to fail under test and more likely to change as the implementation evolves. A loosely coupled interface allows the two applications to be developed more independently. Since the requester and provider often use different technology and, in big implementations, are developed by different teams, this makes a great deal of difference.

The last two analysis points look toward the future.

Flexibility analysis involves thinking about how the system might need to change after the initial release. The technique is to brainstorm possible future extensions to the application. In this example, we would expect this analysis to consider whether the back-end interface is appropriate for other new interfaces, such as orders taken from a call center or from mobile phones. They should also consider what would happen if the application were extended to other kinds of product. Please note, we do not recommend trying to anticipate changes in the code, but we do recommend checking for structural impediments in the design that prevent change.

IT strategy compliance analysis is the final point to consider. It is simply a check that the choices fit the chosen strategy. For instance, if IT strategy is for Java but the project calls for a .NET implementation, then perhaps the technology should be reconsidered. Alternatively, if the reasons for .NET are good ones, then perhaps the long-term strategy should be questioned. The project, especially if it is a big one, might need to be intermeshed with some long-term infrastructure plans such as upgrading the network. Of course, the impact on schedules and budget must be taken into account.

13.4   What makes a good integration design?

We will start by revisiting the concept of loosely coupled and tightly coupled integration.

As discussed in Chapter 6, there is an application and a technical dimension to coupling in integration design. It is possible to have loosely coupled applications, meaning that they can be developed relatively independently, and tightly coupled technology, meaning that configuring the system software correctly is painful and error prone. Observe that tightly coupled applications and loosely coupled technology is also possible, as many organizations are about to discover with their brand new Web services applications. The analysis phase described previously is intended to identify the issues. In particular, the analysis of end-to-end data integrity will help you understand coupling in the application dimension, and the analysis of system management, for example, concerning configuration version control, will help you understand coupling in the technology dimension. The strings keeping the technology tight (so to speak) are considerably looser if your organization is experienced in the technology, so the analyses of ease of implementation and strategy compliance are also significant. This chapter is about application design so, from here on, we concentrate on application-level coupling.

Tightly coupled applications are characterized by many short, real-time messages and complex session state. Practically any application that uses a screen-scraped version of an old application is tightly coupled. An example is a departmental server that provides a front end to order entry and product information, and is tightly coupled with a central order management server because it sets up a new session for each order and sends the order details down line by line. Loosely coupled applications are characterized by a few large messages and no session state. A loosely coupled order entry server would gather all the information about an order locally and ship the completed order to the central server when ready. There are levels of looseness, so to speak. A very loose order entry server would have a local copy of the product information and the customer information. A slightly tighter implementation might have central product and customer information, accessed through real-time messages, but still cache the order locally until it has finished. These gradations of coupling are shown in Figure 13-5.

There are advantages to loosely coupled applications. They are resilient; the order entry server can store orders when the centralized order processing server is down. They are scalable; it is possible to have many order entry servers and one central server. And they perform well; in this example at least, the use of the network is efficient. The interaction with the central order server is stateless, and if the completed order form is in XML, the application allows great flexibility to change any server with minimal impact on the others.

But there are disadvantages, too. Loosely coupled applications work nicely when you can have a local server doing work and shipping data to a central server. It works less nicely when data has to go in the opposite direction, from the center to the local servers. In our order entry example, this would be the case if there

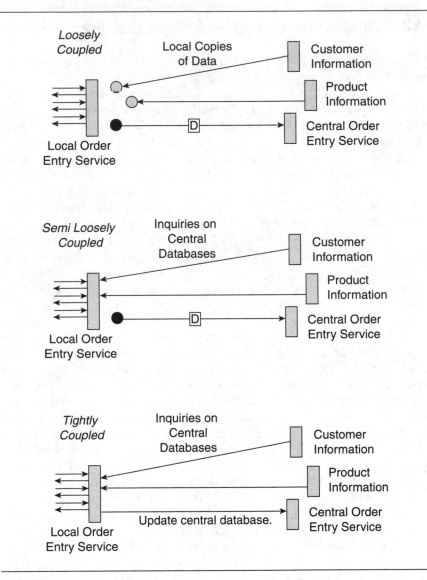

Figure 13-5   Tight and loose coupling

were local copies of the product and customer data. From an efficiency and resiliency point of view, this might work well if the data quantities were not large, and a regular, say nightly, copy of the data were sufficient for synchronization purposes, as long as the synchronization was automated. Broadcasting updates to the customer and product data is also possible but you would have to build in procedures to handle the case of resynchronization of the complete database after a failure. If it becomes necessary for changes to the product or customer information to be visible to all users immediately, then it is probably better to take the semi-loosely or tightly coupled approaches and access that data from central servers. In summary, it comes down to whether the data can be distributed easily.

A more difficult question is, which solution is easier to implement? The loosely coupled solution needs logic for synchronizing the database and reading local copies of the database. The tightly coupled solution requires more integration testing, as noted earlier, but probably requires less code because there is no local database and no synchronization. There is a catch, though. If the nature of the interface to the central server does not suit the requirements of the local server (e.g., it expects an old screen format), then all code-saving gains might be lost. Modernization of existing applications is discussed in a Chapter 15.

But what about tiers? It would be possible to take the loosely coupled design illustrated here and implement the local server with an N-tiered architecture with, say, a presentation tier, a logic tier, and a data tier. Tiers make a great deal of sense as a way to structure program design, but that can be left to the detailed design that follows integration design. To introduce tiers into integration design, they must justify their presence; they must pay their way in terms of introducing additional facilities such as better scalability or better security. Look at Figure 13-6. The N-tiered implementation of the local application, shown at top of Figure 13-6, creates a complex design since two extra tightly coupled interfaces have been introduced. The normal justification for putting the presentation tier in another box is to allow for multiple presentation technologies. If that is what we want to do, it makes more sense to have centralized logic and data tiers. If so, it makes sense to merge them with the central order entry server. If you do all that—centralize the presentation and data tiers and merge back with the central order entry server— you have recreated the tightly coupled solution illustrated in the bottom of Figure 13-5. Thus the loosely coupled solution is a good design only if it makes sense for all the three tiers of the local order entry application to go into one box, in other words, become one application. Does it make sense? There is no scalability issue since the loosely coupled solution gives scalability. The downside of this design is that when you implement a new presentation layer (for a different end-user channel), you must replicate the logic and data layer code. Is this so serious? Only when the complexity of the logic and the data tiers are great. Look now at the bottom of Figure 13-6. Here the logic tier gets the customer and product information directly from the central servers. The benefit of this design is to reduce the complexity of the local order entry application, making the logic and data tiers trivial. In this design it is reasonable to replicate the logic and data tiers for different presentation code. The conclusion from all this rather tortuous argument is that the semi-loosely coupled solution is probably the best as long as the tiers in the local order entry application are all run in the same physical machine.

We hope it is clear that there are many ways to implement a task. In the argument for a semi-loosely coupled solution just presented, it would not take much in

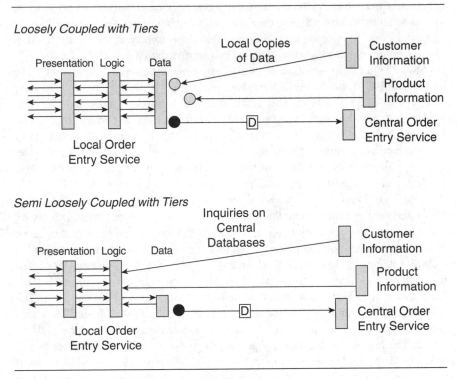

Figure 13-6   Tiers in loosely coupled designs

the way of additional constraints or facts to tip the preferred solution to another solution.

Arguments in integration design range around the use of tiers and the use of tightly coupled versus loosely coupled linkage. If you are finding it hard to reach an agreement, take two or more strawman designs and for each go through the eight analysis points. Hopefully, a clear cut winner will emerge.

13.5   Summary

In this chapter we discuss integration design. Integration design is one of the second-level design tasks; the other very important second-level design task is database design.

Key points to remember:

- Integration design is a short design task used to identify the elements of a distributed solution and ensure that the solution hangs together as an integrated whole.

- The flow of data can be shown in a task/message diagram. This provides a visual prop for understanding and analyzing the integration issues.
- Every task, which corresponds to every use case, should have a task/ message diagram. Often one task/message diagram suffices for many similar tasks.
- The design process consists of, as usual, understanding the requirements, brainstorming solutions, clarifying one or more chosen solutions, and analysis. It might be necessary to loop around steps if the chosen solution is found to be flawed.
- Points for analysis are scalability and performance, end-to-end data integrity, security, system management, enterprise data consistency, ease of implementation, flexibility for future change, and IT strategy compliance.

The next chapter examines some database issues.

14

Information Access
and Information Accuracy

In Chapter 11 we indicate that in our concept of levels of design the task level is the point at which database design should occur. In this chapter, we start by making a few comments on how database design fits in the levels of design scheme and then pick up on two major issues—information access requirements and information accuracy. Especially when it comes to information, almost all organizations are not starting from scratch; databases already exist, often in profusion. A large part of this chapter is devoted to the thorny issue of what to do with existing databases.

During the business process level of design, you identify key data object classes because most IT-intensive business processes are unintelligible unless you have some idea what the tasks are doing to the data. But simply identifying objects is just the very beginning of database design. The act of identifying object types within the context of the processes will, however, start to give you an understanding of the data accuracy requirements. For instance, in our airline check-in example, the seating plan for the flight must be synchronized across the reservation, check-in, and boarding applications. One issue that should have come up in the analysis phase of the business process level design is, what happens if a plane with a different seating plan is substituted for the scheduled plane? The business decision is whether this is handled only in the boarding application or whether the check-in and seat reservation databases are changed to reflect the new reality. Note that decisions can be made about the information without having a database design. If the intent is well understood by all participants in business process level design, then little more is needed except perhaps a glossary of terms.

Task-level design consists of various parallel design activities, one of which is database design. The process-level design tells us what databases need to be defined, whether it is one or many. In practice, the input requirements from database design manifest themselves only as the tasks are examined one by one. What may not be evident from the task descriptions are all the business rules, in particular the data integrity rules. We encourage database designers to participate in the task-level design exercise, but you need a parallel study to gather rules, if only data structure and integrity rules.

There are many, many books on database design, so there seems little point in giving a shortened version in this book. We are assuming that you know how to do this or know a person who does. Instead we focus on four topics that are of keen interest to IT architects because they have such a strong influence on the overall design. They are:

1. Information access
2. Information accuracy
3. Shared data or controlled redundancy
4. Integration with existing databases

14.1   Information access

The requirements for information access differ according to the user. We touch on this subject in Chapter 6, and for your convenience we have duplicated Figure 6-2 in Figure 14-1. In Chapter 6 the focus is on the kinds of middleware. In this section we focus on the design questions of who uses the data and whether they should use a data mart or data warehouse.

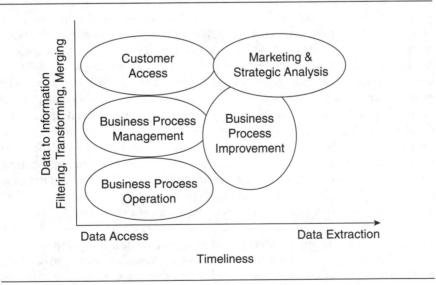

Figure 14-1   Data access users

In the top right corner of this diagram is the territory of data marts and data warehouses. This technology is predicated on copying the data from the production system to the data mart/warehouse system. Before the data is loaded in the target system, it can be processed in several ways:

- It can be reformatted. Internal codes can be changed to meaningful text.
- It can be filtered. Unwanted rows can be thrown out.
- Unwanted attributes can be thrown out.
- Data from several databases can be merged.
- Data from two or more tables can be merged ("joined" in database parlance).
- Summary data can be calculated and the detailed information removed.

The notion of copying and merging from several databases is illustrated in Figure 14-2 (duplicate of Figure 6-4).

Most of these reformatting operations can be done on production data. People want to use a separate database for two fundamental reasons: performance and historical data.

The overhead of doing queries on the production data can seriously affect production performance (discussed in Chapter 8). But the impact on other users is not the only performance concern. Using another database allows the data to be

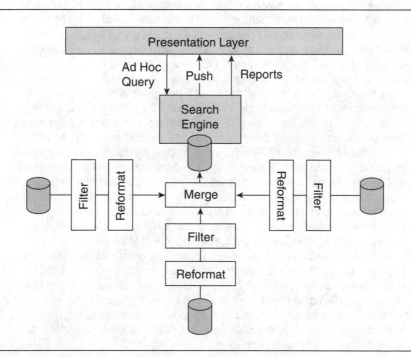

Figure 14-2   Business intelligence server

reformatted more efficiently for access. There is a great deal made in the literature about "denormalization" of data warehouse data. This is largely about turning internal codes into text by joining lookup tables with data tables (e.g., turning a code like "LHR" into "London Heathrow").

A further reason to copy the data is that the query database might hold records for a longer period than the production data. Arguably, there should be an independent archive database since there is often a need to store raw historical data as well as data converted into a format suitable for querying. (As an aside, there is an opportunity for the database vendors to attack the problems of archive data directly. Why not have data such as bank credit and debit records stored once in a special archive database that is visible from both the production database and the data warehouse database?) Note, however, that there are some complex technical issues in searching the archive (see the box entitled "Historical data and format changes").

Historical data and format changes

Over a period of time, the data structure of an object changes—new attributes will be added, changed, and deleted. This creates a problem with existing production data and with data archives.

There are two alternative approaches to this problem: Live with multiple versions or try to convert all the old data to the new format. At an operational level, the second option may not be easy. First, you may have to invent new data fields, and second, the reorganization of large historical collections of data may take an age, especially if a field being changed is used in an index. But even if these challenges are easily overcome, there may be a more fundamental reason not to attempt a reorganization. If, for instance, you make radical changes to the order processing system, it could be that an order from before the change and an order from after the change are so different there is no direct correspondence between many of the attributes.

This is an issue not only with changing the database schema; it could be an issue with the data itself. Suppose you have product table and each product has a style number, and then you decide to repackage the product so components that were part of one style are moved to another style. At the same time, you create a bunch of new styles. A historical search to find out how much of something you sold becomes a difficult query, which can be solved only by someone with an intimate knowledge of the product history.

So what's the solution? You have to make a pragmatic compromise. If the changes are slight and reorganizing the data is feasible, go for it. If the changes are severe, then start a new version of the historic data and have users merge the data from both databases if they want to see the complete picture. It's not a clean solution, but there is no elegant answer. You might want to consider adding a version number to each table in the archive or warehouse in anticipation of change.

We have so far used *data mart* and *data warehouse* synonymously. Many would take violent disagreement to that stance. The thinking behind the concept of a data mart was to have a cheap and cheerful search facility without the enormous effort of creating an enterprise data warehouse. The counterview is that if you create a number of data marts, in the future it will be hard to merge them into a larger data warehouse to create a better enterprise view of the information. Unfortunately, both views are right; their criticism of their opponents is spot on. The consensus view—if there is a consensus—seems to be that you should focus on building a data warehouse carefully and incrementally, and implement any data marts by taking the data from the data warehouse.

We have not mentioned data replication technology. When people discuss data replication, they are usually not thinking of classic data mart or data warehouse applications. Instead, they are thinking about the issues of replicating comparatively small amounts of data to large numbers of users, in particular for mobile users who do not always have access to the production data. Examples are copying product information to a mobile sales force. This problem has unique challenges, and to do it justice requires more room than we are prepared to give it because it is tangential to the main trust of this book.

One way to wend through this morass of different technologies, all vying for our attention, is to build a clearer picture of the users and their requirements. This we now attempt to do.

14.1.1   Basic process information

Everyone in business operations needs access to some basic information, and every one of our object types—tracking objects, resource objects, and plan objects—needs some basic online inquiry facilities. This is to satisfy questions such as: Is this product still available? How much does it cost? What styles do I need? Is this bank account overdrawn?

Some Fourth-Generation Language (4GL) generator products, such as Unisys EAE (Enterprise Application Environment), save large amounts of programming effort simply by generating all these inquiry screens for you.

Currently this kind of information is usually separated from HTML documents available over the Web. In the future there will be more integration. For instance, a button on the product information screen could retrieve the product overview manual or the brochure. Or when products are deleted, the product brochure could be automatically updated with "no longer available" on the front cover.

14.1.2   Process management

This is the basic management information; in the past it was (ok, still is) provided by overnight reports that were (are) printed and distributed in the morning. The kinds of information provided include:

- Status reports, for example, telling a sales manager the orders taken in the last week, month, or year.
- Errors, for example, what orders have errors in them? What invoices haven't been paid? What accounts could not be processed last night?
- Statistics, for example, stock levels, sales figures—how many of each product line have been sold across the company and in each geographical area?
- Trend analysis of key items, which is required for demand forecasting.

All these reports have something in common—they report about what is happening in the business processes. It is information for people monitoring the business processes in contrast to the previous category, which is for people who are part of the business process.

Increasingly, this information is becoming available more online. For instance, the daily report might still be a useful notion but it can come in the form of a spreadsheet sent by e-mail or put into a Web page.

Programming reports is a great deal of work. Furthermore, it is never ending; managers always want something different. There are many products available for report generation, typically built around SQL queries processed directly on the database. Given that networking and disk costs are declining, it is becoming more economical to ship large quantities of data daily to local servers, even to workstations.

One consideration is to use data mart technology. This is not complex data mining—that comes later. Data marts, per se, do not solve all the problems of process management information access; you might still generate and distribute reports, but you would hope that most reports would be replaced by users accessing the data mart directly. They won't do this unless there is a good user interface; these users are not power database query users. But there is not a strong requirement to do extensive reformatting of the data since, for process management, you typically want to see the data as it is seen by the process workers. If they use codes, the process administrator is likely to want to see the same code; after all, the administrator might be responsible for assigning the codes. The advantages of using data marts increase when the raw data is in multiple production databases.

14.1.3   Process improvement

Process improvement starts by analyzing the dynamics of the business process. Questions that need to be answered are, where are the delays? Where is the cost? Where are the errors coming from? The IT system cannot answer all these questions but in theory it could answer them a good deal better than it usually does in practice. For instance, the time taken for the order to be submitted, fulfilled, and distributed could be captured simply by storing a few date and time attributes in the order record. The error rate from orders could be captured. Perhaps this information is being collected and analyzed more than we think, but we suspect people rarely think of gathering basic process improvement data when they are designing a system.

One generic issue is that the business process flow from order, manufacture, and distribution is frequently implemented by sending the data from machine to machine, so there is no picture of the complete process. This isn't implemented in many systems now, but in future business process management products will probably make it easier. In the terminology of Chapter 12, people will start implementing more Copy out/Copy in instead of Pass Through. One reason for this trend is because electronic business is exposing the business processes to the outside world. In our example above, people want to know what's happened to their orders—which brings us to the customer view.

14.1.4   Customer view

With the Web, customers will increasingly want information about products, prices, account status, and the status of their orders. These, in the main, are the same information requests discussed earlier in the section on basic process information.

It is likely for security reasons that you will want to treat customers as a separate presentation channel from internal users. You will probably want to provide some screen that gives a customer-oriented view of the data. The code behind this display may need to process some additional business process logic and also have some additional security checks.

Note that data marts are inappropriate for typical customer access. Customers want to see the most up-to-date data. If they submit an order and then immediately look to see what orders they have in the system, they will be very confused if the order they just submitted is not there.

14.1.5   Marketing and strategic business analysis

Marketing people need access to the data to help them design new marketing programs and to track the program's progress. The facility required for tracking campaign progress is to another process management report, as discussed previously.

An effective marketing campaign must have a well thought-out target, that is, a list of customers to try to sell to. Targets are usually defined by factors such as age, wealth, and particularly what the customer has bought in the past. This relies on good sales records and good customer data.

Strategic business analysis—in other words, deciding the business direction—has much in common with marketing from an information access point of view. Both have a requirement to look at long-term sales trends and analyze them by customer type, by geographic region, by product type, and so on. This is the classic data warehouse type application. The sales data is the central "facts" file and the other data provides the dimensions along which the facts are analyzed. Almost certainly strategic business analysts would also like to do a trend analysis of the kind of data we discuss in Chapter 12 in the category of process improvement. The potential of what you could analyze is almost unlimited.

14.1.6   Summary of requirements for information access

There are several points that come out from this quick review.

- The requirements are varied. They range from access of a single object and simple reports on a collection of objects to highly complex searches over many objects. There is no single solution; you need a blend of strategies for the different requirements.
- The requirements are changing constantly. You can try to stop the continual flow of change requests by giving people the whole data and let them get on with it, but even this may not work; the people may ask for information that isn't in the database, they will ask for explanations of how the data got to be as it is, and they might need help on the query tools.
- Many of the reporting requirements are reports about business processes. The data is a record of current and past business processes, and business management is trying to reconstruct what happened from the data. If there is no understanding in the IT department of the business processes, it will be hard to communicate well with the users.
- If IT support for a single business process is dispersed over several systems, there will be a requirement to bring the data together to create a total view of the process.
- There is a requirement to reformat data to be more understandable, but people want to see the raw data as well.

What this amounts to is that you cannot manage information access projects the same way you build a transaction processing system. It is more volatile. This is a final reason for putting information access on different machines separate from the operational systems; the operational application has much more stringent standards for testing and security, and you don't want to undermine this discipline by having programmers perpetually tinkering with reports.

Sometimes there seems to be an insatiable demand for information. Provide a good service for information access, and you will get many more requests for change.

14.2   Information accuracy

In Chapter 1 we present an example of an organization changing its IT systems to do business on the Web. One of the major issues this highlights was the need for accurate information, consistent across all copies of the data. At last we have gotten around to discussing this subject.

Information access is only as good as the data. One of the largest and most frustrating problems with many IT systems is the inaccuracy of the data.

Information inaccuracies have several sources:

- Information is out of date. The customer's name has changed and no one has updated the database. As a general comment, if the database is telling you a fact, it is useful to know when that fact was recorded.
- Wrong conclusions are drawn from the data. For instance, you might know what you've sold and what you maintain, but neither of these figures tells you who actually uses the product.
- Information is duplicated and you don't know which is the right version.
- Information was input incorrectly.

A subtle example of something halfway between "drawing the wrong conclusions" and "inputting wrong data" is synonyms. Say there is a customer called "Really Big Things Corporation." It might be input in the database as "RBT," "R. B. T.," "RBT Corp," "Really Big Things," and so on. You can't say any are really wrong. Furthermore, if you are dealing with a large organization you are likely to have several customer numbers, many contact names, and several delivery addresses, especially if you are dealing with them internationally. Finally, with all the merger and demerger activity, names change and two customers become one and one becomes two.

But while there are some inherent problems with data accuracy, IT applications often make it much worse. It is very common that most of the information about a business process is gathered right at the beginning of the business process (e.g., renting a car). The person entering the data just wants to get the job done with a minimum of fuss. For instance, the name of the customer may be entered in the order form, hence all the different spellings of the customer's name. Also, if the order has many order lines, the sales person might enter the price for all the items as zero, except one, just because he or she can't be bothered to divide the price among the items. The fundamental problem is that the person entering the data has no incentive to get it right. The solution is to force the data entry to be good but to do it in such a way that the user is being helped rather than hindered. For instance, for the customer name problem, the system could provide a list of customers rather than have the user type the name. Even better, the application could also analyze the name as it was typed and suggest which customers it might be. This is similar to the way most e-mail systems work with names these days. Furthermore, adding a new customer should only be possible from one system (with possibly the information being disseminated to others). The problem of prices in the order lines could be solved by the application picking up the price automatically from the price file. The only price manipulation from the sales staff would then be to fill in the discount field. Unfortunately, these changes add considerably to the complexity of the data entry application and the investment can be hard to justify. (The sales department is happy with the system as it is!)

Many organizations have data duplication, especially of product data and customer data. Customer data is particularly prone to problems. In a financial institution, it is likely that every financial product (investments, loans, mortgages, etc.) has its own customer data. What organizations want now is a consolidated view of all the customers' accounts. This is essential for "customer relationship management" systems, which means understanding the customers better by knowing more about the extent of their dealings with the organization. Suppose there are two customer tables in two different databases, how do you merge the data to form one table of good data? With great difficulty. There are at least three major problems to overcome:

1. How do you know you are talking about the same object? For instance, how do you know that customer "Fred" in table A is the same as customer "Fred" in table B?

2. How do you know whether an attribute is the same? Matching attributes can become quite complex. For instance, an address attribute might be {LINE1, LINE2, LINE3} in one database and {HOUSE NUMBER, ROAD NAME, CITY, STATE, ZIP} in another. (Even if both were in the latter format, you would still have problems with international addresses because they don't have the same structure.)

3. If the data for one attribute of the same object is different in the two databases, what then?

The last problem is unsolvable. The notion of taking the name from one database, the address from another, and the telephone number from a third is laughable. It could be solved in theory if every attribute (yes, every attribute, not every object) has a timestamp that indicates when it was last updated and the latest attribute from all candidate records would be taken. We have never heard of anyone doing this for the obvious reason—it would require a good deal of coding and a massive increase in disk space, and it would incur a considerable processor overhead.

As an aside, this example looks at two databases, but we have heard of a financial organization that had 13 sets of customer records, a Telco that had 65, and a retailer that had a separate customer database in each store—over one thousand of them.

In the next section we examine the issue from the perspective of someone developing a new application. Then we look at the issues of information accuracy in existing systems.

14.3   Shared data or controlled duplication

There are two basic approaches to keeping common data: shared data and controlled duplication. They are illustrated in Figure 14-3.

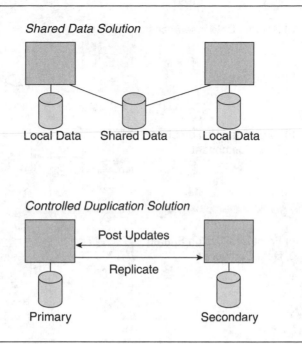

Figure 14-3   Shared data versus controlled duplication

14.3.1   Shared data

The shared data solution implies a common database, typically separate from other databases. There are three ways to implement shared data, which are illustrated in Figure 14-4.

Remote database access has the main application calling the shared data using technology like ADO .NET. While superficially attractive, there are some good reasons for not taking this approach:

- It has poor performance since network traffic is greater than other solutions, especially if SQL commands must be parsed by the database server.
- Some remote database access technology does not support two-phase commits, so updates cannot be synchronized.
- The structure of the shared database is hard coded into many dispersed applications, making schema changes difficult to manage and implement. Put another way, the SQL commands that access the shared data are scattered everywhere.

The first two reasons are why, wherever possible, the database should be on the same machine as the transaction server. The last reason is why for remote

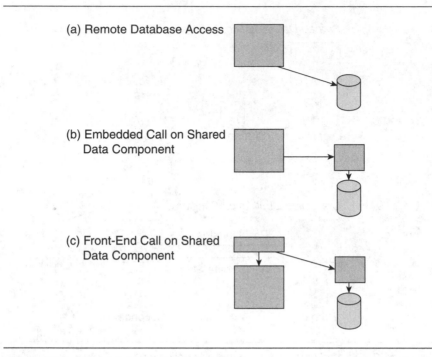

(a) Remote Database Access

(b) Embedded Call on Shared
    Data Component

(c) Front-End Call on Shared
    Data Component

Figure 14-4   Shared data configurations

access you should call a component on the machine that has the database rather than use SQL directly.

The other two solutions, (b) and (c) in Figure 14-4, are similar in that they call a component that manages access to the remote database. The database is hidden behind the component interface and hence can be changed with minimum disruption to the other applications.

The difference between the embedded call and the front-end call is seen in the programs. The embedded call has the shared data component called from within the main application program. The front-end solution has a front-end program, possibly written in a script language like Visual Basic or Java, calling both the shared data component to access the data and the main program to do the main task. The embedded call is the tightly coupled solution; the front-end call is a more loosely coupled solution.

Whether it is better to use an embedded call than a front-end call depends entirely on the application. An embedded call is best when the data is being used in many places. For instance, suppose there is an order entry application and the shared data is product information. The application accesses the product information all over the place—to display data for the user to make a selection, to get the price, to look up the size and weight for calculating delivery costs. A front-end call is best when the data is used in a few places. In this same order entry example, consider a call on shared customer data. It may be that the order entry object itself might need only the primary key (say, the customer number) of the customer data. If so, passing a primary key value through the front end gives flexibility. In one case, the key might come from a customer search screen; in another case the key might come from a charge card. The main body of the order entry processing is the same for both.

Note that in this example, it is desirable to be able to search the order data by customer key value because the application must be able to take some sensible action if the customer disappears. This is an instance of a general rule: With shared data you should always ensure that any references go both ways so you can handle deletions without leaving hanging references pointing at nothing (or even worse, pointing at the wrong thing).

Where possible, though, you should try to standardize on one or a few interfaces to the shared data access routines. You want to be able to move the application around so that if the shared data is accessible through the same interface on many machines, there is no hindrance.

14.3.2   Controlled duplication

Controlled duplication, as its name implies, has the same data in two or more databases. The advantages of controlled duplication are better resiliency and, in many cases, better performance. The disadvantages are that the data is slightly out of date and the application is more complex.

Remember that in this section we are talking about only green-field development, not existing production data (that comes in a later section). In particular, we are assuming all the problems of reconciling data discussed earlier are solved. We assume that you can match an object in one database with an object in another, because they both have the same key. We are also assuming that it is possible to match the attributes, albeit maybe with a bit of reformatting. In short, we are assuming the database schemas have been designed to make controlled duplication possible. If this assumption is incorrect, controlled duplication is not possible.

You will observe from Figure 14-3 that one copy of the data is designated "primary" and the other is "secondary." Many people are tempted to give both copies equal status by allowing updates on both copies, updates that are then propagated to the other copy. The problem with this idea is that the two copies can diverge. Consider the following scenario:

Update "ABC" on object X on copy A.

Update "ABC" sent to the copy B.

Update "LMN" on object X on copy B.

Update "LMN" sent to copy A.

Copy B processes updates from A—object X on B now has "ABC".

Copy A processes updates from B—object X on A now has "LMN".

Sometimes you don't care; if the data is known to have errors in it, one or two more might not hurt. You can of course write a program to arbitrarily fix the data to be consistent.

(A technical aside: The notion of equal status requires that the transformation of attribute from A to B is reversible from B to A.)

It would be possible for both systems to be of equal status by using two phase commits to update all copies of the data. However, the disadvantage of that approach is that if one system is down, then the other system is badly impacted. It would be impossibly clunky to maintain synchronicity across, say, 10 duplicate copies of the data. (We discuss these issues in more detail when we describe the dual active configuration in Chapter 7.) In theory, there are some circumstances where completely synchronous duplication of data is required and two-phase commit would be the solution. In practice, this is rarely, if ever, the case.

So if you don't mind the data being slightly asynchronous but you do need it to be consistent, the solution is to do all your updates on one machine first and propagate the updates using message queuing. The first updated database is the primary. Updates are sent to the secondary, where they are processed in exactly the same order as on the primary. The next question is, are there constraints about how quickly the data must be updated? In most cases, it is desirable for the data to be updated at nearly the same time, but it is better for the system to be up and running with slightly old data than to be down waiting for the updates to come through. This is an ideal application for message queuing.

In the main you can get away with a small timing window for common data because the common data contains resource objects, not tracking objects. Let us give two examples.

Suppose the common data is product data and the price changes. There is a possibility that the order is made after the price change but before the local copy of the price changed on the system. The reason why this does not matter is that there is a much wider window of time between telling the customer the price and sending an invoice. Thus, there will always be prices on the order that do not reflect the current price in the current product database; it is something you have to live with.

For the second example, suppose there is customer data in a Web order processing application and in a delivery application. The biggest danger would be for a customer to change his or her address on the Web application but still get the order delivered to the wrong address. This could happen if the delivery note was sent before the address update got through, but with a message queuing system working well, this is a timing window of less than a second. In any case, given the likelihood of sending the delivery to the wrong address, business processes should already be in place to handle this unfortunate happenstance.

As with shared data, if the primary and the secondary hold exactly the same data, then the interface should be the same. This allows us to move an application from the machine that holds the primary to the machine that holds the secondary without recompilation.

It is possible, though, to have controlled duplication even though the format of the data on the primary and secondary is different. For instance, codes can be converted to text to make them more understandable. For performance, different attributes can be indexed. The simplest solution is to make the primary a complete master copy of all attributes, that is, hold all the data from all the secondaries. In other words, the secondaries can leave out data from the master but not the other way around.

The alternative solution is for the secondary to hold additional data, but the programmer has to know which updates should be sent to the primary first and which are processed in place. It is easy to go wrong, for instance, if an attribute is added to the primary that already exists on the secondary. It helps to stay out of trouble if you put the additional fields into a separate table in the database with a reference to the table loaded from the primary.

14.3.3 Hybrid strategy

It is possible to both share data and have controlled duplication. For instance, you can share data if the two applications are in the same machine but use controlled duplication between machines. Thus, there might be 10 applications on three machines but only three copies of the data, one on each machine. If the interface to the data was the same on all machines, the applications could be moved from machine to machine at will.

14.4 Creating consistency in existing databases

Creating consistency in the data is one of the most important issues facing IT organizations today. It is also one of the most difficult.

The basic assumption of this section is that you want to convert existing applications that have data in silos to use either data sharing or controlled duplication of common data.

There are three problems:

1. A technical problem, converting old programs to use a new component interface or equivalent

2. A data migration problem, moving data from old databases into new databases that may be formatted in a very different way

3. A business process problem, changing the business processes to use the new data

We discuss each in turn and then pull the threads of the argument together.

First, however, the easy way! Many so-called legacy systems have ODBC and OLE DB interfaces and facilities for copying updates to data mart or data warehouse systems. You could choose one production system as the primary and have the others access the data through OLE DB. This is the shared data strategy and has all the advantages and disadvantages of that approach. A further disadvantage is that other existing applications will have to be fixed up to use the shared data. This is the "technical problem" and is explored later. This strategy breaks down in situations such as a large financial institution where data such as customer data is dispersed over many applications. In these situations, the effort of changing so much existing code and the poor performance of the final system mitigate against this solution.

Second, an easy way that sometimes doesn't work! A strategy that has been proposed by reputable authorities is called the Information Broker. It works as follows. When one system updates its customer data, it broadcasts an "update a customer" message to all other systems. This is done by having a grand central station of a system that transforms the data into a standard format ("canonical form" is the technical expression) and then reformats the data for all the destination hosts. This sounds great; assume there are n copies of the data, then instead of "n times $(n-1)$" transformations to maintain, there are "$2n$" (for each host, one in and one out) transformations to maintain.

If you look back at Section 14.3.2 on "Controlled duplication," you will see the problem with this notion. Recall that we had three reasons for data inconsistency: data value inconsistency, inability to match attributes, and inability to match objects. The grand central station idea partially fixes the data value inconsistencies. We say partially because there is no primary copy of the data and, as the example at the beginning of the section on controlled duplication illustrates, there is a problem when the same data is updated at the same time on different databases. On the question of matching attributes, the assumption behind the Information Broker concept is that this is possible. And it is—sometimes. But look at the example given earlier for matching addresses (e.g., does street name equal line one?). Clearly, it is often not simple. Sometimes it is impossible, for instance, if one of the attributes in one system does not exist in another.

The killer problem with the Information Broker is that it does not solve the problem of matching objects. That this is a serious problem is illustrated by a brewery, which wanted to know how many pubs it had (this is England). Three different systems gave three different answers (depending on whether they counted clubs, hotels, pubs that weren't owned by the brewery, etc.). This is a simple example. A much more problematic example is a bank that has many accounts and the customer data stored with the account. In this example, there is no customer number, only names with which to do the mapping. If the address for a "Chris Britton" changes for one account, it would be risky to change the address for a "Mr. C. G. Britton" in another account. In summary, if you have a reliable object identifier key with which to do the mapping from one object to another, you only have a small(ish) problem. If you don't have a reliable object identifier with which to do the mapping, your problem is unsolvable (even by Artificial Intelligence programs because you don't dare take the risk of heuristic rules getting it wrong).

There are two messages from this discussion. First, you cannot avoid changing the applications and the business processes. Second, if you change the grand central station into a grand central database, you have the kernel of something that works. The grand central database would implement the primary copy as in the controlled duplication strategy outlined in the previous section. The next three subsections are built around this idea.

14.4.1   The technical problem

In the green-field scenario, access to common data was hidden behind a component interface. Picture trying to implement the same strategy in an existing COBOL application. The first step would be to try to identify all the code that updates the data in question and put it into a clean interface. This might be extremely easy or impossibly hard depending on how the code was written. Let us suppose it is done; the extracted code has been put into a COBOL copy library and the rest of the code fixed to call the copy library instead of using the data directly. The process must be repeated on all applications that want to use the same data. It is highly desirable that all applications use the same copy library for the shared data, but that might mean much greater changes to the applications. The next step is to decide which application has the primary copy of the data. The copy libraries in the secondaries then need to send messages to the primary to make the updates on the primary database, and the primary needs to send messages back to all the secondaries to update the database copies.

If it is possible to create a component interface for data access, should you go for a shared data strategy or a controlled duplication strategy? It might be possible to implement a shared data strategy, but there is a wrinkle. It could be that the updates to the shared data are embedded in transactions that do something else as well. This means that splitting off the shared data would require converting a simple transaction into a distributed transaction. Some COBOL environments cannot easily support a program initiating a subtransaction on another machine.

So what if creating a component interface is too difficult? An alternative often available is to use the transaction interface. Say there is an existing system that has customer data. There are likely to be existing transactions for creating, updating, and deleting customers. The messages from grand central database to the local system can become calls on these existing transactions. It is advantageous for performance and resiliency to send the messages through a message queue, so you need a small program to read the queue and call the transactions. You then have to ensure that the existing user interface for updating the customer data does not call these transactions. Instead they must send a message to the grand central database and allow the updates to be propagated back as described above.

14.4.2   The data migration problem

If you have a grand central database for common data (and you want it only for common data, not everything), then you will be able to migrate applications to the use the new database one at a time rather than all at once.

There is obviously a logistical problem of converting the data, loading it into the new database, and putting in the new application at the same time. The logistics can be alleviated to some extent if there is a time period when the old application updates its old data and, at the same time, sends updates to the grand central database. This way you can do the data migration before the application migration and, for a while, be able to do parallel running on the old and new databases.

The problems of converting the data and loading it to the new database are not too bad for the first application, but for subsequent applications there is the issue of trying to match data to see if it refers to the same object. You probably will need to load the old data into the new database and then do a manual reconciliation job in the new location. You might want to develop a program that identifies possible matches. You may find that the grand central database needs to record aliases rather than always eliminating one object in favor of another.

14.4.3   The business process problem

The point about a grand central database is to turn it into the primary and only authority of that piece of information. Inevitably this changes the business process. Information accuracy is a business process issue, and no amount of technology will change that. However, one reason we are so keen on having a primary copy of the database is that it provides a focus for business process change. For instance, if it is customer data being consolidated, the grand central database of customer information will ultimately become the one and only way to maintain customer details, which is just how it should be.

Observe that this strategy implements the notion of business processes controlling resource data, illustrated in Figure 12-3.

14.5   The information controller

Data administration is frequently seen as the systems manager for the databases, the person who runs recovery and reorganization routines and actually types in the schema changes. This worked fine with traditional silo application development. Each silo had its database, and the design of the database was entirely the responsibility of the silo application development manager. But with integrated applications that is no longer possible. Someone must take responsibility for the data layer as a whole to ensure consistency and quality; otherwise, it won't happen.

This wider role we shall call the *information controller*. Many organizations would call this role the database administrator, but in other organizations, the database administrator has no design responsibilities. Other terms—such as *data god!*—have been proposed but none has widespread acceptance. So to avoid confusion (we hope) we have coined a new title, information controller. The information controller's responsibility can be easily stated; he or she is responsible for information access and information accuracy. Exactly what that means in practice includes the following:

- Data mart and data warehouse development
- A say in online inquiry development (to resolve issues about when to use a data mart)
- Control of the database schema
- Control of the development of data access interfaces and components
- A say in the application development to ensure systemwide data quality

In other words, when a designer wants a change made to shared data or someone in the organization has a complaint about the quality of the data, they go to the information controller.

Note that the information controller is looking after common data, not all data. Otherwise, the job would be just too big and get in the way of everybody else. What we suggest is that the information controller gradually take control of data as the common data is synchronized. In other words, if there are 10 customer databases, the information controller takes command of the customer databases one by one as they are bought into a control of the common data strategy.

But before taking control of the data, the information controller needs to understand the severity of the problem. Repositories and modeling tools are important aids. The repository should hold the schema information from the various databases and the new object models of the common data. It could also hold all the interface definitions. Modeling tools could be used to give a pictorial representation of the objects and the business processes.

As noted earlier, many of the issues of data quality can best be fixed when the data is input, which means that the information controller is not some backroom administrator but a very visible member of the IT management team.

A key skill of the information controller must be a deep understanding of the difference between an information access project and a transaction development project. In an information access project there may be little or no programming because off-the-shelf tools meet most of your requirements. But in spite of that, these projects are not easy. For instance, you can forget about a clear statement of requirements. Also, what tools will be successful will depend on training the end user, but are the end users willing to be trained? Even at the business level, the typical manager will very clearly tell you what data he or she needs but, when it is provided, will immediately change his or her mind. The information controller needs to communicate well and have excellent interpersonal skills.

The final point is that information access and accuracy is not a one-time fix. It will be a slow incremental process of improvement. Any single project will tend to be short, but there will be many of them. Information controller is a challenging job.

14.6   Summary

This chapter discusses some architectural aspects of database design.
Key points to remember:

- There is no one fix for data access; different users have different require-ments. Some want canned reports, some want inquiry screens, others want to do ad hoc queries. Some need up-to-date information, others don't mind so much. A good place to start is to position the user on the timeliness/data to information chart.

- There is tight coupling between the transaction service and the database. If direct SQL access to the database is widespread, there are major problems with changing the database schema. The solution is to have a designated primary update service for the database with direct access to the database and to ensure that all secondary inquiry and update access is through a component interface.

- There are two strategies for common data such as customer data or product data: Either share the data or have controlled duplication. For controlled duplication, always have a primary database, and update the primary before propagating the updates to the secondaries.

- For common data in existing databases, migrate the common data to a central primary store one at a time, and implement either a shared data or a controlled duplication strategy.

- Someone in the organization should take the role of information controller, who has the responsibility of information accuracy and information access.

The next chapter looks at more aspects of evolving existing applications to become part of the architecture.

15

Changing and Integrating Applications

There is plenty of literature about implementation design for new applications. There is very little on the very real problem of implementation design where applications already exist. This chapter is about changing existing applications, in particular, transaction applications. We also take a look at batch programs because they remain significant in many environments.

In Chapter 14, the subject of changing existing applications was addressed in the context of the data tier. In this chapter, the concern is the presentation and processing tiers; this chapter is about programs, not data.

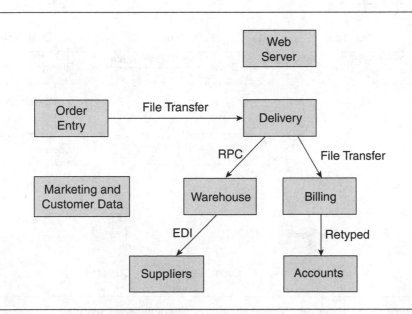

Figure 15-1   Example of order processing before changes

We will start by discussing again the order processing example used in Chapter 1. First let us recall the "before" state, as shown in Figure 15-1.

From a business process perspective, what we are trying to achieve is illustrated in Figure15-2. The figure shows that order entry processing, delivery, and billing are part of one large business process; let us call it the order-handling process. In the terminology used in Chapter 12, the Order Tracking object is the tracking object for the order-handling business process. Figure 15-2 also illustrates the need to maintain Product and Customer resource objects. Finally, the figure shows real-time and deferrable links between the applications.

Figure 15-2 is only a process view. It does not show the data inquiry requirements. To show, this we will redraw the diagram to include the customer's interaction with the system. This is shown in Figure 15-3. It shows that the customer has a Fixed inquiry link to the customer, product, and order-tracking data. Calling these links "Fixed inquiry" links indicates that the inquiry is tailored to the customer's demands. (Other situations might call for specifying "Ad hoc query" links and "Push" links.)

If this is what is needed, how can we get there?

Clearly a major issue is that multiple applications share data. This is discussed at length in the previous chapter, so we won't discuss further the synchronization of customer and product data.

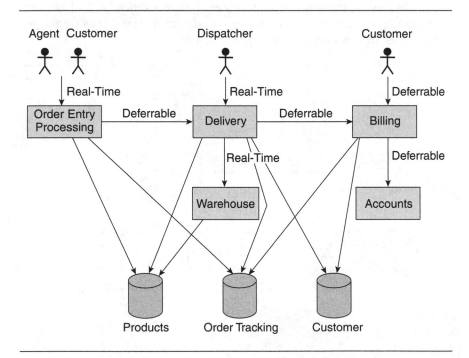

Figure 15-2   Example of order processing with high-level integration requirements

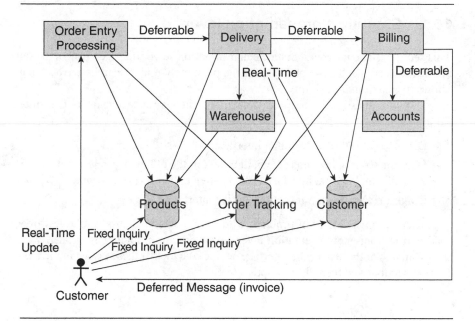

Figure 15-3   Example of order processing from the customer's viewpoint

In Figures 15-2 and 15-3 the order-tracking data is represented as a disk file and hence as a passive data source, but this is not necessarily the case. As previously described, it is usually best if the logic for updating the data goes with the data, and with the order-tracking objects would go the logic for such complex issues as multiple deliveries and replacement deliveries. Put another way, this logic is the order-handling business process logic.

In this example, there are four sizeable projects:

1. The implementation of order-tracking data and an order-handling process

2. The consolidation of product data

3. The consolidation of customer data

4. The creation of a Web interface

The first priority is probably number 4 because as soon as the others are ready, the Web interface can quickly be adapted to make use of them. It's likely that numbers 2 and 3, the consolidation projects, need to be split into smaller deliverable chunks, one chunk for each consolidated application; the alternative of doing the whole thing as one large project would mean a long wait for delivery.

Note that one skill in the evolutionary process is splitting the work into small projects that deliver the most benefit early on. This sometimes means implementing interim solutions that have short lives. That's all right because early functionality is a benefit to the organization.

15.1 Creating a presentation layer

This section is about carving out a clean transaction server interface from existing applications so that a new interface for the presentation layer can be created that allows for maximum flexibility.

The first question is, to what degree should we make changes? Consider Figure 15-4:

- Diagram (a) is the old terminal interface.
- Diagram (b) is a new interface built to talk to the old interface without changing the original interface. This is often called *screen-scraping*.
- Diagram (c) shows a transaction service interface.

There are two classes of problem with screen-scraping. It puts a large workload on the front-end presentation layer, and there are problems associated with the mismatch of the size of the interface device. We look at these issues in the next two subsections and then discuss option (c).

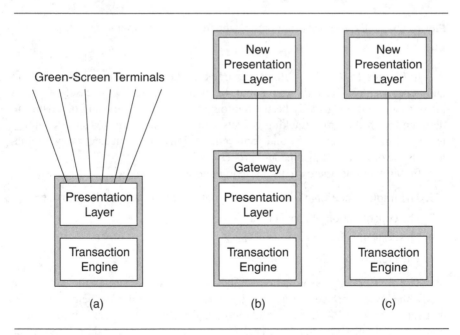

Figure 15-4 Adding a presentation layer to an existing application

15.1.1   Screen-scraping task

Consider a front-end Web server calling an existing application by screen-scraping. In addition to sending and receiving the data for inquiries and transactions, it must also do the following:

- Log on to the back-end system.
- Do any menu traversal required.
- Reformat the data into a string of text that precisely conforms to the format expected by the existing application.
- Take out the fields from exactly the right place in the received message.
- Keep track of the position in the dialogue (i.e., the current screen) of many end users simultaneously.

Error handling makes these problems more difficult because the screen output may indicate the field in error by positioning the cursor in front of it and sending a highlighting character to make the field blink or stand out in bold. On the other hand, if the error is a network error, the front-end program may have to log on again and go through all the menus again.

The impact of screen-scraping is to set the existing application in concrete since any change to the screen layout now has ramifications for the front-end program. This is an instance of what Gerald Weinberg calls the "Fast-Food Fallacy," which states that "No difference plus no difference plus no difference plus no difference . . . eventually equals a clear difference." (The name comes from the notion that reducing the number of sesame seeds on a bun from 100 to 99 is not noticeable, likewise 99 to 98, 98 to 97, . . . 51 to 50. But the reduction from 100 to 50 is collectively a clear difference.) In this case, screen-scraping on one screen won't be noticeable, but screen-scraping on even ten screens will be a major headache. And we have encountered cases where exactly this has happened.

15.1.2   Interface size mismatch

Some error-handling situations are even harder to implement. Figure 15-5 illustrates the problem of large messages. A large message from the Web may correspond to many terminal-sized messages to the production system. Say a large message corresponds to five messages at the back end and, while processing the third message, the transaction aborts. Now the front-end program must undo the work of the first two messages, which had completed without a hitch. The simplest solution is to process the entire large message in one two-phase commit transaction (probably on one database); however, if you are emulating a terminal, you are unlikely to have a two-phase commit capability. Instead you have to review what the human operator would do in a similar situation. In some cases, such as updating a record on the system, there could be no clear answer—the human operator makes a value judgment that some of the updates are ok and some

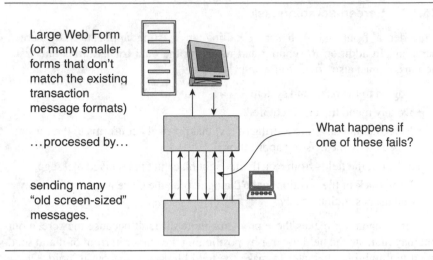

Large Web Form (or many smaller forms that don't match the existing transaction message formats)

...processed by...

What happens if one of these fails?

sending many "old screen-sized" messages.

Figure 15-5   The device size problem

aren't. He or she might even resubmit the input but leave out the single field that caused the error. The Web server is unlikely to know enough to make these judgments, so it must reverse all the completed transactions. In the worst case, there may be no explicit reversal transaction types.

15.1.3   Turning existing applications into services

Thus, there is a strong case for moving to option (c) in Figure 15-4—a transaction service. We will look at this issue from three angles:

- What needs to be done to the existing production code
- Wrapping the old technology with new
- The impact on the business processes

In this section we look at the first of these. The next subsection looks at wrapping, and the impact on business processes gets a whole section to itself.

Changing the existing code is largely a process of elimination. Obviously the presentation code—building the screen messages—can go because a service interface needs to send only raw data. Most security checking code can go as well since the user will be authenticated at the presentation layer. Security information is required by a transaction server only if the application itself is doing additional security checks, perhaps giving different users access to different customers. In that case, the ideal solution is to add input fields for the user and role identifiers to messages for the transaction server.

Menu traversal code can go. In many terminal applications, the applications guided the user, but now the presentation layer does all the guiding; the transaction server should process only inquiry and update transactions without regard for the ordering.

Unfortunately, many existing online transaction processing applications do have ordering dependencies. The programmers knew the terminal screens would be submitted in a certain order and have exploited this fact. For example, one screen might locate a customer or add a customer, and a later screen adds an order. The customer identifier might be stored in local storage and used in the new order transaction without doing further checks.

Storing the customer identifier in local storage is an example of the session holding state. Note that state is being held on a per-terminal dialogue basis. Typically the transaction monitor has facilities for storing small amounts of data in the output message. This data is never sent to the user but can be retrieved by any application that receives the next input from the same terminal.

Before leaving this example, observe what happens when there is a failure: The session state is lost. The user must therefore start the session from the beginning, hopefully, finding the customer on the database rather than adding it again. When reimplementing the application using a different presentation layer, it may not be possible or desirable to carry this recovery strategy forward. In this example, the simplest solution is to store the customer identifier in the client and pass it as a parameter to the transaction server. That way, on any server failure, the client can go straight in and carry on processing where it left off.

Ordering dependencies are one reason to store state. Two other common reasons are security, discussed previously, and temporary data gathering. An example of the latter is an order entry application that stores all the order information locally until the final "It's done" command is sent, when all the data is stored in the database in one transaction.

Sometimes these problems turn out to be nonproblems. Look again at Figure 15-5 and the issue of the mismatch of sizes of the channel. With a transaction server, there is an easy solution without a two-phase commit: Create a new transaction that takes all the data and calls the existing code within one transaction. There is no need to collect data in the session state because all the data comes in one transaction. If there is still a problem, the session states should be stored in the database, as discussed in Chapter 7 on resiliency.

Let's summarize the argument so far. Think of it as a three-step process.

1. The terminal forms-handling code and the menu traversal are taken out of the application.

2. Security code is taken out of the application.

3. Any remaining session state must be reviewed and if necessary stored in the database.

With these steps accomplished, the application is ready for wrapping.

How difficult is this whole process? It depends. (You knew we were going to say that.) Sometimes it is easy—sometimes there is no code to change. Sometimes

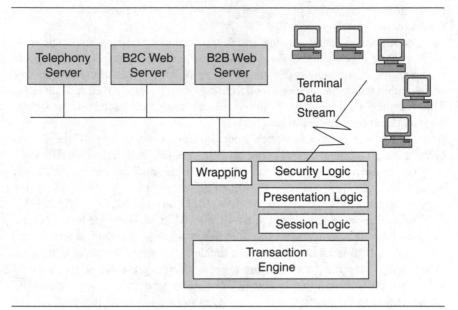

Figure 15-6   The old and the new presentation layers

it is hard. The only way to find out is to let a programmer try. Even if it turns out to be hard to make comprehensive changes, all is not lost. Often the old must coexist with the new, as in Figure 15-6.

The number of transaction types that need to be wrapped is often very small, maybe five or ten transaction types out of a total population of several hundred. It is not very difficult to clone the few transactions that need to be changed, change them, and leave the rest alone.

Of course, if wrapping transactions really does turn out to be difficult, then it is time to consider replacing the complete application. Even so, the old must coexist with the new. If we added a new order entry process to our example at the top of this chapter, the result would be Figure 15-7. This shows how an alternative order entry application can be introduced without changing anything else.

15.1.4   Wrapping

Wrapping is the name for creating a new interface for an application by installing some software that converts the old interface to the new interface.

The technology aspect of taking a mainframe transaction processing application and giving it an interface to the world of components is relatively straightforward. For instance, in Unisys you can run transactions under an implementation of Open Group DTP in the Unisys OS2200 and MCP environments. It is similar to Tuxedo, but there are some differences, specifically, the protocol used when

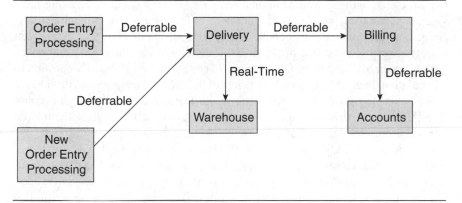

Figure 15-7   Example of two order-entry processes

transaction managers communicate: Tuxedo to Tuxedo is not the exactly the same protocol as Open Group DTP to Open Group DTP. Tuxedo applications can work with Open Group DTP applications using a product called eLink OSI-TP, which acts as a gateway between the two protocols. Unisys also supports wrapping of Open Group DTP applications by Microsoft COM+ components, which is part of the functionality of the Distributed Transaction Integration product. Putting this together with eLink OSI-TP allows communication between Microsoft and Tuxedo, including support for two-phase commit capability across Tuxedo, COM+, and Open Group DTP applications. For IBM MVS, the Microsoft product COMTI wraps CICS transactions with COM+.

There are similar products for Enterprise JavaBeans. BEA Systems itself has all the links from Tuxedo and its eLink products to Enterprise JavaBeans. The bottom line is that, technically, wrapping is not difficult. The catch with all these technologies is that the applications on the mainframe transaction monitor must be stateless. In most cases, this is inevitable. Because there is no terminal and because a Web session is so different from a terminal session, all the baggage that comes with a terminal interface must be eliminated.

15.1.5   Building a middle tier

A key issue is the complexity of the wrapping. Should it be a minimal wrapping, simply converting one technology to another with minimal overhead, or should it create a new object view of the interface?

The second approach is advocated by both the Microsoft and J2EE three-tier architectures, which perpetuate a strange conceit that transaction logic implemented on mainframe systems is part of the data tier, in contrast to transaction logic implemented in .NET Enterprise services or EJB, which is part of the middle tier. In practice, the middle tier often turns out to be little more than a gateway to the back end, perhaps with additional code for security checking, routing messages, and workflow management. Putting an object interface on old online transaction applications is usually not difficult. If you look at an online transaction, you almost always see that one of the fields is something like "account number" or "product number" and identifies an object. The transaction call easily converts to an operation on an object by taking the rest of the transaction input and turning the input fields into parameters. For instance, all transactions that change account details become operations on the account object. The actual code in the middle tier is typically little more than calls on the old mainframe applications.

Sometimes the logic in the middle tier becomes more complex. For instance, the data you want to expose may be physically located in several back-end transaction systems. Another complex scenario is trying to make a batch system look like an online system by storing a local copy of the data that is more up-to-date than the data on the back-end system (a notion referred to as *pseudo updating* or *memo updating*). When you are faced with difficulties such as these, you have to ask whether you want to add complex code to the middle tier or whether it would be better to fix up the back-end systems to be more supportive of the new functionality.

The disadvantage of creating an object-oriented middle tier is that the objects have to be designed with care. Some organizations have developed good solutions using non-object middleware, such as Tuxedo and MQSeries. Having some common middleware-based infrastructure seems to be a more important factor for success than having an object foundation.

In spite of the difficulties, there are now many examples of successfully creating a transaction service interface from existing applications.

15.2   Business processing change with new interfaces

Let us return to the order-handling process and look at the details of the order entry application. It is very common that old terminal-based applications are rigid. The order form screens are presented in a fixed order, customer information such as shipping address and billing details must be retyped for every order, and if the user finds that some information is missing, the complete order is aborted. It does not have to be like that. A flexible solution is illustrated in Figure 15-8.

When we discussed business processes in Chapter 12, we contrasted on the one hand, a military process—doing it by numbers—and on the other hand, a flexible rule-based definition of a process. A similar idea applies at the task/dialogue level because the starting point for developing a flexible interface is an understanding of the fundamental rules of the task. Suppose there are several channels; for instance, order entry might have a Web interface, a call center, and a traditional terminal interface. All of these channels share the fundamental logic of order entry, illustrated in Figure 15-8. But they may have a more rigid interface, may

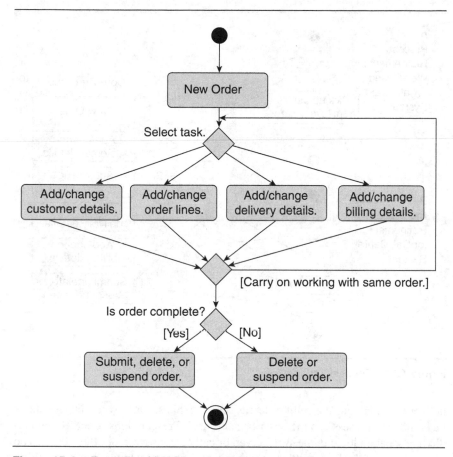

Figure 15-8   Example of flexible order entry

impose additional rules, or may implement additional features. For instance, the call center might have a script that guides the telephone user through the steps of the ordering process, and the script imposes an order that isn't there in the most general case. The core process should implement the flexible rule-based definition of the business process, while the specific presentation channels might impose some military order to the process. Furthermore, the call center may be available only for specially registered customers for which the customer, delivery, and billing details may have already been entered, so some steps may be missing. The notion of a general, flexible process and specific, presentation-based processes is illustrated in Figure 15-9.

There are various ways to implement Figure 15-9. One extreme is to implement the core process activities as a transaction server. All the different activities would map to one or more operations on an Order object. Within the Order object there would need to be status flags that indicate whether the customer details, the

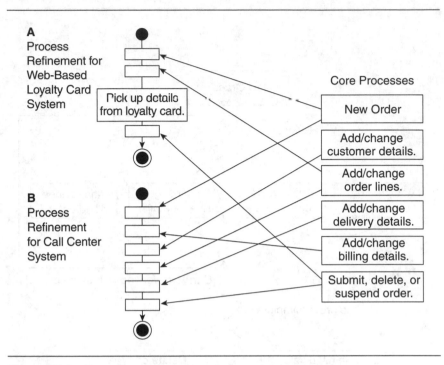

Figure 15-9 Process refinement

delivery details, and the billing details have been set. Only when all the status flags indicate success can the order be submitted. Presentations A and B are handled by separate logic in the Web server, or call center server, or other server. The logic in A and B calls for little more than handling the dialogue flow and calling the core process activities. We call this style of implementation the *core server model,* and it has several advantages:

- The core server itself is a stateless server, which, you have probably realized by now, we like.
- Core process rules are implemented in one place and, once implemented, immediately apply to all kinds of data entry.
- It is not difficult to mix presentation modes. For instance, the order can be initially entered over the Web, suspended, and then changed by a telephone call.
- Different core activities can be physically located on different servers. Any customer details updates may be actually implemented on the customer data server.

The alternative to the core server model is the *reuse model.* Each presentation layer refinement is implemented as a separate application and, instead of calling the core processes, the core processes are incorporated into the application. To avoid developing the core processes multiple times, reuse is used. Two forms of reuse are relevant in this model, component reuse and class library reuse. (Component reuse is reuse of run-time components and class library reuse is reuse of program language source files.) The key characteristic of the reuse model is that each application has its own private data.

The advantages of the reuse model are:

- It is fast—data is stored locally for the duration of the dialogue.
- Processes are easier to change since you don't have to ensure that your changes are compatible with the core process implementation.

But there are disadvantages:

- Processes are easier to change only because there is no control to ensure consistency among the different forms of the process.
- It is impossible to mix presentation modes in the business process under consideration.
- It may be hard to reuse components and modules because different presentation servers may be using different technology, for instance, one may need .NET components, the other Java Beans.

Which model is best? In general, the core server model has better control and flexibility but it is more complex. (We are aware of cases where this approach has been very successful.) For order entry processing, the core server model allows mixing of presentation channels, which is an attractive feature. But take another example, such as the new car rental process discussed in Chapter 12 where there is no possibility of mixing up the presentation channels, the reuse model may be a better solution.

So what should be done about existing applications? Typically, existing applications combine a single implementation of the core process activities and one process refinement for one presentation channel. The ideal solution would be to pick a clean core server model out of the code.

15.3   Changing the middleware between transaction servers

You probably noticed that in Figure 15-1 the "middleware" used is file transfer and remote procedure calls (RPC). Figure 15-2, in contrast, has the messages between the applications described as deferrable and real-time. The implication is that file transfer is used to implement deferrable messages and RPCs are used to implement real-time messages. In the early chapters of this book, we describe message queuing as the best solution to deferrable messages and transaction component middleware as the best solution for real-time. Is it important to introduce the new middleware? Why? And how should it be done?

The tasks required to move from a file transfer implementation to message queuing include training, installation, configuration, development of operating procedures, and program changes to the existing applications. It is a task of sufficient size not to undertake without significant benefits. The benefits of moving to message queuing are in the areas of responsiveness and integrity. The responsiveness benefit is a result of the messages being sent immediately rather than when the next file is transferred. The downside is that sending all data immediately is likely to have more overhead than batching it up for later delivery. The integrity benefits come as a result of message queuing's built-in mechanism for ensuring that messages are sent and sent only once. File transfer usually requires manual procedures to ensure both these conditions are met. Many organizations have implemented file transfer solutions, which work well if nothing goes wrong; but if there is a failure during file creation, file transfer, or file processing, messages can be lost or processed twice. Obviously, in our order processing example, lost orders and duplicate orders have a serious business impact.

Similarly, there is a case for moving from RPCs to transactional component middleware, the chief benefits of which are:

- The use of components helps reuse in the server.
- The use of object interfaces may simplify the client code.
- The use of distributed transactional processing makes it possible to call many operations in one transaction.
- TCM software has performance features, such as connection pooling, that may make your application go significantly faster.

But in the conversion from RPC to transactional component middleware, all these advantages are in the box marked "possible future benefits" rather than a box marked "immediate return on investment." The reality is that something—possibly the need for integration to a Web server—needs to be added to the project before it will be justifiable.

A further difficulty with moving to transactional component middleware is that, in contrast to message queuing and RPC, the client must be written in an object-oriented language, or at least use a gateway that is written in an object-oriented language. In our example in which RPC is being used between the Delivery application and the Warehouse application, this could be a serious concern if the existing applications aren't object-oriented.

Even in a newly developed system, we would expect several forms of middleware, for instance, message queuing, transactional component middleware, and remote database access for ad hoc queries. In a real organization, there are a number of other middleware products and various ad hoc solutions, such as file transfer, so we are looking at an environment of considerable complexity that is not likely to become much easier anytime soon.

Web services technology, specifically SOAP, adds new possibilities. Depending on the underlying transport mechanism, SOAP can be used both for RPC-like and deferrable messages. The effort required to implement SOAP connections to applications should be roughly comparable to introducing message queuing.

When changes are made, it is advisable to put in mediator components, in other words, to have a layer of software screening the application logic and the infrastructure. Change will be that much easier in the future.

15.4   Batch

We should not lose sight of the fact that batch processes remain a very significant part of the operation of many enterprises. For example, some banks have batch processing at the heart of their system—from a business perspective, they are not real-time banks. All account updates are collected during the day and processed against the accounts during an overnight batch run.

Of course, it is not so simple; the bank must prevent someone going around from ATM to ATM taking money out. One solution is simply to prevent more than, say, $200 being taken out during one day. This does not help with Internet banking, telephone banking, and using debit cards. There are so many ways these days of extracting money that the bank is more exposed than ever. Unless the bank is going to offer a seriously limited service (or allow very large overdrafts), the only solution is to have real-time bank balances. Some banks still run their batch processes but calculate a "pseudo real-time balance" by updating an account balance when the data is input without doing a full debit/credit on the account.

Another difficulty with processing accounts in batch is more subtle. Suppose a bank product is set up to move money from a checking account to a savings account when the checking account's balance goes above a certain limit, and also to move money from a savings account to reduce the mortgage (additional to monthly repayments) when it goes above another limit. There are four batch updates: a debit on the checking account, a credit on the savings account, a debit on the savings account, and a credit on the mortgage account. But the batch run may not process all these kinds of transactions in that order; for instance, all savings account updates may be done before checking account updates. Therefore, a whole day passes between posting the money from the checking account and updating the savings account. There may be another day's delay before the mortgage account is updated. Therefore, not only is the service slow, but also, from the customer's perspective, money is debited from one account one night and not credited to another account for 24 hours. (And the day's interest is foregone—but banks might view this as an advantage.)

From a technical point of view, there are advantages and disadvantages to batch processing. A major performance advantage is that totals can be calculated during the batch run (being careful to capture any running totals in the restart area). In an online transaction, calculating totals would require an update to statistics stored in a database record or posting the data to another application. Also, bank IT operations have become very comfortable with recovery procedures that rely on a consistent copy of the account data after the batch run is complete.

A major concern for large batch runs is the time it takes. As business becomes more and more a 24-hour affair, the batch window—the time set aside for running batch programs—becomes shorter and shorter. The problem is illustrated in Figure 15-10.

There are four approaches to shortening the batch window: shorten or eliminate the batch administration tasks; shorten the batch application's elapsed time; run batch applications alongside the online process; and eliminate batch applications, replacing them with online applications. All four can be done; you need to attack the problem of the batch window from multiple angles.

The first approach, shortening the administration, is discussed in Chapter 7, which covers resiliency.

The key step in the second approach, shortening the batch process, is usually running many programs in parallel. Conceptually, this is usually simple: Split your input data into multiple inputs. The difficulties are merging running totals and, more problematic, long transactions. The most common reason long transactions exist in batch is not because the business processes require them, but to simplify restart code. Programs can recover only to a point where they are out of

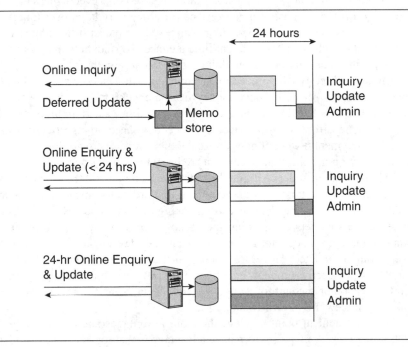

Figure 15-10   The shortening batch window

transaction state (after a commit). It is much easier to update a whole file in one transaction because it doesn't require writing restart code to reposition the program in the middle of the file. Most of these long transactions can be eliminated, albeit with a bit of work.

The second approach is simply to run batch alongside the online processing, and this too can be done—as long as the transactions are short. Ideally, there is a throttle mechanism, so batch can do more or less work according to how busy the online processing is. This is easier to do using message queues than files, since you can put all your input into one queue and have multiple programs processing the queue. The number of programs can be increased or decreased according to the load. A program reading a queue is also easy to recover by putting the dequeue operation in the same transaction as the database updates.

Sometimes, though, the batch program requires the database to be frozen. Many of these cases are a convenience rather than an absolute requirement. For example, suppose a financial system needs a new set of interest rates every day. At some point, you need to give the system the new data, and the easiest way is to replace the old file and restart the system. Obviously, it is possible to implement an online change of the data, but with additional effort. Typically moving to a 24 by 7 operation requires making very many of these kinds of changes.

But some cases of frozen databases are real. Reports are one case, for example, closing the accounts at the end of a quarter. The time can be minimized. For example, you can use disk subsystem technology in which disk volumes are mirrored and then broken off as snapshot copies of the data. This can be done online, but you must close the database to ensure that the database buffer pool is all written to disk to ensure a clean copy of the database. The copy can then be used for reports.

The third approach, replacing batch applications with online programs, can also be done sometimes. But, as we have noted, batch cannot be eliminated entirely because some business processes are triggered by time events (e.g., payroll or regular accrual of interest payment).

Changing a process from batch to online is not just a change of technology; it is a change to the business process (almost always for the better, unless the performance hit is too high). It may not be easy. A batch application and its online equivalent usually consist of the same basic operations but they may be processed in a totally different order. This is illustrated in Figure 15-11.

In many ways a batch run is like a giant transaction, and this allows subtle optimizations. A group of operations that in business terms are one transaction, and must be implemented as one transaction in an online implementation, can be rearranged in a batch run. Thus the online transaction to move money from a savings account to a checking account may update both accounts in one transaction; the equivalent batch application has two input files, one for checking account updates and another for savings account updates. Furthermore, all the updates to one account, which in business terms were separate transactions, are implemented as one transaction in the batch process to improve performance.

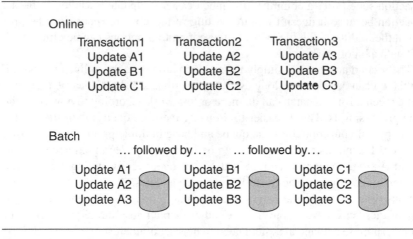

Online

Transaction1	Transaction2	Transaction3
Update A1	Update A2	Update A3
Update B1	Update B2	Update B3
Update C1	Update C2	Update C3

Batch

... followed by...   ... followed by...

Update A1   Update B1   Update C1
Update A2   Update B2   Update C2
Update A3   Update B3   Update C3

Figure 15-11   Batch processing versus online transactions

Clearly, in some circumstances there may be no simple way to change a batch program to an online program. The best you will achieve is to salvage some of the code.

In general, therefore, it is not possible to eliminate batch, but it is often possible to have it run alongside the online system. The result is a set of transaction routines that are written with short transactions and are essentially the same as online transaction routines. The eventual goal should be to have one set of routines callable from either batch or online. This is illustrated in Figure 15-12. Essentially the model is a transaction server with a bunch of feeder programs. You can think of batch as a weird type of presentation layer if you like.

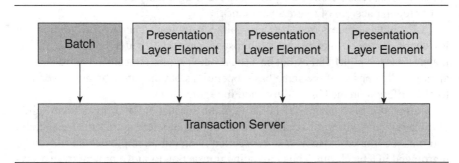

Figure 15-12   Batch as a presentation layer

15.5 Summary

In this chapter, we discuss changing existing applications into service applications. Key points to remember:

- Start from a high-level business process model of the complete system and the mapping from that to the current IT applications (as in Figures 15-2 and 15-3). From this information you will be able to identify necessary shared data and the integration dependencies (real-time and deferrable) between the applications.
- Use this analysis to decide on the business priorities for change. We anticipate that most changes will be in the areas of data consolidation and adding a presentation layer channel.
- Having focused on a particular application, you need to extract from the task dialogue the fundamental logic of what's required. From that you can identify the core process activities. And from this analysis you can explore various options for changing the code.
- The only way to really understand how easy it is to change code is to try. In most cases, you will find that only a few transactions need to be adapted to support a new presentation layer channel.
- Wrapping and gateways are effective technologies for interfacing new technology with old mainframe applications. The presentation logic, security logic, and session control logic in these programs will have to be removed, typically by creating new transaction types from the old code rather than changing existing transaction type code.
- Batch continues to remain important, but the batch window is shrinking. We discuss various techniques for reducing or eliminating batch.

Changing existing applications isn't easy, but it is often easier and less risky than rewriting from scratch. (Whether it is better to rewrite or to change the existing application is discussed in Chapter 1.) If you are going to rewrite, a good first step is to turn the existing application into a number of separate services, which can then be replaced one at a time.

16

Building an
IT Architecture

We argue strongly in this book that architecture, which we define as high-level design, is an essential starting point for any IT project. The majority of IT projects involve some integration of varying amounts of new and existing applications, and architectural models must take this into account. Using an architectural framework, business requirements can be reviewed in terms of the interactions between the architectural components needed to satisfy them. This leads to decisions about the appropriate technology to use, and then to choices of product. The critical technology is middleware, which has evolved over a number of years. We believe that service-oriented middleware, including but not limited to Web services, is a promising technology for constructing future distributed systems.

We also argue that it is not enough just to consider functional requirements when developing an IT architecture. There is another set of requirements, which we call nonfunctional to distinguish them from functional requirements. They are concerned with the resilience, performance, manageability, and security of the resulting system, and they are every bit as important as the functions the system must perform. Failure to consider them during design and implementation can easily lead to a system that does what is required functionally but is operationally unusable. We therefore use the architectural model as a framework for exploring both the functional and nonfunctional requirements early on, because both influence choices of technology and product.

The resulting architectural model should be used to guide implementation, modified if necessary during the life of a project; it is not something to develop and then put on a shelf. The place to start is at the top, establishing a framework and then refining it to ensure that all factors, both functional and nonfunctional, are considered. We stress that it is important that architects work with those who understand the business requirements, with applications designers, and with technicians who understand what can and cannot be done with specific technologies and products. Not doing this is likely to lead to disappointing results, as the number of failed IT projects suggests.

This final chapter provides some case studies, which we hope will illustrate the value of the architecture-based approach we are advocating. All are examples of successful projects. Following the case studies, there is a brief look at what the future may hold—we're sticking our necks out—and finally there is a summary of the key points we hope you will remember after reading the book.

16.1   Case studies

Case studies are instructive for anyone considering a new project. They provide models for the architecture and detailed design, which can be very valuable. They may also provide guidance on other aspects of running a project—what to do and what not to do. Such guidance can be very helpful in setting realistic expectations about implementation effort and schedules, and reducing risk.

We include three examples, which range from a project that was predominantly concerned with providing an integration infrastructure for existing applications to one that developed a new application. All are based on real cases. Although two have been adapted slightly, they remain realistic. We also include remarks on some of the common mistakes made when going about a project. These are useful in that lessons can always be learned.

16.1.1   Case 1: Providing an integration infrastructure

The organization concerned is referred to as Company A. Because of history, including mergers and acquisitions, the company had a mixture of hardware and software environments, which formed the environment at the start of the integration infrastructure project discussed here. They included Unisys ClearPath mainframes, a leading UNIX variant, Windows, and IBM OS390 systems. The existing applications comprised custom implementations in a variety of languages and packages, including SAP and Peoplesoft, and used various databases.

Some integration was in place, using file transfer and some other proprietary technology. However, experience had shown that this rather ad hoc approach, where each problem was solved as it arose, was unacceptable. The requirement was for a comprehensive integration infrastructure able to satisfy both immediate and anticipated requirements. Specific requirements included providing for application integration, defining a multitier architecture to facilitate addition of access channels and applications, based on a service-oriented approach, and providing appropriate levels of systems management. The use of generally accepted open standards wherever possible was mandatory.

These requirements, together with the starting environment, are typical of a great number of organizations in all sectors of business, as well as the public sector. The architecture developed is therefore relevant in a wide variety of cases.

The approach taken was to develop an architecture based on the notion of a middleware bus. Figure 16-1 shows the elements of the architecture as they would appear in the application systems.

The applications using the middleware bus may be written in a variety of languages, including C, C++, VB, Java, and COBOL. Many, of course, had already been written at the start of the project. The infrastructure has to support the languages used.

The elements defined by the middleware bus architecture are shown in box labeled "Defined in Architecture" in Figure 16-1. The lowest-level element is the *standard middleware transport.* An analysis of the requirements revealed a need for deferrable communications, with options for guaranteed, nonduplicated delivery. The chosen technology was message queuing, with MQSeries as the product, because it was available on all the required and anticipated platforms.

A further analysis showed a need for real-time interaction, with the option of global transactions across more than one system and database, in particular between Windows and the Unisys ClearPath environments. Technology and product choices were COM+ (and .NET in the future) in the Windows environment and a Unisys implementation of the Open Group DTP standard, named Open DTP. COM+ and Open DTP can interact using a Unisys connector product called Distributed Transaction Integration (DTI). This product converts between the two standards and allows either end to initiate distributed transactions involving the other, including support of two-phase commit, if required. Open DTP provides

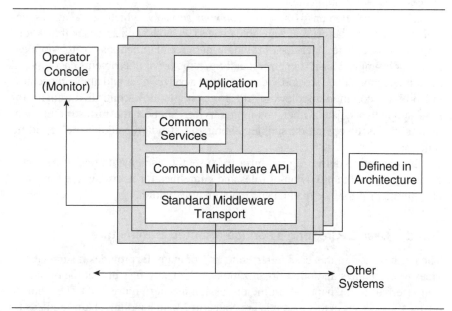

Figure 16-1   Middleware bus architectural elements

the transaction management within the ClearPath system. DTI also allows Web clients to interact with Open DTP using the IIS Web server and COM+, as well as thick (rich) clients running under Windows.

Open DTP provides an additional service for MQSeries in the ClearPath environment. It allows database and queue updates to be managed under transactional control when running under the same operating system image. When a transaction completes, it is either committed and both database and queue updates are performed, or it is aborted and any database or queue changes rolled back. This is two-phase commit within the same platform. Most implementations of MQSeries provide this feature, so it is used in other systems in the environment discussed here.

Although the applications could have interfaced directly with the middleware transport, using the APIs provided by the middleware, it was decided to implement two additional elements between the applications and the middleware transport, providing a number of extra facilities in the middleware bus. The first element is the *common middleware API*. This offers the applications a middleware API that is abstracted to a higher level than the standard middleware transport API, isolating the applications from the specifics of the implementation. This approach allows the standard middleware transport to be changed to a different technology should it be desirable, although any replacement would have to support the same capabilities, for example, guaranteed delivery or two-phase commit (it may add more). The common middleware API is implemented in all the attached platforms, so all the applications use the same interfaces, and supports the various languages used by the applications.

The second element is a set of *common services,* which are again implemented across all platforms and are able to interface with applications in the various languages used. These services provide a number of functions for the applications, for example, to assist in error handling in the event of problems encountered in an interaction. They also provide additional services over and above those provided by the common middleware API, for example, flow-controlled transfer for large amounts of data. Other common services support the infrastructure that reports events to operators, supplementing the standard middleware reporting functions.

In addition to delivering the infrastructure, the implementation of the architecture included the provision of rules and guidelines for its use, in the form of a programmer's reference manual and other documentation.

16.1.2   Case 2: Creating a service-oriented architecture

The organization in this case, referred to as Company B, provides insurance services to companies and other organizations. (Company B is in fact the organization referred to in Chapter 4, in the discussion around Figure 4-3.) The primary business processes in this example are concerned with handling claims and ensuring that subsequent payments are made into the claimants' banks.

In the market concerned, service quality means speed and accuracy of claim processing. Company B's business requirement was to move the company into the leading position in a highly competitive market by applying sophisticated, automated workflow and process management combined with high-performance and reliability. A goal of the implementation was to do this in a way that allowed a great deal of flexibility to respond to future changes, both within the insurance market and from external sources (e.g., a result of legislation). A final goal was to optimize the cost of each processed claim. The motivation for the project was thus very much business, not technology, driven.

Claims arrive on a variety of media, including paper, diskette, CD, and e-mail. Increasingly, however, they are delivered electronically over a network, especially from the bigger clients, using an extranet. Standards have been designed for electronic submission, using Web services technology. The simplest—and the ideal—case is that a claim arrives electronically and is verified automatically (i.e., without human intervention), and the payment is executed automatically. This can be done by applying rules for validation and by defining criteria for authorization of automatic payments, thus ensuring no human intervention.

There are, however, a number of cases where human intervention is required. Apart from claims arriving on media needing human processing, the other cases include the following:

- There are errors or other exceptions in the claim, which require some level of intervention to correct. Company B's staff make the corrections and return the claim to the processing flow. In extreme cases, the claim has to be returned to its originator and resubmitted after correction.
- The claim is of a type or size that requires human approval. It cannot be processed automatically, even if there are no errors.

At the start of the project, Company B was using a mainframe-based application implemented in a Unisys ClearPath system. The application had been in operation for some time and provided a terminal (green-screen) interface to its users. The application was developed in a Unisys 4GL, Enterprise Application Environment (EAE, formerly called LINC). Its run-time environment was the standard transaction monitor on the ClearPath platform concerned. Since the application was stable and functionally rich, it was decided to adapt it to run into a set of independent services, which could then be used in the new environment.

The new architecture follows a tiered, or layered, model:

- The top layer, *access channels,* comprises workstations and other channels (the users of the system).
- The next layer is the *process layer,* which defines the various processes executed, defined in a workflow management system. Each step in a workflow definition identifies the (external) services needed to perform it.
- The external services defined in the process layer are executed by internal services in the next layer, which is called the *service layer.* An external

service may be executed by one or more internal service components, and an internal service may be invoked by one or more external services. The internal services are not aware of the characteristics of whatever is calling them; they simply provide a function or functions to the requester.

- The final layer is the *data layer.* The persistent data about customers, claims, and so on resides in databases in this layer

Figure 16-2 shows this architecture. Internal users use workstations with a client offering a GUI to the user. External access channels currently include Web browsers and Web services, with a facility to add channels if required. The central environment is accessed through a user interface depending on the type of equipment used, for example, a workstation that contains client software or a browser.

The process layer contains a set of services, which are executed by the various users. The required services are either explicitly selected by a user or defined by the workflow manager as representing the next step in processing the claim. In this model, applications are effectively constructed using a table-driven approach in the process layer to define the external services, which in turn use a set of internal services to implement the logic and database operations. The internal services

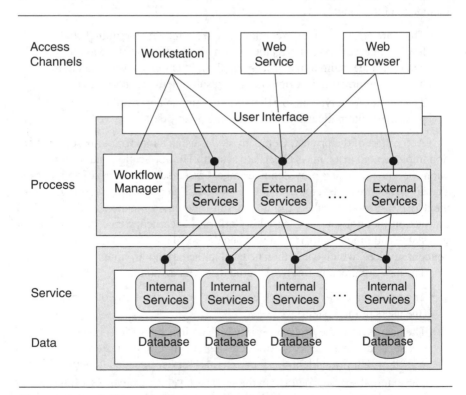

Figure 16-2 Architectural tiers

are self-contained and reusable. In principle, they may be relocated among platforms, if desired, without changing the external services using them. In addition, new internal services, perhaps required by new or extended external services, can be implemented anywhere. The external service that invokes them from the process layer needs to know only the functions offered and the interface.

In the implementation, the service and data layers are within the Unisys ClearPath environment and attached storage subsystems. The original EAE, green-screen application has been adapted and generated to run as a set of Open Group DTP services. This is a generation option provided by the EAE 4GL environment.

The process tier is implemented in a UNIX environment, with a workflow management package and an application generator, which produces the PC client application for users in Company B and defines the external services and the external-to-internal service mapping. The external services invoke the required internal services using Tuxedo, which provides a middleware backbone. A gateway product converts the Tuxedo APIs to the appropriate Open Group DTP APIs (they are very similar). The Web browser and Web service interfaces are implemented using BEA's WebLogic J2EE application server, which integrates with Tuxedo.

The architecture and the middleware chosen—Open DTP on the ClearPath system, Tuxedo in the process tier, and WebLogic—integrate well. Two-phase commit, for example, is supported and used across databases in the process tier and the data tier. Further, the specific products used allow future implementation of services in a J2EE environment, should it be required.

Although Company B decided to retain its mainframe application and restructure it into a service-oriented model, the new structure would also allow the application to be moved in stages if business needs suggested it. Redeveloping the application would therefore be a less risky venture than rewriting from scratch. We strongly recommend this approach for cases where business considerations really do suggest a rewrite. This leads to the final example, which concerns the development of a new application, which would in some cases have to integrate with an existing application, which it was designed to replace in steps. In addition, the new application would have to interact with other applications. The new product was therefore designed very much with integration in mind.

16.1.3   Case 3: Developing a new application

The final case study concerns the development of a new application product suite for passenger services in the airline industry. This product suite, AirCore™, is a Unisys development. A few words of background explanation are required to put the business rationale and architectural approach into context.

The airline industry was just about the first to use online transaction processing, starting in the late 1950s. The business motivation was simple and powerful: The major airlines had reached the limit of handling reservations with manual processes, and so they could not expand passenger numbers without automation.

The most urgent, immediate requirement was for a relatively simple transaction processing system to book passengers on flights, although additional functions and applications quickly appeared. For the first decade or so, the applications were custom built, typically joint developments between the airlines and their IT suppliers. Because the IT industry was still in relative infancy, the developments usually included operating systems and other support software, and required the definition of standards for communication as well.

Although some airlines sold applications to others and new airline projects often made use of software developed for earlier projects, there were no application packages available from IT or other vendors. In the early 1970s, Unisys (Sperry Univac at the time) embarked on the development of airline application packages under a family name of USAS. The company had been active in the airline industry from the start, so the decision to move toward packaged applications was a natural one. USAS applications are used by many airlines across the world and have been progressively enhanced to meet new requirements and to take advantage of rapid improvements in technology and standardization.

Some 25 years after the introduction of USAS, it was decided that the original business model for handling passenger services had changed sufficiently for a new model and implementation to be developed. Among many factors changing the business model, the Internet revolution was taking off, enabling new marketing and sales channels. The resulting new application suite is called AirCore.

In developing the AirCore architecture, a number of factors were taken into account. First, the new applications had to be able to integrate with existing systems internally in an airline. For USAS users, the goal was to allow new AirCore modules to be phased into production alongside USAS, selectively replacing existing functions, to minimize risk. And since most airlines, like other large organizations, had a variety of other systems as well, the architecture had to allow for integration with various other platforms.

Second, external integration with other airlines and partners was a feature of airline environments; they had been doing it for decades. AirCore therefore needed facilities to allow it to interwork with other, external systems around the world, many of which would require standards developed by the airline industry through bodies such as IATA (we mention this in Chapter 2, where we discuss the origins of middleware). So although preferences would be to use new standards for cooperation, for example Web services, there was a requirement to provide facilities to integrate old technologies, because an external organization such as another airline could not be forced to change its system interfaces.

Finally, AirCore was (and is) a continuing development, with new features and applications services being added to meet business requirements. The system had therefore to be easily expandable by adding new modules.

The resulting architecture, in a simplified form, is shown in Figure 16-3. This is a logical view, which can be deployed in a variety of physical configurations.

The technology chosen for the implementation was J2EE. This would allow deployment on a variety of hardware and software platforms, to suit customer

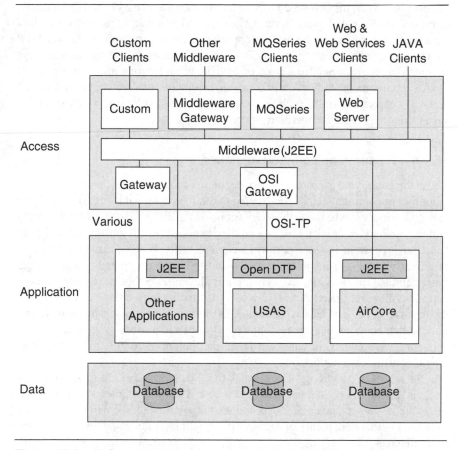

Figure 16-3 AirCore architecture

preferences. In addition to the portability possibilities, the J2EE architecture and Java language were widely used, so trained resources were available. The J2EE environment used for the applications providing the AirCore services is shown at the lower right in Figure 16-3. The external clients are shown at the top. Any Java client can access the applications using technology such as RMI. Other external interfaces require some form of gateway or connector to the environment. Web technology, such as browsers and Web services, enter through a Web server. MQSeries clients enter through MQSeries, which then connects to the Java environment. The middleware gateways include connections to other middleware standards, for example, Tuxedo and CORBA. Finally, the custom gateway includes various airline industry standards for interworking and allows the development of any special gateways that may be required.

As noted earlier, a typical airline has a variety of systems, including USAS for those airlines using it. The AirCore applications therefore had to be able to connect to USAS; they could do this through a gateway. One of the USAS developments implemented some time earlier was to provide an industry-standard means of access. The applications were adapted to run in an Open Group DTP environment, so a gateway using OSI-TP could be used to provide access. This permitted a progressive introduction of AirCore modules for a user starting with a USAS environment. Other application environments can be accessed through gateways of various kinds, such as message queuing and Web services, or native Java technology if they are written using J2EE.

16.1.4   Remarks on common mistakes

These three cases are examples of successful projects. Although they are different, a number of common factors contributed to their success. All were driven in large part by business needs, not technology for its own sake. All spent time developing and maintaining an architecture as a guiding framework. All took account of non-functional requirements (i.e., performance, scalability, systems management, etc.) at an early stage. All involved people with the necessary spread of knowledge, both technical (application and software/middleware) and business. Proof of concept activities were used extensively to verify technology choices. Performance testing was done, particularly in case 3, at an early stage, using modules developed at that point, to measure and tune the system and provide guidelines for subsequent developments. In other words, all paid attention to the kind of activities we discuss throughout this book.

So what can go wrong? The reasons that IT projects fail are many and various, and are discussed in great detail elsewhere. The level of interest in the causes of failure is obvious, given the costs and the money wasted. We will not name any failures, but there are plenty of examples! We will mention just a few of the common mistakes.

First, the wrong place to start defining an architecture is at the bottom, by drawing up a list of preferred products and technologies and then working upward. Starting at the bottom often results from quasi-religious preferences for certain technology without regard to its appropriateness in the context in which it will be have to be used, and it ignores what is in place. Centralized government IT strategy organizations in the public sector often dictate technologies and products to be used in different departments or agencies.

Second, failing to get the right people involved early in a project can be a disaster, something we have seen more than once. The right mix of people includes both application and technical designers. A failure to take sufficient account of the characteristics of technology frequently leads to functionally complete but unusable systems, most often from a performance point of view. Two examples of performance problems are an inability to scale sufficiently and long response times. The latter problem may result from poor application performance or, in a number of cases we have seen, wide area network overloads. The network problems often occur when using Web browser technology because unless care is taken, it is easy to generate very large messages. This problem can be acute when replacing green screens with browsers; circuits with plenty of bandwidth for the relatively short green-screen messages can be seriously inadequate when browsers replace them. For example, we have seen green-screen messages of a maximum of 2KB replaced by browser outputs up to 60KB or more. This problem is relatively easy to avoid in design but can be very difficult to fix after implementation be-cause it has significant ramifications for the way the application works.

The final point we will mention is a failure to start measurements at an early stage. Without measurement, it is difficult or impossible to predict what may hap-pen, where potential problems lie, and how they can be fixed. It is essential to identify and quantify performance metrics early on and to measure the system to determine the values of the metrics as soon as possible. Tuning and refinement follow the measurement, followed by more tests; it is an iterative process. The results of this activity can then guide the remaining development, for example, in guidelines for efficient use of applications servers and databases. Test drivers are an essential component of this activity to manage costs and to ensure repeatability of the tests.

16.2   What does the future hold?

In the spirit of reckless endeavor, we thought we would end by guessing what the future might hold in the area of IT architecture and middleware.

Large changes to the IT industry come about only when a technological change makes possible a new way of doing business. The most recent example is the Web; the Web enabled a new way of reaching and selling to customers and enabled some new kinds of business. Previous examples are OLTP, which allowed organizations to start automating manual processes and provided remote access (this was really the first e-business), and the introduction of the PC, which enabled computing for the masses. Counterexamples are the rise of UNIX in the 1990s and the rise of OO programming. These made not a bit of difference to the world out-side computing but changed a great deal within. Changes driven by business com-bined with technology have been pervasive. Changes driven by technology alone have been less so. The UNIX revolution never killed off the mainframe as it was meant to and, in spite of the OO revolution, the language with the most lines of code is still COBOL.

What kind of change is Web services?

Two business changes happening now, if speeded up, could have a massive impact on IT. One is the extension of the Web to mobile technology and beyond; the other is the breakup of organizations through outsourcing.

We are on the verge of seeing the Web mark 2—the mobile Web—and, further into the future, the Web mark 3—the embedded computer Web (network-connected household goods, cars, and even clothes). Most of the technology for the mark 2

Web is already there; all that is holding it back is the lack of cheaper devices and people to use them creatively. The main open question is, how long it will be before these devices reach beyond the early adopters, the gadget lovers, to the masses? In both these future Webs, Web services play an important role because instead of using a browser, client programs will be downloaded into the device. As the person or vehicle moves around, the mobile devices may stop some applications and reload new ones. Adaptive reconfiguration could be important. For example, real-time communication such as video conferencing depends on acceptable networks being available. The video-conferencing application may seek to improve its QoS by selecting a network transport protocol suited to the underlying network infrastructure (wireless LAN, long-distance Internet, etc.) and the bandwidth available. It may also respond to the equipment used for display, reconfiguring itself according to the devices available. Applications running in a mobile device may also need to adapt to whatever service is available, perhaps even reading a UDDI directory and building a new interface to access a service it knew nothing about previously.

The second important business change currently under way is the move to outsourcing and using offshore resources for cost reasons. More and more organizations, both commercial and governmental, are handing over part of their operations to third parties. They are eliminating whole departments: Sometimes the employees are taken on by the new organization and sometimes they are reassigned to other work or laid off. It seems possible that in the future many businesses will be little more than a brand and a head office and everything else—production, delivery, research, sales, marketing, accounts, billing, and so on—will be outsourced. Normally, the IT that supports the department goes with the department; indeed, doing IT better is a major reason given that the outsource supplier can work more efficiently. From an architecture perspective, outsourcing implies many loosely coupled applications, probably using Web services technology. An interesting question is, what happens to common data such as product and customer information? It is possible that controlled duplication over the Web will be implemented, possibly using choreography software to control the flow and integrity of updates. Alternatively, Web services may be implemented that give access to shared data. Personal data is a particularly interesting case because both data privacy and antiterrorist legislation can have an impact. There are dire predictions that e-mail will be extinct in the near future because of the abuse by junk mailers. It seems more likely that people will have multiple e-mail addresses and eventually multiple identities on the Web. Perhaps handling personal information will become so complex that it will be entrusted to a few specialist organizations. This is to some extent what Microsoft is trying to do, with limited success, with .NET Passport.

Suppliers make money by servicing many organizations. They want to optimize the usage of their resources and that is likely to mean clients sharing resources. They also want to respond quickly to changes in the client's business volumes, which implies the service supplier will either grow or shrink their clients' resource allocation according to need. We expect the IT industry to respond to this demand in two ways: grid computing and adaptive software. We have already discussed adaptive software. Practical examples of grid computing today exist largely in the compute-intensive worlds of some scientific research, such as searching for alien life (e.g., see www.seti.org) and climate change (e.g., see www.climateprediction. net). These examples are essentially grid computing using spare cycles on desktop PCs. Much more difficult is grid computing across a number of independently managed data centers. The vision is, first, for applications to be moved automatically to run in their optimal location and, second, for resources to be combined to be able to do tasks that would be beyond any one of them. The infrastructure to tie all this together is, of course, middleware.

Most IT professionals these days live with the fear that their lives might be turned upside down by IT outsourcing. IT outsourcing puts a legal contract between the user and the provider. For operational activities, it can work well. For instance, a contracted-out network may have good reliability and good performance for a reasonable cost. A common challenge is knowing what is going on. For instance, if response times are slow, it can be hard to figure out whether the server or the network is at fault. The network provider is reluctant to share network configuration and performance information; it would much rather monitor service levels itself. It seems likely to us that this will drive major changes in the system management area. Users will want to monitor suppliers, suppliers will want to monitor users. When a fault is reported, it becomes more and more important to pin down the cause quickly.

Outsourcing of application development is more difficult. In many ways, application development is more like a research project than a production line. You can set the cost, set the deliverables, and set the time period, but not all three. The outsourced developer must therefore pad estimates simply to offset the considerable risk. Furthermore, lacking intimate contact with the client is a huge problem because of the difficulty in finding and understanding requirements. At the moment, there are places in the world where people with good skills are earning low wages, but this is only effective for medium to large projects with well-defined specifications.

Big IT projects have (we're being charitable here) a mixed record of success. We see more emphasis in the future on more evolutionary approaches. As noted in an earlier chapter and illustrated in this one by a case study, this does not mean never rewriting. But it does mean rewriting in stages and mixing old and new applications.

Most of the developments we anticipate in IT are, from a technical perspective, evolutionary rather than revolutionary. If there is an area that needs a revolution, it has to be application development. For years people have lamented the high failure rates of application development projects. It's not that there haven't been attempts at revolution. The history of application development has been one failed coup after another.

Where will this revolution come from? Three approaches to better application development are being touted today: better programming, model-driven development, and frameworks. Better programming means better tools for programming, agile methodologies, and more features provided by operating systems, databases, and middleware. Model-driven development, especially combined with business rules, is an interesting approach with great potential. It's early though. There is very little practical experience in using business rules intensively when defining large-scale applications, and virtually none in automatically generating applications from the rule base. This is a problem with frameworks as well. Frameworks have been around for a while but have never taken off in a big way. One reason is that with the framework, you get an architecture whether you like it or not; and if that architecture conflicts with your current architecture, it is hard to integrate what you have with what you want.

Our major concern for all three approaches is that, assuming they work, they are all are good at generating silo applications and poor at generating integrated applications, especially when integrating with existing applications. Thinking about integration all the way from requirements, through modeling, to implementation still hasn't become central to application development, and it needs to be.

To summarize, Web services and loosely coupled applications will become increasingly important but will not replace all other forms of middleware. Tightly coupled systems will remain. Systems management software and security software are active areas where we anticipate many improvements, in particular, software becoming more and more adaptive. Application development will remain in turmoil. Whatever happens, a key factor for success will be developing and maintaining the IT architecture.

16.3   The key points to remember

If you have read this book all the way through, no doubt you will be pleased to reach the final section of the final chapter. We will leave you with the key points we believe to be important. Overall, there is no magic approach, no single technology, which can be used to guarantee success when building IT systems. There never has been and, in our opinion, there never will be. The silver bullet does not exist.

What can be done, however, is to attack the problems systematically, following something like the principles we have attempted to explain in this book, and paying attention to detail. The case studies in this chapter all did just that; the success of such projects has acted as the main source of our views. And, of course, less successful projects have provided valuable lessons. The main points to remember are stated next, grouped under the four major sections into which the book is organized.

16.3.1   Middleware technology alternatives

There is a great deal of different middleware technology around. Broadly, it can be classified into request-response (or synchronous), message queuing (or asynchronous), and remote database access. Each has its role. Request-response middleware has had a particularly active history, mainly because of the later introduction of object interfaces and components.

Distributed transaction processing is important, not only to synchronize transactions across a network but also within one machine to synchronize database activity with reading and writing to message queues. It does have a performance penalty but this can largely be mitigated if the most performance-critical server (typically the central database) is updated last.

Web services and associated technology have made a big splash in the industry, and in some quarters they are seen as the latest solution to all IT problems; the results could prove disappointing. That said, we believe that service-oriented architectures in general, and Web services in particular, are a very good way of designing and building distributed systems. The notion of service orientation is easy to understand. Web services standards promise to make heterogeneous system interconnection an easier prospect than it has been because the standards are widely accepted and publicly owned, by the W3C among others.

16.3.2   IT architecture guidelines

For the purposes of building an application, middleware has two roles. One is to provide real-time, request-response semantics; the other is to provide deferrable, or send-and-forget, semantics. It is possible to build real-time semantics using message queuing and deferrable semantics using request-response middleware such as RMI, but this requires additional programming. It is also possible to use a hub to provide real-time and deferrable messages across multiple middleware types, but again this does require careful design. Putting a hub in the architecture adds complexity, so it should be avoided unless it can "pay its way"; in other words, it provides a good solution to a concrete problem.

The notion of loosely coupled and tightly coupled concerns the degree to which one application depends on another application. It has a technical and application dimension.

On the technical dimension there are, broadly speaking, three large-scale architectures: message bus architecture, hub architecture, and Web services architecture. The message bus architecture is the most tightly coupled but has the best performance, security, and resiliency. (For instance, automatic switching to backup is inherently tightly coupled.) The Web services architecture is the most loosely coupled and the hub architecture is somewhere in between. The hub is ideal when routing is required, particularly if multiple channels need routing to multiple servers. There is no best architecture; each has a role.

From an application perspective, a tightly coupled solution is one where there are many short messages and each end of the dialogue must remember the state of the dialogue. A loosely coupled solution is one with a few large messages where the dialogue is stateless. Tightly coupled applications only run well in a message-bus technical architecture, but loosely coupled applications can run well everywhere.

Stateful sessions make performance and resiliency much harder to implement. Physical distribution of data (e.g., splitting accounts by account number ranges) introduces a great deal of additional complexity and is unnecessary for all but the largest applications.

16.3.3   Distributed systems technology principles

We pay quite a lot of attention in this book to technical requirements that must be addressed early on when developing systems—we call them the nonfunctional requirements. Failure to consider them can result in systems that are not usable. We considered four subject areas: resilience, performance, systems management, and security.

The degree of resilience required of any system, like many other things, is determined by the needs of the business and the impact of system failure: How much does it cost to be off the air? Online stock exchanges invest heavily in backup systems because the cost of downtime is huge. In other areas, the cost of lack of availability may be very high but measured in potential loss of life rather than money. Some defense and air traffic control systems are examples. Good practice principles include simplicity of design, anticipation of errors, exhaustive testing, and a backup strategy and configuration that are regularly tested.

Performance is always a concern, even given the tremendous growth in the power available. Key points to remember include defining the requirements carefully, ensuring that the architecture, technology, and product choices are consistent with the required performance, and measuring, followed by tuning.

System management becomes more important in the complex environments that are arising. IT environments are becoming increasingly distributed, with elements of the environment (networks, for example) under the control of some other organization and with required cooperation among enterprises. Effective management requires an ability to monitor the behavior of the whole environment so that the overall system ramifications of problems in any component can be determined. As much automation as possible should be another goal. It takes time and effort to make this happen, and it is never complete, but it is worth the effort, not only for cost reasons but also for quality of operation.

Security needs careful design mainly to decide where access control is going to be implemented. The increased use of the Web services is leading to changes in security technology with a greater dependence on encryption and security tokens.

16.3.4   Distributed systems implementation design

Design is done at multiple levels. In this book we discuss the upper levels, which we call business process level and the task-level design.

Business process level design concerns aligning the applications and the data with the business processes. At this level, four patterns can be mixed and matched.

They are Single Centralized server, Multiple Centralized servers, Pass Through, and Copy out/Copy in. Pass Through and Copy out/Copy in are more loosely coupled but require more implementation effort.

It is common that some key pieces of data need to be widely distributed, for instance, customer data and product data. There are two strategies: shared data and controlled duplication of data. Shared data needs less implementation and the data is immediately up-to-date. Controlled duplication is often more efficient and allows the local data to be restructured for the local application. For controlled duplication of data, it is best to have primary copy.

Task (or dialogue) design is sometimes trivial but needs careful attention when the application is distributed. Our approach is to draw task/message diagrams, which we then analyze to ensure there aren't design problems like performance and potential loss of data.

Our final key point is that the purpose of the process-level design and the task-level design is to provide a framework for the technical architecture specialists and the application architecture specialists to work together. Whatever you think of this framework, we hope you agree that bringing the technologist and the application analyst together early in the project is vital for the project's success.

Appendix: Acronyms

This book, like most books on IT, contains a lot of acronyms (including IT!). This appendix contains expansions of them, for quick reference. In a few cases, the acronym has become a name; the expansion has dropped out of use for some reason. This may be because it is a product name, which at one time was an acronym for which the expansion is not now generally used. This applies typically to products such as operating systems, for example, Unisys MCP. In other cases, the expansion has ceased to be useful because it no longer reflects the true meaning of the acronym, but because it is widely used, changing the name to something else would be difficult and not worth the effort. A prominent example is SOAP, which originally meant Simple Object Access Protocol, but since it is neither that simple not specifically to do with objects, the expansion has been dropped. (Name) will be used to indicate that the acronym is generally used as a name, followed by a very brief indication of what it stands for. The name or acronym in brackets at the end of the definition defines the source of the acronym, usually a vendor or a standards-making body.

4GL: Fourth-Generation Language

ACID: Atomicity, Consistency, Isolation, and Durability. These are properties of a transaction.

ADO: Active Data Object [Microsoft]

API: Application Programming Interface

ASCII: American Standard Code for Information Interchange

ASP: Active Server Page [Microsoft]; Application Service Provider

ATM: Automatic Teller Machine (banking); Asynchronous Transfer Mode (telecommunications)

ATMI: Tuxedo API set [BEA]

BNA: Burroughs Network Architecture [Unisys]

B2B: Business-to-Business

CICS: (Name) Transaction processing system [IBM]

CIM: Common Information Model [DMTF]

CMP: Cellular MultiProcessing [Unisys]

COBOL: Common Business-Oriented Language

COM: Component Object Model [Microsoft]

COMS: Transaction Processing Environment [Unisys]

COM+: (Name) An umbrella name covering a number of related technologies: COM, DCOM, MTS, etc. [Microsoft]

CORBA: Common Object Request Broker Architecture [OMG]

CPU: Central Processing Unit

CRM: Customer Relationship Management/Manager

C2B: Consumer-to-Business

DCA: Distributed Communications Architecture [Unisys]

DCE: Distributed Computing Environment [OSF]

DCOM: Distributed Component Object Model [Microsoft]

DES: Data Encryption Standard [FIPS]

DHCP: Dynamic Host Configuration Protocol [IETF]

DMTF: Distributed Management Task Force [Vendor consortium]

DMZ: Demilitarized Zone

DNA: Distributed interNet applications Architecture [Microsoft]; Distributed Network Architecture [DEC]

DNS: Domain Name Service [IETF]

DRDA: Distributed Relational Database Architecture [IBM]

DTD: Document Type Definition. [Part of XML]

DTI: Distributed Transaction Integration [Unisys]

DTP: Distributed Transaction Processing

EAE: Enterprise Application Environment [Unisys]; used to be called LINC

EAI: Enterprise Application Integration

EBCDIC: Extended Binary Coded Decimal Interchange Code

EDI: Electronic Data Interchange

EJB: Enterprise JavaBean, part of J2EE

FML: Forms Markup Language, part of Tuxedo

FTP: File Transfer Protocol

GPI: Generated Programming Interface

GUI: Graphical User Interface

HTML: HyperText Markup Language [W3C]

HTTP: HyperText Transfer Protocol [W3C]

IATA: International Air Transport Association

IDL: Interface Definition Language

IETF: Internet Engineering Task Force

IIOP: Internet Inter-ORB Protocol [OMG], part of CORBA

IL: Intermediate Language [Microsoft]

IP: Internet Protocol [IETF]

IPSec: Secure Internet Protocol

ISO: (Name) International Organization for Standardization

ISP: Internet Service Provider

IT: Information Technology

JCL: Job Control Language

JDBC: Java DataBase Connectivity, part of J2EE

JDO: Java Data Object, part of J2EE

JIT: Just-in-Time

JMS: Java Message Service, part of J2EE

JNDI: Java Naming and Directory Interface, part of J2EE

JSP: JavaServer Page, part of J2EE

JVM: Java Virtual Machine.

J2EE: Java 2 Enterprise Edition [Sun]

KDC: Key Distribution Center, part of Kerberos

LAN: Local Area Network

MCP: (Name) Unisys Operating System

MDA: Model Driven Architecture [OMG]

MIB: Management Information Base, part of SNMP

MSMQ: MicroSoft Message Queuing [Microsoft]

MTS: Microsoft Transaction Server [Microsoft]

MVS: (Name) IBM operating system (later became OS390, then zOS)

.NET: (Name) an operating system platform or framework [Microsoft]

NFS: Network File System [originally from Sun]

ODBC: Open DataBase Connectivity [Microsoft]

OLE: Object Linking and Embedding [Microsoft]

OLE DB: Object Linking and Embedding DataBase [Microsoft]

OLTP: On-Line Transaction Processing

OMG: Object Management Group

ONC: Open Network Computing [originally from UNIX International]

OO: Object-Oriented

ORB: Object Request Broker [OMG]

OSF: Open Software Foundation

OSI: Open Systems Interconnection [ISO]

OSI-TP: Open Systems Interconnection-Transaction Processing [ISO]

OS2200: (Name) Unisys operating system

OTM: Object Transaction Manager

OWL: (Name) Web Ontology Language [W3C]

PCI: Peripheral Component Interconnect

PIM: Platform-Independent Model, part of MDA

PNR: Passenger Name Record

PSM: Platform-Specific Model, part of MDA

RAD: Rapid Application Development

RDBMS: Relational DataBase Management System

RFC: Request For Comment (an IETF standard or working paper)

RM: Resource Manager, part of the Open Group DTP model

RMI: Remote Method Invocation, part of J2EE

RPC: Remote Procedure Call

RSA: (Name) RSA Security Inc.

RTT: Round Trip Time

RUP: Rational Unified Process [IBM]

SAA: Systems Application Architecture [IBM]

SGML: Standard Generalized Markup Language

SITA: Société Internationale de Télécommunications Aeronautiques

SMTP: Simple Mail Transfer Protocol [IETF]

SNA: Systems Network Architecture [IBM]

SOA: Service-Oriented Architecture

SOAP: (Name) Originally, Simple Object Access Protocol [W3C]

SPO: Single Point Operation [Unisys]

SQL: System Query Language

SSL: Secure Sockets Layer [Netscape]

SWIFT: Society for Worldwide Interbank Financial Telecommunication

TCM: Transactional Component Middleware

TCP: Transmission Control Protocol. TCP/IP is a combination of the separate standards TCP and IP, and is also used as a name for the whole set of related standards. [IETF]

TGT: Ticket Granting Ticket [Kerberos]

TIP, HVTIP: (Name) TIP is a transaction processing system; HVTIP is High Volume TIP [Unisys]

TLS: Transport Layer Security [IETF]

TM: Transaction Manager, part of the Open Group DTP model

TPC: (Name) Transaction Processing Performance Council

TPC-C: (Name) One of the TPC transaction processing benchmark specifications.

tpmC: Transactions Per Minute, Type C

TX: Open Group DTP API set

TxRPC: Open Group DTP API set

UDDI: Universal Description, Discovery, and Integration [W3C/UDDI.ORG. Note that UDDI.ORG is the name of the organization, not simply its Web address.]

UDP: User Datagram Protocol [IETF]

UML: Unified Modeling Language [OMG]

URI: Uniform Resource Identifier [W3C]

URL: Uniform Resource Locator [W3C]

USAS: Unisys Standard Airline System [Unisys]

VB: Visual Basic [Microsoft]

WAN: Wide Area Network

WAP: Wireless Application Protocol

WBEM: Web-Based Enterprise Management [DMTF]

WS-CAF: Web Services Composite Application Framework (proposed standard from consortium of vendors)

WS-CF: Web Service Coordination Framework, part of WS-CAF

WS-CTX: Web Services Context, part of WS-CAF

WS-TXM: Web Transaction Management, part of WS-CAF

WSD: Web Services Definition

WSDL: Web Services Definition Language [W3C]

WWW: World Wide Web

W3C: World Wide Web Consortium

XA: Open Group DTP protocol for distributed database coordination

XACML: XML Access Control Markup Language

XATMI: (Name) Open Group DTP API set

XML: eXtensible Markup Language [W3C]

XP: eXtreme Programming

Index

Unisys Series

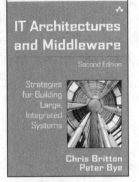

0321246942

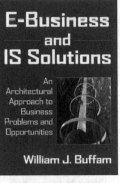

0201708477

0201379384

0201575922

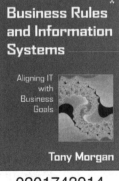

0201743914